LATIN AMERICA AND ITS PEOPLE

Cheryl E. Martin
University of Texas at El Paso

Mark Wasserman
Rutgers University

PEARSON
Longman

New York San Francisco Boston
London Toronto Sydney Tokyo Singapore Madrid
Mexico City Munich Paris Cape Town Hong Kong Montreal

Senior Acquisitions Editor: Janet Lanphier
Senior Marketing Manager: Sue Westmoreland
Supplements Editor: Brian Belardi
Media Supplements Editor: Melissa Edwards
Production Manager: Stacey Kulig
Project Coordination, Text Design, and Electronic Page Makeup: Electronic Publishing
    Services Inc, NYC
Cover Design Manager: John Callahan
Cover Designer: Maria Ilardi
Cover Illustration/Photo: Scenes from religious ceremony with richly dressed priests,
    musicians, and masked dancers, 1948. Watercolor by A. Tejeda, reconstruction of
    Mayan frescos in Chamber 1 of Bonampak, Chiapas, Mexico (detail). The Art
    Archive/Archaeological and Ethnological Museum Guatemala City/Dagli Orti.
Photo Researcher: Jody Potter
Senior Manufacturing Buyer: Dennis Para
Printer and Binder: R. R. Donnelley and Sons
Cover Printer: R. R. Donnelley and Sons

For permission to use copyrighted material, grateful acknowledgment is made to the
copyright holders on page 276, which are hereby made part of this copyright page.

Library of Congress Cataloging-in-Publication Data

Martin, Cheryl English,
  Latin America and its people / Cheryl E. Martin, Mark Wasserman. -- 2nd ed.
      p. cm.
  Includes bibliographical references and index.
  ISBN 0-205-52053-7 (single vol. ed.) -- ISBN 0-205-52052-9 (v. 1) -- ISBN 0-205-
52050-2 (v. 2) 1. Latin America--History. I. Wasserman, Mark, II. Title.
  F1410.M294 2007
  980--dc22
                                  2006102296

Please visit us at www.ablongman.com

ISBN 13: 978-0-205-52053-4 (single-volume edition)
ISBN 10: 0-205-52053-7
ISBN 13: 978-0-205-52052-7 (volume one)
ISBN 10: 0-205-52052-9
ISBN 13: 978-0-205-52050-3 (volume two)
ISBN 10: 0-205-52050-2

1 2 3 4 5 6 7 8 9 10–DOC–10 09 08 07

To the students of Rutgers University
and the University of Texas at El Paso,
who have inspired us.

CONTENTS

1

THE FIRST PEOPLES OF THE AMERICAS 1

2

AMERICANS AND IBERIANS ON THE EVE OF CONTACT   35

3

THE EUROPEAN CONQUEST OF AMERICA   72

The Europeans Arrive   73

4

THE IBERIANS' NEW WORLD   110

5

THE AMERINDIANS' CHANGING WORLD   144

6

A NEW PEOPLE AND THEIR WORLD   177

7

THE SHIFTING FORTUNES
OF COLONIAL EMPIRES   212

8

THE NEW NATIONS
OF LATIN AMERICA   245

LIST OF FEATURES

LIST OF MAPS
AND COLOR PLATES

Maps

Color Plates

Gulf of Mexico

BAHAMAS

Nassau

Havana

CUBA

Mexico City

DOMINICAN REPUBLIC

PUERTO RICO

HAITI

JAMAICA

Kingston

Port-au-prince

Santo Domingo

San Juan

VIRGIN IS.

ST. KITTS & NEVIS

ANTIGUA & BARBUDA

GUADELOUPE

DOMINICA

MARTINIQUE

BARBADOS

ST. LUCIA

ST. VINCENT

THE GRENADINES

GRENADA

TRINIDAD & TOBAGO

BELIZE

Belmopan

GUATEMALA

Guatemala City

HONDURAS

Tegucigalpa

EL SALVADOR

San Salvador

NICARAGUA

Managua

San Jose

COSTA RICA

Panama City

PANAMA

Carribean Sea

Caracas

L. Maracaibo

Orinoco

VENEZUELA

Bogotá

COLOMBIA

GUYANA

Georgetown

Paramaribo

Cayenne

SURINAM

FRENCH GUIANA

ATLANTIC

OCEAN

GALAPAGOS
ISLANDS

Quito

ECUADOR

Amazon R.

BRAZIL

São Francisco R.

Lima

PERU

L. Titicaca

La Paz

BOLIVIA

Brasília

PACIFIC

OCEAN

Paraguay R.

Paraná R.

PARAGUAY

Asuncion

São Paulo

Rio de Janeiro

CHILE

Cordoba

Santiago

Buenos Aires

URUGUAY

Montevideo

ARGENTINA

FALKLAND/MALVINAS
ISLANDS

Tierra del Fuego

National Capitals

PREFACE

Our aim in writing *Latin America and Its People* has been to provide a fresh interpretative survey of Latin American history from pre-Columbian times to the beginning of the twenty-first century. The millions of "ordinary" Latin Americans are the central characters in our story. We look at the many social and political institutions that Latin Americans have built and rebuilt—families, governments from the village level to the nation-state, churches, political parties, labor unions, schools, and armies—but we do so through the lives of the people who forged these institutions and tried to alter them to meet changing circumstances. The texture of everyday life, therefore, is our principal focus.

THE TEXTURE OF EVERYDAY LIFE

Life has not been easy for most Latin Americans. Poverty, hard work, disease, natural calamities, the loss of loved ones, and violence have marked many people's lives. Many have lacked educational opportunities and the chance to speak their political opinions openly. In the chapters that follow, we will devote a lot of attention to the daily struggles of men, women, and children as they faced these difficult challenges and adapted to changing times. We are also interested in how people managed to find meaning and enjoyment in their lives. Even in the midst of hardship and tragedy, they came together as families and communities to celebrate, to dance, to eat and drink, to flirt, to marry, and to pray. Our readers will meet the people of Latin American history "up close and personal," in their houses and on the streets, on the shop floors and in the fields, at work and at play, for it is the texture of everyday life that makes the history of Latin America so fascinating and compelling.

THE DIVERSITY OF LATIN AMERICA

Latin Americans are a very diverse people. They have spoken Spanish, Portuguese, Nahuatl, Quechua, Maya, Aymara, Guaraní, and scores of other languages. Their ethnic and cultural roots can be traced to the indigenous civilizations of the Americas and to many generations of European, African, and Asian immigrants. A few have been very rich, but many more have been very poor. They have adapted to many climatic zones, some at altitudes as high as 11,000 feet above sea level. Many Latin Americans have lived in rural areas, but they have also built some of the world's most sophisticated cities, from the Aztec and Inca capitals of Tenochtitlan and Cuzco to such modern industrial giants as São Paulo, Brazil, and Monterrey, Mexico, to cosmopolitan urban centers like Mexico City and Buenos Aires. Following their independence from Spain and Portugal, they have experimented with a variety of political regimes—monarchy, liberal democracy, oligarchy, socialist revolution, and brutal military dictatorships, to name a few.

Despite this diversity, Latin Americans have faced certain challenges in common. European conquest and subsequent shifts in world economic and political configurations have shaped the region's history over the past five centuries. Latin America's rich natural resources have attracted foreign investors who have profited handsomely, while the people who worked in the mines and oilfields have seldom garnered an equitable share of the bounty. The region's ability to produce a stunning variety of agricultural staples has shaped patterns of landholding and labor throughout the region, again to the detriment of the many and the benefit of the few. How to achieve political stability in nations divided by class, ethnic, and regional differences has been an enduring conundrum for Latin Americans, even if they have tried many different means of resolving that dilemma.

Our goal, then, is to explore Latin Americans' common history without losing sight of their diversity, and to compare how the many different peoples of the region have responded to similar situations. We have therefore organized our text thematically rather than proceeding country-by-country. There are too many countries and too much time to cover for us to thoroughly document the history of every Latin American nation. No doubt, some country specialists will feel their area slighted, but textbooks are as much about the choices of what to exclude as they are about what to include. Unlike many other texts on Latin American history, *Latin America and Its People* interweaves the history of Brazil with that of its Spanish-speaking neighbors, rather than segregating it in separate chapters, while also pointing out the special features that distinguish it from other Latin American countries. Volume I includes coverage of those portions of the present-day United States that were once part of the Spanish colonial empire.

Our underlying assumption is that, in order for our students to gain an introductory (and, we hope, lasting) understanding of Latin America, it is best not to clutter the narrative with too many dates and names. We believe that students will remember the major themes, such as the struggle to control local affairs, the impact of war, the transformation of women's roles, and the social changes wrought by economic development. And students will remember, perhaps even more clearly, that many Latin Americans lived and continue to live in overwhelming poverty.

VOLUME I

Volume I of *Latin America and Its People* looks at the ways in which people have continually reinvented the hemisphere that Europeans called the "new world." This world was first "new" for the nameless ancestors of today's Native Americans, who migrated across the Bering Strait and fanned out across North and South America over the course of many millennia. Generation after generation, they adapted to the many different climatic zones of the hemisphere and gradually accumulated the surpluses necessary to found the great civilizations of the Aztecs, the Inca, the Maya, and so many others. Chapter 1 is devoted entirely to the long trajectory of cultural development in the Americas down to the year 1400 C.E., while Chapter 2 includes an extensive comparative discussion of the Aztec and Inca empires and the simultaneously emerging national monarchies of Spain and Portugal.

Spanish and Portuguese colonists not only found this world very different from what they had known; they also remade it as they discovered its potential for yielding silver, gold, sugar, and other commodities of value to them. The changes introduced by European conquest and colonization profoundly altered the world of the indigenous peoples of the Americas. Over the course of three centuries, the hemisphere witnessed the rise of a new people, the biological and cultural offspring of native peoples, Europeans, and Africans, who yet again made this world something new. Chapters 4, 5, and 6 explore the constantly changing worlds of Latin American peoples under Spanish and Portuguese rule.

The most important theme of Volume I is how ordinary people built these successive new worlds and continually renegotiated the complex and overlapping hierarchies of class, ethnicity, political status, and gender that supposedly governed their lives. Native peoples endured military and political conquest, catastrophic epidemics, highly oppressive labor regimens, and the imposition of a new religion. Yet, despite these enormous challenges, they survived and rebuilt their communities, selectively incorporating cultural elements introduced by the Europeans along with traditional practices and beliefs as they formed their new society.

Against what might seem like insurmountable odds, Africans brought to the Americas as slaves managed to retain something of the life they had known before, especially in places where their numbers were sufficiently great that they could form some kind of identifiable community. Some found ways to escape the bonds of slavery and passed that freedom to successive generations of descendants. Like the indigenous peoples, they too borrowed selectively from European cultures.

Throughout three centuries of Spanish and Portuguese colonial rule, Latin Americans of all races and social classes contested, sometimes successfully, sometimes not, the many "rules" that dictated how men and women should behave and how people in subordinate social positions should render deference to those who supposedly ranked above them. Volume I argues that it was not just kings and priests and other authority figures who built the world of colonial Latin America. Men, women, and children of all classes had at least some say in the outcome, even if the colonial state sometimes wielded enough power to silence the most vocal among them.

VOLUME II

The overarching theme of Volume II is how ordinary people struggled over the course of two centuries to maintain control over their daily lives. This meant that they sought to determine their own community leaders, set their local laws and regulations (especially taxes), establish and keep their own traditions, practice their religion, supervise the education of their children, live by their own values and standards, and earn a living. This endless struggle came to involve more than just the narrow view and experience of their village or urban neighborhood or their friends and neighbors. Rather, it brought ordinary people and their local lives into constant, not always pleasant and beneficial, contact with the wider worlds of regional (states, provinces, and territories), national, and international politics, economy, and culture. Although the local struggle forms the backbone of the narrative, we must include summaries and analyses of the contexts in which these struggles occurred, as well. Because all Latin Americans, regardless of country, participated in this struggle, the economic and political narratives proceed thematically and chronologically.

Volume II offers three chapters (10, 13, and 15) that describe the everyday lives of Latin Americans at different points in time. We want students to know what people ate and drank, how they had good times, how they worshipped, where they lived, and what their work was like. The descriptions are individual and anecdotal and collective and quantitative. Thus, it is our hope that students will remember how a Brazilian small farmer raised cassava, or the tortuous efforts of Chilean copper miners. Perhaps, readers will remember the smells of the streets of nineteenth-century cities or the noises of late twentieth-century megalopolises. The struggle for control over everyday life and the descriptions of daily life are related, of course, for the struggle and its context and the reality were joined inseparably. Students should know what the lives were like for which so many bravely and often unsuccessfully fought.

There are other themes interwoven with that of the struggle for control over everyday life. Unlike many other texts in the field, our book gives full and nuanced coverage to the nineteenth century, incorporating the most exciting new scholarship on that period. In the nineteenth century, we assert, chronic war (external and internal) and the accompanying militarization of government and politics profoundly shaped the region's economy and society. We maintain, as well, that race, class, and gender were the crucial underlying elements in Latin American politics. Moreover, warfare, combined with the massive flow of people to the cities, most particularly transformed the place of women.

In the twentieth century, conflict between the upper, middle, and lower classes was the primary moving force behind politics. No ideology from either Left or Right, nor any type of government from democracy to authoritarianism, has brought other than temporary resolutions. We also follow the continued changes in the role of women in society and politics in the face of vast transformations caused by technology and globalization.

It is also our belief that the history of Latin Americans is primarily the story of Latin America and not of the great powers outside the region. To be sure, Europeans and North Americans invested considerable sums of money and sometimes intervened militarily in Latin America. Their wars and rivalries greatly affected Latin America's possibilities. We do note the importance of such key developments as Mexico's loss of half its national territory to the United States in 1848, the impact of the Cold War on Latin America, and the training that right-wing Latin American military establishments received at the hands of United States military forces in the late twentieth century. But we prefer to keep the spotlight on the people of Latin America themselves.

SPECIAL FEATURES

In addition to the main narrative of our book, we have included three separate features in each chapter. Each chapter offers a feature called "Latin American Lives," a biography of an individual whose life illustrates some of the key points of that chapter. Some of these are famous figures such as Simón Bolívar and Frida Kahlo, but others are much less well known. Chapter 2, for example, highlights Tanta Carhua, a young woman sacrificed to the Inca sun god in Peru, while Chapter 4 discusses a seventeenth-century Spaniard who made a fortune mining silver in Bolivia. We also give a "Slice of Life" for each chapter—a vignette that takes students to the scene of the action and that illustrates in detail some of the social processes under discussion. We include, for example, deliberations of the Spanish cabildo at Cuzco, Peru, in 1551, living conditions in Chilean copper mining camps in the late nineteenth century, and the circumstances that provoked Mexico City's so-called "Parián Riot" of 1828.

We hope, too, to convey a sense of the methods that historians have used in bringing that texture of everyday life to light and the many debates the intriguing history of Latin America has generated. Each chapter therefore includes a piece entitled "How Historians Understand," designed to give readers better insights into the way that historians go about their work or the ways in which historical knowledge is used and transformed according to the concerns of a particular time and place. Chapter 5, for example, describes how historians have measured Indian acculturation under colonial rule by analyzing the incorporation of Spanish words into indigenous language sources. In Chapter 9, we show how changing political conditions in Mexico are reflected in the many myths and interpretations that have arisen concerning the life of President Benito Juárez.

AIDS TO LEARNING

Because students are at the heart of this enterprise, we have included a number of aids to learning. A glossary explains technical terms and Spanish and Portuguese words used in the text. Discussion questions at the end of the special features Latin American Lives , Slice of Life, and How Historians Understand are intended to stimulate classroom discussion and individual research projects. We have also included suggestions for further reading at the end of each chapter. In keeping with our emphasis on everyday life in Latin American history, we have chosen books that give readers especially clear views of "ordinary" men, women, and children as they went about their daily lives and made Latin America what it is today, at the beginning of the twenty-first century.

ACKNOWLEDGMENTS

Textbooks are inherently collective enterprises. In synthesizing the work of other scholars we have come to an extraordinary appreciation for the remarkable researches and analyses of our colleagues all over the world. We have tried to use the best old and new discoveries to illuminate Latin America's past. The list of those to whom we are beholden is endless. Because space constraints forced us to eschew scholarly apparatus, we have not presented formal recognition of these contributions. Many will recognize their work on our pages. They should regard this as our highest compliment. Some, but by no means all, we mention in our "Learning More about Latin Americans" at the end of each chapter. But the latter include only books in English that primarily pertain to everyday life, so it is incomplete.

We would like to thank the editors at Longman, especially Erika Gutierrez, whose patience and encouragement fostered the project. Thanks, too, to Danielle E. Wasserman, who read and commented on the chapters in Volume II, and to our colleagues Sandra McGee-Deutsch and Samuel Baily for their helpful suggestions. To Marlie Wasserman and Charles Martin, our gratitude for putting up with us, during the years that this book was in the making. Special thanks to the many students who have taken our courses at Rutgers University and the University of Texas at El Paso over the last quarter-century. Their questions and their enthusiasm for learning about the people of Latin America helped inspire this book.

Finally, we would like to thank the following reviewers for their helpful comments and suggestions:

Evelyn Powell Jennings, *St. Lawrence University*

Greg Hammond, *Oberlin College*

Kevin Gannon, *Grand View College*

Joan Supplee, *Baylor University*

David Burden, *Angelo State University*

Cheryl E. Martin

Mark Wasserman

ABOUT THE AUTHORS

Cheryl E. Martin has taught Latin American History at the University of Texas at El Paso since 1978. A native of Buffalo, New York, she received her bachelor's degree from the Georgetown University School of Foreign Service and her M.A. and Ph.D. from Tulane University. She studied at the Universidad de Cuenca, Ecuador, on a Fulbright Fellowship and was a visiting instructor at the Universidad Autónoma de Chihuahua, Mexico. Her publications include *Rural Society in Colonial Morelos* (1985) and *Governance and Society in Colonial Mexico: Chihuahua in the Eighteenth Century* (1996). She also co-edited, with William Beezley and William E. French, *Rituals of Rule, Rituals of Resistance: Public Celebrations and Popular Culture in Mexico* (1994).

Professor Martin has served on the council of the American Historical Association and on the editorial boards of the *Hispanic American Historical Review*, *The Americas*, the *Latin American Research Review*, and H. Borderlands. She has received two fellowships from the National Endowment for the Humanities and Awards for Distinguished Achievement in both teaching and research at the University of Texas at El Paso. In her spare time, she likes to ice skate.

Mark Wasserman is a professor of history at Rutgers, The State University of New Jersey, where he has taught since 1978. Brought up in Marblehead, Massachusetts, he earned his B.A. at Duke University and his M.A. and Ph.D. at the University of Chicago. He is the author of three books on Mexico: *Capitalists, Caciques, and Revolution: The Native Elite and Foreign Enterprise in Chihuahua, Mexico, 1854–1911* (1984); *Persistent Oligarchs: Elites and Politics in Chihuahua, Mexico, 1910–1940* (1993); and *Everyday Life and Politics in Nineteenth Century Mexico: Men, Women, and War* (2000). He also coauthored the early editions of the best-selling *History of Latin America (1980–88)* with Benjamin Keen. Professor Wasserman has twice won the Arthur P. Whitaker Prize for his books. Professor Wasserman has received research fellowships from the Tinker Foundation, the American Council of Learned Societies/Social Science Research Council, the American Philosophical Society, and the National Endowment of the Humanities. He has been Vice-Chair for Undergraduate Education of the Rutgers Department of History and Chair of the Department's Teaching Effectiveness Committee. Professor Wasserman was an elected member of the Highland Park, New Jersey, Board of Education for nearly a decade and served as its president for two years. He is an avid fan of Duke basketball and enjoys hiking and travel.

1

THE FIRST PEOPLES OF THE AMERICAS

WHEN WE THINK of the pre-Columbian past of North and South America, the images that come most readily to mind are perhaps the spectacular empires of the Aztecs of Mexico and the Incas of Peru, whose splendid architecture, art, and social organization so dazzled the Spanish conquistadors of the sixteenth century. But the Incas and the Aztecs had risen to prominence little more than a century before the first Europeans arrived. They succeeded in building their great cities and their empires only because they could draw upon the technical and cultural achievements of previous societies in the Americas.

For thousands of years, human beings had occupied the lands that would one day be home to the Incas and the Aztecs. Through a long process of trial and error, they had learned how to make those lands productive enough to feed growing numbers of men and women who devoted their energies and intellects to endeavors beyond mere subsistence. They observed the movements of stars and pondered what cosmic forces were responsible for the origins and sustenance of human life. They discovered also how to organize growing populations into complex but cohesive units capable of building monuments to their gods and palaces for their leaders. In this chapter, we will explore how these early Americans learned to harness the resources of their natural environment and how they built their communities, refined the cultural legacies of their ancestors, and transmitted those legacies to their descendants.

THE FIRST AMERICANS

The first human inhabitants of the Americas had no sense that they were entering a "new world" when they walked across the frozen Bering Strait from Siberia to Alaska, or paddled small canoes along the coast, probably in pursuit of mammoths, mastodons, bison, antelope, caribou, and wild horses. Nor, of course, did they think of themselves as "Americans." Each person probably identified only with the small group of people with whom he or she traveled. Only much later would they begin to identify with larger communities. Not until Europeans arrived in this hemisphere, just over 500 years ago, was the word "America" even coined, in honor of the Italian navigator Amerigo Vespucci, one of the first to proclaim this hemisphere a "new" world. Many more years elapsed before the people for whom this was a very "old" world came to call themselves "Native Americans." But for want of better terminology, we shall speak of these people as the earliest Americans.

Coming to America

The timing of the earliest migrations to the Americas is subject to debate, but most authorities believe that they probably began sometime after the emergence of the human species as we know it today, more than 35,000 years ago, and continued until about 14,000 years ago. Then the climate began to warm, and the ice bridge gradually melted. Although some theorists claim to have found evidence of occasional contact between the two hemispheres after that time, the "new world" remained separated from the "old" for more than ten millennia. The migrants spread throughout North and South America, adapting to the changing ecological conditions they found. Again, scholars dispute the chronology of this movement. Some cite evidence of human habitation in northeastern Brazil as many as 30,000 years ago, and many others assert that the Andean highlands of South America have been occupied for over 15,000 years. Virtually all experts agree that human beings had reached southern Chile by at least 10,000 and perhaps as many as 14,000 years ago.

Subsistence Strategies and the Development of Agriculture

These early Americans were foragers, subsisting on fish, leaves, eggs, insects, lizards, nuts, and fruits, as well as whatever large and small game they managed to trap and kill. People in central and southern Mexico, for example, obtained animal protein from deer, foxes, gophers, rabbits, and tortoises. These hunters and gatherers of aboriginal America moved from place to place as food supplies fluctuated with the changing seasons, sometimes stopping to camp a while, or even permanently, where foods were abundant in one place. Foraging also

WESTERN HEMISPHERE	EASTERN HEMISPHERE
35,000 BP–14,000 BP Migrations from Siberia to North America	
10,000 BP Human settlements in southern Chile	
	7000–4000 BCE Spread of agriculture in the Middle East
6500–3500 BCE Transition to agriculture in Mesoamerica	
5000–2000 BCE Transition to agriculture in Peru	**2600 BCE** Building of the first great pyramid in Egypt
2000 BCE Fully sedentary communities and first ceremonial centers found in Mesoamerica and Peru; pottery use widespread throughout the Western Hemisphere	**1796–1750 BCE** Rule of Hammurabi in Babylon
1500 BCE Metalworking in Peru	**1000–970 BCE** King David in Israel
1200–400 BCE Olmec civilization in Mexico	
900–200 BCE Chavín de Huantar in Peru	**470–430 BCE** The height of Greek civilization at Athens
500 BCE–700 CE Monte Albán in Oaxaca, Mexico	**27 BCE** Augustus founds the Roman Empire
300 BCE–800 CE The Classic Maya	
250 BCE–1000 CE Tiwanaku in Bolivia	**476 CE** The fall of Rome
100 BCE–750 CE Teotihuacan, Mexico	**700–800 CE** Spread of Islam
100–750 CE The Moche and Nazca in coastal Peru	
500–850 CE The Wari Empire, Peru	
700–1200 CE Mixtec ascendancy, Oaxaca, Mexico	
800–1517 CE The Post-Classic Maya	
900–1200 CE The Toltecs, central Mexico	**1066 CE** Norman Conquest of England
1150–1532 CE The Chimu Kingdom, Peru	

provided fibers that could be fashioned into baskets, fishnets, and textiles; animal hides that were used for clothing and shelter; as well as dyestuffs, stimulants, and hallucinogens.

Gradually, aboriginal Americans discovered that they could plant seeds at propitious locations and return later to harvest a crop, and that they could carry seeds with them to new places. Like their ancestors who had unwittingly crossed into a "new world" thousands of years before, they began supplementing their diets with a few incidental cultivated plants without making a conscious "transition to agriculture." After all, farming involves hard work and a delay between the planting of crops and the consumption of food, while foraging offers more instant gratification. Only when hunting and gathering yield sufficient food can people afford the luxury of labor that is not immediately productive. Thousands of years passed before these early Americans derived the bulk of their nutritional needs from crops they had planted and nurtured. The gradual extinction of mammoths, horses, and other large game after about 8000 B.C.E. gave them an extra incentive to find new sources of food.

People in Mexico and Central America—what archaeologists call Mesoamerica—developed some of the earliest complex agricultural systems. Gourds were evidently the first plants to be cultivated, perhaps as early as 6500 B.C.E. Next came squashes, beans, peppers, and avocados. With the domestication of maize by about 3500 B.C.E., the Classic Mesoamerican diet was born. These crops supplied essential carbohydrates, vegetable proteins, fats, and vitamins, which ancient Mesoamericans continued to supplement with animal protein from small game and fish. Meanwhile, they also began cultivating cotton.

Agriculture began developing in parts of South America by 5000 B.C.E. In the Peruvian Andes, people cultivated potatoes and lesser-known tubers such as oca and ullucu. High in caloric content, these crops could be grown even at altitudes above 10,000 feet. At lower elevations, they grew maize, a grain known as quinoa, and various legumes. By 3000 B.C.E., early Andean peoples as far south as Chile had also domesticated guinea pigs for food, llamas as beasts of burden, and alpacas as a source of wool. These larger animals also provided manure to fertilize their fields. Images of llamas and alpacas appear in the rock art of these ancient Americans.

The development of agriculture in coastal Peru shows how ancient Americans gradually added cultivated plants to a diet based on resources readily at hand. The ocean, full of fish carried by the Humboldt Current, was the prime "hunting ground" of these early Peruvians. They ate anchovies, sardines, and larger fish, as well as mussels, clams, crabs, sea lions, and marine birds. Beginning perhaps about 4000 B.C.E., they began growing crops a few miles inland on the flood plains of rivers that flowed from the Andes to the coast. In addition to such edible plants as squash, beans, peppers, sweet potatoes, and manioc, they grew cotton that could be woven into fishnets and gourds that were used as flotation devices for the nets. But only after 2000 B.C.E., as they added maize to their list of crops, did more of their diets come from agriculture than from hunting, gathering, and fishing.

Maize cultivation had spread over a wide area by 2000 B.C.E., from the interior of Brazil to parts of what is now the southwestern United States. It reached eastern North America during the following millennium and the Caribbean coast of what is now Colombia by the year 1 C.E. Elsewhere, hunting and gathering persisted even longer as the primary mode of subsistence, in some cases until well after the arrival of Europeans in the hemisphere.

Sedentary Communities and Ceremonial Centers

Once they could cultivate or otherwise obtain sufficient food in one place, early Americans became more sedentary. The establishment of permanent villages usually accompanied the domestication of plants, and fully sedentary communities appeared throughout Mesoamerica and the Andes by 2000 B.C.E. In coastal Peru and Chile, however, fishing provided so much nourishment that a sedentary lifestyle developed long before agriculture provided more than an incidental source of food. Analysis of human remains has concluded that in some communities people obtained more than 90 percent of their diet from the sea.

The establishment of sedentary communities and the growing productivity of agriculture and fishing created pools of labor that could devote a portion of their energy to purposes beyond mere subsistence. As some individuals assumed positions of command and orchestrated collective construction projects, the ancient Americas witnessed the development of public architecture—structures that served purposes beyond minimal shelter for humans and storage of food supplies. Most often, these buildings were dedicated to religious rituals aimed at tapping the power of the supernatural.

Some of the earliest monumental structures, found in coastal Peru, date from between 3000 and 2000 B.C.E., roughly contemporaneous with the Old Kingdom pyramids of Egypt and the ziggurats of Mesopotamia. The Huaca de los Sacrificios and the Huaca de los Idolos at Aspero, some 100 miles north of present-day Lima, are sloped stone platforms measuring about 100 by 150 feet at their bases. Atop the platforms sit multi-roomed structures, their interior walls adorned with friezes and niches.

Other projects that required collective labor also began to appear in Peru and elsewhere by the second millennium B.C.E. Most important were irrigation canals in the arid coastal lowlands and agricultural terraces on the steep slopes of the Andes. Such technical improvements increased agricultural yields, allowing larger populations to thrive and permitting some men and women to dedicate even greater time to non-subsistence pursuits. The people of coastal Ecuador, Colombia, and perhaps the Amazon lowlands had learned to make pottery as early as 3000 B.C.E., and by 2000 B.C.E. potters could be found in many

How Historians Understand   ARCHAEOLOGY, LITERACY, AND THE STUDY OF HISTORY

Our discussion of early American societies has relied heavily on archaeological evidence—temples, tombs, and homes; the murals and carvings that adorned these structures; and the artifacts left behind by the men, women, and children who lived, died, worked, played, and worshipped at these sites. Through painstaking study of everything from tiny fragments of pottery to enormous pyramids, archaeologists have deduced much about the lives and worldviews of these people. They have even analyzed coprolites (fossilized human feces) to learn what early Americans ate.

New archaeological discoveries are constantly adding to our knowledge, yet enormous gaps remain. For most early American civilizations, we can only give approximate dates, even for specific events such as the founding of Monte Albán or the dedication of Quetzalcoatl's temple at Teotihuacan. Indeed, we do not even know what language was spoken at Teotihuacan, or what its residents called their splendid city. We know much more about their European contemporaries, the ancient Romans. For Rome, we have the names of specific individuals and very precise dates, the kind of data that are the historian's traditional stock in trade. We know, for example, that Julius Caesar was assassinated on the Ides of March in 44 B.C.E., and his writings allow us to share, word for word, his perspective on his military and political exploits.

Thus, we can speak of Julius Caesar and the Romans as "historic" peoples in the sense that we know their names, their deeds, and their dates, while Americans of Caesar's time remain "prehistoric." It is not that they had no stories to tell, nor even that they did not record them for posterity. But instead of using alphabetic script, most of them used pictures and stylized designs that appeared on temple walls, textiles, and pottery. Their priests and rulers knew the meaning of these symbols and used them as memory aids or illustrations in explaining concepts or events, rather like a public speaker might refer to lecture notes and display images on a screen for the audience. What is missing is the kind of verbatim transcripts that we have

balam

Maya writing combined symbols that stood for whole words as well as symbols that represented syllables. In this example, the first of the two signs—a picture of a cat's head—represents the word "jaguar" (*balam* in Maya). But scribes added syllabic symbols to distinguish the jaguar from other spotted cats. The element to the left of the cat's head stands for the sound "ba," while the symbols beneath the head signify the sound "ma."

ba - balam - ma

for the famous orators of ancient Greece and Rome. We can only speculate what the ritual specialists of Chavín de Huantar and Monte Albán might have told their listeners.

The Classic Maya and the Mixtecs and Zapotecs of southern Mexico are something of an exception. They left detailed pictures and symbols that expressed abstract ideas, and the Maya developed a form of writing that reproduced human speech. For these people, we can identify specific rulers, their lineages, and the precise dates of their reigns. The glyphs identifying King Pacal of Palenque are phonetic, so we even know what people called this great Mayan lord of the seventh century C.E. In other words, we can speak of the Maya and a few other societies as "historic" peoples. Even so, they remain much more obscure to us than their contemporaries in Europe.

Our understanding of the ancient societies of the Americas is limited not only by the absence of true writing systems in many societies, but also by events that followed the arrival of Europeans in the sixteenth century. Native priests who might have provided some clues as to the meaning of symbols recorded by their ancestors died in the conquest or were driven underground, so much of their knowledge was lost to future generations. Sometimes Spanish priests ordered the destruction of indigenous writings and artifacts, believing that they were the work of the devil. At other times, some of these same missionaries wrote down their observations of native society and religion, providing a valuable view of indigenous culture, at least from the perspective of sixteenth-century Spaniards and their native informants.

The archaeological record itself became obscured over the course of many centuries, as important pre-Columbian sites suffered the ravages of weather, earthquakes, and looters. Even today many sites remain unexplored. But it is important to remember that the people who built Chavín de Huantar and Teotihuacan were as culturally sophisticated as their contemporaries in Greece and Rome.

Questions for Discussion

Does the absence of written texts about most ancient American societies affect the way we think about their descendants in our own times? How would our attitudes toward classical Greece and Rome be different if we only had the archaeological remains to tell us about them?

parts of the Americas, manufacturing utilitarian items for storing and cooking foods, as well as figurines and drinking vessels used for ritual purposes.

The many different styles of ceramics and other artifacts offer evidence of the artistic creativity and cultural diversity of ancient Americans. Textiles featuring colored designs appeared in Peru and elsewhere. By about 1500 B.C.E., Peruvians began working metals, hammering out thin sheets of copper and gold that have been found in the burial places of men and women who evidently held positions of high status within their society.

CEREMONIAL CENTERS IN MEXICO AND PERU

Toward the latter half of the second millennium B.C.E., more complex societies developed in some parts of Mesoamerica and the Andes. Farmers now produced surpluses sufficient to enable many people to become full-time construction workers, artisans, rulers, and ritual specialists. The result was an increase in the building and use of ceremonial centers, which in turn was accompanied by remarkable advances in art and architecture. Religious practices became more elaborate, and social divisions among people of different occupations widened.

The Olmec: "Mother Culture" of Mexico?

One of the first groups in Mesoamerica to develop large ceremonial complexes were the Olmec, who lived in what are now the states of Veracruz and Tabasco, along the tropical coast of the Gulf of Mexico. Fertile soil and abundant rainfall allowed farmers to harvest maize and other crops twice a year, freeing others to build and embellish temples. Of the several dozen known Olmec ceremonial centers, San Lorenzo and La Venta have received the most attention from archaeologists. Although some of the cultural remains found at San Lorenzo date as far back as 1500 B.C.E., it reached its greatest splendor between 1200 and 900 B.C.E., while La Venta flourished somewhat later, between 900 and 400 B.C.E. The people who built La Venta were the contemporaries of the ancient Greeks.

La Venta is situated on an island encircled by marshland. Its most remarkable monument is a cone-shaped mound more than 100 feet high, with a base diameter of over 400 feet. The entire site of San Lorenzo rests on an artificially created earthen platform. Neither center had a resident population of more than about 1000, so they must have drawn on the many surrounding villages for the labor necessary to construct these works.

The first Mesoamerican people to carve bas-reliefs and statues in the round, the Olmec crafted giant basalt heads, more than 8 feet high and weighing 20 tons or more. The facial features of each head are so distinctive that historians theorize that they were actually portraits of specific individuals. The stone used for these figures came from more than 50 miles away and was probably rolled on logs and then transported on wooden rafts along the region's many rivers. The Olmec also used large blocks of serpentine stone to create huge mosaics, measuring 15 by 20 feet, in the form of jaguar masks. They excelled in carving smaller pieces, such as ceremonial axes, jewelry, and figurines from jade and other semiprecious stones. Already evident at San Lorenzo by 1150 B.C.E., their distinctive artistic style often depicted beings that combined human and jaguar-like features. Spindle whorls found at San Lorenzo also indicate that they were experts in textile production.

Because the Olmec showed many cultural traits that reappeared in later civilizations in Mexico and Central America, scholars have often portrayed them as the "mother culture" of Mexico. They were evidently among the first to play the Mesoamerican ball game, a ritual that had profound religious overtones. Rubber is abundant in the Gulf Coast area, and indeed the name "Olmec" (literally, "people of the place with rubber") is what centuries later the Aztecs would call those who lived there. The Olmec began manufacturing rubber balls as early as 1200 B.C.E., eventually exporting them throughout Mesoamerica. Their 260-day ritual cycle was still central to Mesoamerican religion when Europeans arrived some 2500 years later. They also had a rudimentary writing, in the form of glyphs using dots and dashes. Although archaeologists have not succeeded in deciphering these symbols, they were probably calendar notations.

Another very important cultural innovation that apparently developed in various parts of Mesoamerica during the later stages of the Olmec era was the tortilla. Although Mesoamericans had eaten maize for several millennia, it was in the form of roasted ears or a gruel known as *atole,* both of which were perishable and not easily portable. Production of tortillas–grinding the maize and shaping it into flat pancakes and toasting them on a ceramic griddle called a *comal*–was highly intensive labor, usually performed by women. And tortillas, unlike atole and roasted ears of corn, lasted for several days and were easily transported. Archaeologists surmise that they served as a convenient "fast food" for merchants or armies in transit and may have had a significant impact on the economic and political transformation of Mesoamerica.

Whether or not the Olmec in fact were the originators of Mesoamerican culture, they maintained extensive contact with their contemporaries as far south as El Salvador. Olmec influences are especially apparent at sites located at strategic points on ancient trade routes. Some of their jade came from the state of Guerrero in western Mexico, and they acquired obsidian from Oaxaca in the south. Evidence has been found of an Olmec colony at Chalcatzingo in Morelos, just south of modern-day Mexico City, dating from about 900 B.C.E.

Ancient Mesoamerica

Chavín de Huantar in Peru

At about the same time that Olmec civilization was developing in Mesomerica, the Andes entered a new cultural phase with the rise of the ceremonial site known as Chavín de Huantar, located in northern Peru at an altitude of more than 9000 feet. Established in the tenth century B.C.E., Chavín reached its peak between 400 and 200 B.C.E. Like San Lorenzo and La Venta in Mexico, it served primarily as a center of religious observances, with a resident population that never surpassed 3000. It stood at the juncture of natural travel routes in the Andes, and pilgrims from a wide area came to consult its oracle and attend religious rituals held at its Old Temple. This structure contained more than 1600 feet of internal drainage and ventilation ducts. Water draining through the canals must have produced impressive acoustic effects to enhance its aura. An interior staircase enabled priests to emerge at the top of the mound. The temple complex formed a "U" shape, with the open end facing the rising sun in the east. A sunken courtyard in front of the temple was large enough to hold 500 people. Best known of its monuments is the Lanzón, a 15-foot-high granite sculpture that combines human and feline features, perhaps reflecting the priests' belief that they could transform themselves into jaguars. Religious observances at Chavín evidently employed hallucinogens, intoxicants, ritual cannibalism, and sacrificial offerings of llamas and guinea pigs.

Material culture at Chavín suggests the importance of long-distance trade. Chavín art features images of snakes, jaguars, caymans, and other jungle fauna, as well as tropical crops such as manioc and peanuts, suggesting contact with the Amazon basin east of the Andes. Luxury items found at Chavín include lapis lazuli from as far away as the Atacama Desert of northern Chile and cinnabar (mercuric sulphide, which produces a brilliant red dye), probably from the mountains of southern Peru. Large strombus shells from coastal Ecuador were fashioned into trumpets used in religious ceremonies. The people of Chavín used tools made of obsidian, obtained from more than 250 miles away. These items and goods such as coca, chile peppers, salt, and dried fish were carried to Chavín on the backs of llamas.

Artisans at Chavín were well known for their expertise and innovation in textile design. They combined llama and alpaca hairs with cotton fibers and wove them into fabric. Their tapestries and other textiles featured multicolored designs, some of them painted on and others achieved through techniques similar to tie-dyeing and batik. Metalworkers at Chavín learned soldering techniques and produced silver, gold, and copper alloys. They were evidently the first to craft three-dimensional objects from metal. Like the Olmec sites, Chavín exerted cultural influence over a wide area along the coast of Peru and in the highlands as well. Pilgrims visiting the shrine probably brought ritual and utilitarian objects home with them, providing models that could be replicated by artisans who had never been to Chavín.

After 200 B.C.E., the Chavín cult began to decline, perhaps because of widespread droughts. Building of monumental structures stopped throughout its sphere of cultural influence. Localized artistic designs replaced Chavín motifs on ceramics and other media. But the memory of Chavín de Huantar lived on. Sixteenth-century Spaniards marveled at the old temple, and a stone bridge that crossed the nearby Wachesqa River remained in use for nearly 3000 years, until a landslide destroyed it in 1945.

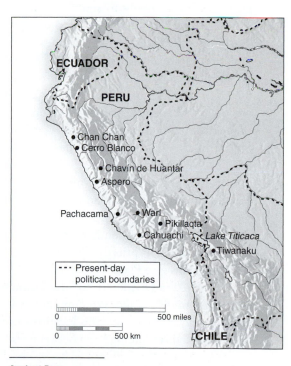

Ancient Peru

THE CITIES OF CLASSIC MESOAMERICA

The monumental public architecture of early Mesoamerica and the Andes served important ceremonial purposes, but sites such as San Lorenzo, La Venta, and Chavín de Huantar cannot be considered true cities, because their permanent populations remained small and probably consisted primarily of religious specialists and highly skilled artisans. In the latter half of the first millennium B.C.E., however, the size and occupational diversity of a few places in Mexico and Central America took on proportions that warrant their designation as genuine urban centers. Social hierarchies became more sharply defined, and systems of government began taking on the multiple layers of power and authority characteristic of modern states. The ascendancy of these centers inaugurated a 1000-year epoch known as the Classic Period.

Monte Albán

The first of these great population centers was Monte Albán, just outside the present-day city of Oaxaca in southern Mexico. Founded by the Zapotec people in about 500 B.C.E. at the center of the three-pronged Valley of Oaxaca, the city dominated the surrounding area for more than 1000 years. Archaeologists theorize that Monte Albán owed its existence to the deliberate decision of valley settlements to establish a capital on a neutral site, perhaps for defensive purposes but more likely to settle disputes among themselves. In this respect, Monte Albán has been compared to newly created modern capitals such as Washington, D.C., or Brasilia. Nobles from communities throughout the valley took up residence at Monte Albán.

By about 250 B.C.E. the city's population reached 15,000, and at its height in the sixth century C.E. it was home to as many as 25,000 people. These figures are, of course, rough estimates based on surveys of structures that, in their design or the distribution of artifacts found within them, suggest they served as dwellings for "ordinary" households. Archaeologists have discovered what they believe are 15 separate residential subdivisions at Monte Albán, many of them situated on carefully created terraces on the sides of mountains. The city's main ceremonial structures sat atop an artificially flattened mountain that towered 1300 feet above the Valley of Oaxaca. They include a pyramid with an internal staircase leading to the top, numerous sacrificial altars, a ball court, and palaces that probably housed its priestly elite. A defensive wall protected the city on its north and west sides (see Plate 3).

Monte Albán evidently collected tribute in the form of food and other supplies from many smaller communities in Oaxaca. Hieroglyphics adorning the palaces may refer to specific locations under its dominion. One of its most famous structures, dating from between 500 and 250 B.C.E., is the Palacio de los

Danzantes (Palace of the Dancers), named for the 150 bas-reliefs of naked, contorted male figures that adorn its exterior walls. Archaeologists now believe that these images represent not dancers but rather prisoners captured in battle, perhaps being tortured, or the corpses of sacrificial victims. The hundreds of stelae (pillars carved with hieroglyphics) found at the site show Zapotec rulers standing on symbols said to stand for conquered territories, also suggesting that their influence spread through military force.

Archaeologists have explored nearly 200 Zapotec tombs at Monte Albán. These enclosures have highly decorated entranceways covered with hieroglyphics, and frescoes can be found on some of their interior walls. One particularly impressive tomb features the Zapotec god of maize wearing an elaborate headdress of serpents and feathers. Pottery funeral urns and lavish grave offerings can be found in many of the tombs.

There are many signs of Olmec influence or cultural kinship. The facial features of the "dancers" depicted on the Palacio de los Danzantes resemble Olmec styles. The people of Monte Albán used a form of glyphs, probably associated with calendrical signs and the 260-day ritual calendar, that again are reminiscent of the Olmec. But they built on cultural traditions closer to home as well. A site known as San José Mogote flourished in the northern branch of the Valley of Oaxaca between 1350 and 500 B.C.E. Its archaeological remains feature figures similar to the danzantes.

Monte Albán's decline set in after 600 C.E., as it lost access to merchandise coming from the great central Mexican city of Teotihuacan (see below) and the Zapotec rulers could no longer use these commodities to buy the loyalty of chiefs from other valley communities. By the year 700 C.E., the population of Monte Albán had shrunk to about 4000, and the political unity of the valley fragmented.

Teotihuacan

Meanwhile, urban centers on an even grander scale arose in the Valley of Mexico, not far from today's Mexico City. Cuicuilco, at the southwestern edge of the valley, grew in population to more than 10,000 by 300 B.C.E., but its continued development was interrupted around 50 B.C.E., when volcanic eruptions destroyed the agricultural lands on which it depended and created the lava beds that residents of Mexico City today call the *pedregal.* Cuicuilco's decline opened the way for the city that centuries later the Aztecs would call Teotihuacan, "the place of the gods," to dominate the entire valley. Teotihuacan's population had already topped 40,000 by 100 B.C.E. At its peak 600 years later, it had well over 100,000, and by some accounts as many as 200,000 residents, making it one of the largest cities anywhere in the world at the time. Its ethnically diverse population included a colony of Oaxacans and another of people from Veracruz. At least a third of the city's residents worked at pursuits other than farming.

Teotihuacan is today one of Mexico's leading tourist attractions, and justifiably so. The city's territorial expanse covered about 12 square miles, and everything about it was of monumental proportions. It had about six hundred pyramids, including the massive Pyramid of the Sun, more than 215 feet high and measuring half a million square feet at its base, as well as the smaller but equally impressive Pyramid of the Moon. The central promenade, now called the Street of the Dead, is 150 feet wide and more than 2 miles long. More than 100 palaces housed priests and other dignitaries.

The facades of the Pyramids of the Sun and Moon were once covered with brightly colored stucco designs. Another exquisitely decorated structure, the Temple of Quetzalcoatl, bears carved images of both the feathered serpent deity found at many Mesoamerican sites and another identified as the rain god. Pilgrims evidently came from great distances to participate in rituals at Teotihuacan. The city was a haven of artisan and mercantile activity, with a huge market complex and hundreds of workshops for the manufacture of ceramics and obsidian tools.

Archaeologists speculate that about 2000 apartment complexes, laid out on a grid pattern and dating from the fourth century C.E., housed the city's working population. Excavations of these compounds have given us a glimpse of everyday life in Teotihuacan. Household artifacts include numerous comales, so the preparation and consumption of tortillas was evidently common. Cooking of other foods was done on small braziers, probably in open-air patios scattered throughout the apartment structures. Also found within the residences were numerous incense burners and ceramic figurines, suggesting that religious rituals were part of the domestic routine.

Although scholars once depicted Mesoamerica's Classic Period as a "golden age" of peace and artistic advance, it is now clear that Teotihuacan used military force to extend its influence throughout central Mexico. Large numbers of men were conscripted into its armies. Military motifs appear in murals and ceramics with increasing frequency, especially after 650 C.E. Soldiers from Teotihuacan were evidently the first Mesoamericans to use the type of quilted cotton body armor—as much as 2 or 3 inches thick—that Aztec armies wore when they confronted the Spanish in the sixteenth century. Enemies captured in battle became sacrificial victims. Mass human sacrifices marked the dedication of the Temple of Quetzalcoatl around 150 C.E. Their corpses were buried beneath the pyramid, along with their military accoutrements. It is likely too that some of the city's spectacular population growth can be attributed to the forced relocation of conquered peoples.

Teotihuacan's cultural and economic influence spread even further than its military reach, thanks to its monopoly on obsidian, the sharpest material known to Americans before the introduction of European steel. Its trade networks extended to what is now the southwestern United States and southward to Central America. At the Maya highland center of Kaminaljuyu in Guatemala, many public buildings dating from the early sixth century resembled structures found at Teotihuacan. The art and architecture of Monte Albán also show Teotihuacan influences, and the Zapotec elites became fond of luxury goods imported from the north.

By the sixth century C.E., Teotihuacan evidently began losing population, and ultimately it suffered a fate similar to that of Monte Albán. The center of the city was destroyed and burned about 750, probably by its own people, though perhaps by semi-nomadic groups invading the valley from the north and west. The decline of Teotihuacan probably contributed to the demise of other Mesoamerican sites, whose elites lost access to the goods they had obtained from the great city in the valley of Mexico.

Following the collapse of Teotihuacan, a substantial portion of its population dispersed throughout central Mexico. As many as 30,000 residents remained in place for years to come, but the days of Teotihuacan's glory had clearly passed. Several hundred years later, however, the Aztecs believed that a race of giants had lived there, and that it had been the birthplace of the "fifth sun," the universe as they knew it.

Maya Civilization in the Classic Era

The lowland rainforests of southern Mexico, Guatemala, Honduras, and Belize witnessed the rise of another great civilization of the Classic Era, the Maya, beginning in the third century B.C.E. and peaking about 1000 years later. One of the Mayas' greatest cultural achievements was the development of a true system of writing. While other early American peoples used pictorial symbols that sometimes came to stand for abstract ideas and occasionally even sounds, Classic Mayan writing is phonetic—that is, many of the glyphs we see on their carved stone monuments, and in their few surviving books, stood for sounds. The Maya could record the spoken word far more accurately than any other pre-Columbian civilization. Their writing system was, in the words of Maya scholars Linda Schele and David Freidel, "a rich and expressive script, capable of faithfully recording every nuance of sound, meaning, and grammatical structure in the writers' language."

Over the last few decades, archaeologists and art historians have succeeded in deciphering close to 90 percent of the Mayan glyphs. Many Mayan writings record the genealogies of local ruling classes, and the Maya are the earliest Americans for whom we can identify specific individuals and exact dates. For individuals such as Pacal, lord of Palenque in southern Mexico, we can reconstruct full biographies and genealogies. But Mayan script also reveals much about religious rituals and the lives of warriors and artisans as well as kings and queens.

LATIN AMERICAN LIVES

PACAL THE GREAT, KING OF PALENQUE, 603–683 C.E.

PALENQUE (THE WORD COMES from the Spanish word for stockade) in the southern Mexican state of Chiapas is one of the most frequently visited Mayan sites. Situated on the western fringe of the Mayas' cultural sphere, it rose to prominence during the final two centuries of the Classic Era by extending its influence over the surrounding region through military conquest and marriage alliances with local rulers. References to Palenque at Tikal, and to Tikal at Palenque, show a particularly strong connection between these two great Mayan cities. Palenque's most distinctive building, a palace that evidently served as an administrative center and a residence for members of its ruling elite, features a four-story square tower that commanded a stunning view of the city's environs. Archaeologists have found a glyph representing the planet Venus on one of the tower's interior walls, suggesting that it also functioned as an observatory.

Palenque reached its peak in the seventh century, during the reign of King Pacal the Great. Pacal received the throne in 615 from his mother, Queen Zac-kuk, and ruled for nearly 70 years until his death in 683. Painted relief sculptures on many of Palenque's structures chronicle his genealogy and the elaborate rituals that accompanied his funeral. When Pacal was about 70 years old, work began on the Temple of the Inscriptions, the pyramid that would eventually serve as his tomb. Among its carved images is one depicting Pacal's passage from this world to the next.

An interior staircase led from the summit of the Temple of the Inscriptions to Pacal's subterranean crypt. There he was entombed in great splendor, along with half a dozen people sacrificed as part of his funeral rites. His corpse was adorned with a collar, headpiece, earspools, rings, and bracelets all made of jade. A mask fashioned from jade, shells, and obsidian covered his face. These and other goods interred with him can today be seen at Mexico City's famous Museum of Anthropology and History. His sarcophagus and the walls of his tomb featured likenesses of Pacal, his mother, and his oldest son and successor Chan Bahlum ("Serpent Jaguar"). These images suggest that in death and perhaps in life Pacal had come to be identified with the Sun god and that his mother was the mother of all the gods.

Great construction projects and important architectural innovations continued during the reign of Chan Bahlum, which officially began 132 days after Pacal's death and continued until the year 702. Especially worthy of note is the Temple of the Cross, built to commemorate Chan Bahlum's accession to the throne. It too contained images of Pacal, again showing him as the Sun god, and the passing of royal authority from father to son. The temple was positioned so that light struck these images only at sunset on the day of the winter solstice.

The builders of the Temple of the Cross intended that Pacal's rule would be remembered for many years to come. Pacal himself probably encouraged them to think in this way, for he left an inscription proclaiming that his successors would celebrate the anniversary of his coronation eight days following the end of the Mayan calendar's 8000-year cycle. In our calendar, that day will come more than 2700 years from now, on October 15, 4772.

Questions for Discussion

How did King Pacal use monumental architecture to enhance his own power? How do you think Mayan commoners would have responded to these building projects? Is there evidence that the rulers of other communities discussed in this chapter used similar methods of promoting themselves?

Mayan civilization had no single dominant center comparable to Teotihuacan or Monte Albán. Instead, there were more than 50 politically autonomous but interdependent city-states, each drawing tribute from a hinterland that probably extended no more than a day's travel distance from the center. With a population that neared 50,000, Tikal in Guatemala was one of the largest and most powerful Mayan cities, and one of its most spectacular as well. It boasted several artificial lakes and the tallest known Classic Mayan structure, at 230 feet. Its ruling dynasty was established in 219 C.E. Copán in Honduras may have had a sphere of influence comparable in size to Tikal. Glyphs referring to Tikal have been found at Copán, and vice versa, indicting that the two cities had considerable contact with one another.

Each separate Mayan polity had its *ahau,* or king, and nobility, and these upper classes lived in style. In the summer of 2000, archaeologists discovered a splendid palace at Cancuén in Guatemala. Before the excavations began, it resembled a hill covered with dense jungle foliage. The absence of visible pyramids at the site caused previous researchers to overlook it. Covering an area larger than two present-day United States football fields, the structure contained 170 rooms and 11 courtyards. Inscriptions date the palace from the reign of King Tah ak Chaan, who ruled at Cancuén from 740 to 790 C.E. Even Cancuén's commoners were relatively well off, as evidenced by the many objects of jade found in their graves. Archaeological finds at Palenque show that the burial places of Mayan kings were lavish.

Scholars once thought that the Mayan city-states lived in relative harmony with one another, but the images on their monuments suggest otherwise. Recent research has shown that Tikal and the city of Calakmul, some 60 miles to the north, engaged in a protracted conflict, with smaller communities often serving as pawns in this contest of Mayan superpowers. Brilliantly colored murals at Bonampak in Chiapas, Mexico, show captives taken in battle undergoing torture (see Plate 1). The ruling classes of the city-states cemented alliances with one another through marriage, but resorted to warfare when such tactics failed. Fighting evidently consisted of small-scale raids of one community against another, for the jungle terrain of lowland Mesoamerica prohibited the movement of the large armies fielded by highland centers such as Teotihuacan. The extent of warfare among the Classic Maya nonetheless remains subject to debate. The palace of Cancuén, for example, shows no evidence that its rulers engaged in war.

Most lowland Mayan communities had similar resource bases, so trade was not particularly important in their relations with one another. Glyphs at Tikal and other locations suggest that they did carry on long-distance exchanges with Teotihuacan, however. Obsidian from central Mexico and Teotihuacan-type pottery have also been found at numerous Mayan sites, including the kingdom of Kaminaljuyu. The people of Cancuén evidently derived a significant portion of their wealth by serving as intermediaries in the obsidian trade. In exchange, the Maya exported slaves, feathers, chocolate, and animal skins.

The Maya excelled in mathematics, using a system based on units of 20. They were apparently the first people to develop the concept of zero–the Hindus began employing the zero in their calculations in the fifth century C.E., while Europeans learned it from the Arabs some 800 years later. The Maya had both a 365-day solar calendar and a 260-day ceremonial calendar. They reckoned time in millions of years. Centuries later, by contrast, most Europeans saw the world as no more than 6000 years old. Their knowledge of astronomy was also considerably ahead of that of Europe at the time. Craft specialists, including jewelers, featherworkers, painters, carvers, and sculptors, could be found in the larger centers. Most Mayan sites featured ball courts. The murals at Bonampak show that the Maya were also musicians, using drums, rattles made from tortoise shells and gourds, and trumpets, flutes, and whistles made from shell, bone, or wood.

Blood-letting was an important part of religious observance for many Mesoamericans. The woman kneeling on the right side of this Mayan stone relief is pulling a thorny cord through her tongue.

A volcanic eruption that occurred about 600 C.E. near Cerén in present-day El Salvador left a Mayan village buried in ash. Recent excavations have uncovered homes, a steam bath, and a civic center, giving archaeologists a rare glimpse of how ordinary men, women, and children lived and worked in Classic times. The people of Cerén evidently lived in nuclear family households. In gardens next to their dwellings, they grew manioc, medicinal plants, and the agave cactus that yielded fiber that could be fashioned into textiles. Storage facilities contained large quantities of beans and other seeds, and strings of chile peppers hung from the rafters of their houses. Their diet also included maize and a fermented beverage made from it, as well as squash, avocados, and chocolate, and the meat of deer, dogs, and other animals. Artifacts found in village homes included *metates* used for grinding maize and sharp obsidian blades. Households had large numbers of ceramic pots for cooking, storing, and serving food.

Mayan city-states suffered a devastating collapse beginning around 800 C.E. Building of temples and carving of stelae halted, abruptly in many centers, more gradually in others. Construction ceased at Tikal after 830, and the last carved date at Palenque is 799. The ceremonial cores of many cities were abandoned to squatters, and the populations of major sites such as Tikal shrank by as much as 90 percent.

Numerous factors have been cited to explain the decline of the Classic Mayan sites. A likely hypothesis points to accelerated population growth and resulting food shortages. Competition for scarce resources in turn exacerbated conflicts among city-states and between working classes and privileged elites. In particular, the conflict between Tikal and Calakmul seems to have contributed substantially to the collapse of many Mayan centers. Intrusions from central Mexico may have further upset an already delicate ecological balance. The deterioration of trade links with Teotihuacan probably also played a role.

PERU AFTER CHAVÍN

The cultural unity fostered by the cult of Chavín de Huantar fragmented in the second century B.C.E. Within two centuries, however, new regional centers emerged, more urban in their population size, economic diversity, and social stratification than Chavín. A number of these cities extended their cultural influence and political control over wide areas. The methods they used to dominate growing populations included warfare, intermarriage with local elites, and political tactics that clearly foreshadowed those later adopted by the Incas. Archaeological sites from this period show growing numbers of fortified villages and defensive bastions stocked with stones that could be hurled at approaching enemies.

The Moche

Contemporaries of the builders of Teotihuacan in Mexico, the warlike people known to archaeologists as the Moche built South America's most important societies during this period. The Moche inhabited the river valleys along the arid north coast of Peru. Their influence extended for more than 300 miles, and eventually over a population that ranged in the hundreds of thousands. Scholars once thought that some kind of centralized empire controlled the entire area, but recent work suggests that at least two separate political entities existed. The Moche people were excellent engineers, building impressive public works, such as flat-topped pyramid mounds, fortresses, roads, and complex irrigation works. They enhanced the productivity of their agriculture by fertilizing their fields with bird guano, a substance that became an important export from Peru in the nineteenth century.

Two of the most impressive ceremonial structures of their society, the Huaca del Sol and the Huaca de la Luna, can be found at a site known as Cerro Blanco. Building of these works began around 100 C.E. and continued for several centuries. The largest structure in the Western Hemisphere for its time, the Huaca del Sol measured 500 by 1000 feet at its base and was 130 feet high. It probably served as a palace and a mausoleum for deceased rulers. Some 143 million molded adobe bricks were used in its construction, many of them bearing an identifying symbol, perhaps signifying which group of people made the brick as part of their tribute obligation. The settlement surrounding these two structures may have housed as many as 10,000 people. Near the Huaca de la Luna, archaeologists have unearthed a pottery workshop dating from between 450 and 550 C.E.

The Moche lacked a system of writing comparable to that of the Maya. On

Moche pottery vessel showing a healer and patient.

the other hand, they were exceptionally skilled artists, producing splendid ceramics, carvings, and textiles, as well as highly detailed murals and friezes that tell us much about their society and ritual practices. A recurrent motif in Moche art is a deity that archaeologists call "the Decapitator," a fearsome fanged creature who holds a knife in one hand and a human head in the other. Further evidence of human sacrifice can be found at the Huaca de la Luna, where more than 40 skeletons of young men have been unearthed. Thick layers of sediment surrounding the corpses suggest that they were sacrificed during a time of excessive rainfall. Excavations of Moche tombs show that sacrifices of llamas and humans accompanied the burials of notable men and women.

Moche art also shows humans going about daily activities, from domestic routines, hunting and fishing, to sexual practices and childbirth, giving us some of the most detailed information that we have about gender roles in early American societies. Their portraits of sick people are so realistic that we can even specify their ailments, and we can see detailed drawings of medicinal plants used to treat them. The Moche left images of the elaborate costumes and fine jewelry worn by nobles on ritual occasions, a feature confirmed by rich caches of gold, silver, and copper ornaments and jewelry made from Chilean lapis lazuli found in Moche tombs (see Plate 2). Indeed, the Moche were expert metalworkers, mastering the art of casting objects such as tools and weapons from molds. Moche society began its decline between 600 and 750 C.E., due at least in part to drastic climatic fluctuations, as severe drought alternated with devastating floods that destroyed homes, monuments, and irrigation works.

The Nazca

Contemporaries of the Moche, the Nazca flourished for several hundred years in five separate river valleys along the southern coast of Peru, probably under the aegis of a small-scale confederacy. Their environment was even drier than that of the Moche, and they too excelled in hydraulic engineering. In the sixth century C.E., they constructed elaborate aqueducts that enabled them to tap underground streams. Remnants of this system continued to be used down to the twentieth century. Their most famous shrine, known as Cahuachi, was located where the Nazca River surfaced after flowing underground for a considerable distance. Pilgrims came from afar to worship and to bury their dead during the period of Cahuachi's ascendancy, from about 100 to 500 C.E.

The importance of water to the Nazca can be seen in their geoglyphs, the archaeological feature for which they are best known today. These were large designs, often measuring five or more miles in length, traced on the desert plains north of the Nazca River. Still visible from the air today, and perhaps originally intended to be visible to the sky gods, the geoglyphs depict animals, people, and abstract shapes. The Nazca made these markings by scraping away the layer of manganese and iron oxides that covered the ground, so that the lighter-colored soil below could be seen. Scholars once thought that the geoglyphs were aligned with astronomical phenomena, and some people have even seen them as evidence of extraterrestrial contact. Recent research has suggested that the markings pointed to sources of water. One clearly visible line leads from Cahuachi to what appears to have been their most important settlement.

One example of the Nazca lines.

The Nazca were expert artisans as well. They excelled in textile production, using alpaca fiber obtained via trade with the highlands as well as cotton grown along the coast. Their textile designs often featured fibers dyed in many shades of the same color. Nazca pottery also employed many different colors. Given the harsh climate of their homeland, the Nazca failed to achieve the population densities of their contemporaries in Mesoamerica or elsewhere in Peru, and their temple mounds and other architectural achievements were more modest in size.

Tiwanaku

Meanwhile, other important centers of South American civilization were developing at much higher inland elevations. One of the foremost of these was Tiwanaku, near Lake Titicaca in present-day Bolivia. Founded in about 250 B.C.E. at an altitude of almost 13,000 feet above sea level, it flourished between 100 and 1200 C.E., extending its influence to southern Peru, coastal Chile, and eastern Bolivia through trade and military conquest. At its peak, the city of Tiwanaku covered more than 1000 acres and had a population estimated at between 20,000 and 40,000.

Tiwanaku's most imposing buildings were erected between 100 and 700 C.E. The structures were fitted together without mortar in a manner later copied by the Incas, using large stones transported across Lake Titicaca by boat. The principal ceremonial center sat on an island surrounded by an artificially created moat separating it from the rest of the city. Soil that was dug up to form the moat was then used to create a cross-shaped multi-level platform known as the shrine of Akapana. From its summit, one could see Lake Titicaca and the surrounding mountains that were sacred sites in local religion. Subterranean and surface drainage channels drew water away from the platform and may have produced sound effects similar to those created at Chavín de Huantar many centuries before.

The people of Tiwanaku excelled in weaving, pottery, bone carving, and masonry. Brightly colored stucco designs adorned the walls of ceremonial buildings and the palaces of the elite. One of its most impressive monuments was a 24-foot-high sandstone carving of an elaborately dressed human figure representing either a god or a ruler that today stands in a plaza in La Paz, capital of Bolivia. Tiwanaku's rulers evidently exacted labor from conquered provinces in order to build these structures, much as the Incas would later do.

Extensive irrigation works and raised fields made the area surrounding Tiwanaku far more fertile than it is today. People also herded llamas and alpacas and harvested fish and aquatic plants from the lake. Colonies established in outlying areas from southern Peru to eastern Bolivia gave them access to chile peppers, coca leaves, and other produce from different ecological niches. Long-distance trade extended southward to the Atacama Desert in coastal Chile, 500 miles away. Deteriorating environmental conditions, most notably reduced rainfall after about 950 C.E., contributed to the eventual decline of Tiwanaku. The city was abandoned by the year 1200.

The Wari Empire

The sixth century C.E. witnessed the rise of the Wari Empire, centered near today's city of Ayacucho in Peru and eventually extending over 400 miles to the north, southeastward to the plateau around Cuzco, and to the Moche and Nazca areas on the coast. Its capital city, also called Wari, was located 430 miles northwest of Tiwanaku. It served as both a ceremonial center and an administrative hub, and housed as many as 35,000 residents–perhaps even more–who lived in large rectangular compounds separated by narrow streets. Some archaeologists have suggested that Wari began as a colony of Tiwanaku and later asserted its independence. In any event, there is evidence of significant cultural contact between the two cities. The people of Wari also maintained ties with Pachacama, an important pilgrimage site on the coast, dedicated to the god Pachacamac, that flourished between 800 and 1000 C.E.

The rulers of Wari employed administrative tactics later used so effectively by the Incas. They used *quipus* (knotted cords) to record and transmit information, relocated subject peoples to consolidate their dominions, established centralized control over agricultural production, ordered the terracing of mountainsides to increase the amount of land under cultivation, and maintained large storehouses for maize and other essential commodities. A network of roads, with rest stops at strategic points along the way, linked its various provincial capitals.

Archaeological research at the Wari outpost of Pikillaqta suggests that Wari administrators put the local population to work in return for providing them with food. A separate barracks at Pikillaqta was evidently reserved for female workers who prepared *chicha* (maize beer) and other foods consumed on ritual occasions. Like Tiwanaku, the Wari empire began its decline about the year 850, when its capital was abruptly abandoned.

MESOAMERICA AND PERU, 900–1400 C.E.

Following the collapse of the Classic centers in Mesoamerica and the Tiwanaku and Wari empires in the Andes, both regions entered a period of political instability that ended only with the spectacular rise of the Aztecs and the Incas 500 years later. The political turmoil of the times was accompanied by increased warfare and mounting human sacrifice. New cities appeared, but they were generally smaller, controlled less territory, and lasted for shorter periods of time than those that preceded them. For several centuries, the pace of cultural and technical advance slowed as well, with the notable exception of metalworkers in Mexico and Central America, who finally caught up with their South American counterparts. Mesoamericans also continued their practice of recording their histories and genealogies in symbols carved in stone or painted on animal skins, so we are able to identify even more specific individuals from these centuries than from the Classic Era.

The Toltecs

Following the fall of Teotihuacan, many groups migrated into central Mexico from the north and west. Native histories characterized them as warlike hunter-gatherers who gradually adopted the more civilized lifestyles they encountered as they settled in their new homes. The Toltecs, builders of the city of Tula some 50 miles from Teotihuacan, were among the most prominent of these migrant groups. Their rise to prominence began sometime after the year 800 C.E., especially under the leadership of the legendary ruler Mixcoatl. Tula was evidently settled by refugees from Teotihuacan as well, reaching a population estimated at between 35,000 and 60,000 at its peak. Tula's urban planning was far less sophisticated than that of Teotihuacan, however.

Tula's dominance, like that of Teotihuacan before it, rested in part on its command of the obsidian trade, but warfare also contributed heavily to its success. Toltec militarism is evident in a series of carved stone warriors over 15 feet tall that can still be seen at Tula today. Murals painted on the walls of Toltec tem-

Stone warrior statues at Tula.

ples also depicted legions of soldiers ready for battle. Skull racks and stone figures holding basins thought to be receptacles for human hearts suggest that
human sacrifice figured prominently in their ceremonial life.

The cult of the more peaceful plumed serpent god Quetzalcoatl assumed
great importance at Tula as well. Quetzalcoatl apparently demanded only sacrifices of flowers and butterflies instead of the bloody offerings made to most other
Mesoamerican deities. Mixcoatl's son and successor Ce Acatl was an ardent
devotee and eventually assumed the god's name for himself. Mesoamerican legend holds that his political enemies overthrew him and expelled him from Tula
sometime in the late tenth century. He reportedly headed east, and some
accounts say that he headed across the sea. Others hold that he and his supporters ended up in Yucatán, and many signs of Toltec cultural influence there
tend to support this hypothesis.

Tula collapsed in the twelfth century, again for reasons disputed by specialists, and its population dispersed to other towns throughout the valley. But its

cultural influence extended not only to Yucatán, but also south to Guatemala. The Toltecs' fame and legacy endured throughout central Mexico down to the eve of the Spanish conquest. Later societies, especially the Aztecs, credited them with great cultural and technical achievements, from the development of maize cultivation to the ability to cultivate cotton that came in many colors, although in fact they merely borrowed what previous societies had developed. The highest compliment that an Aztec artist could receive was that he or she worked "like a Toltec." For centuries, ruling dynasties in city-states throughout central Mexico legitimized their position by marrying into families that claimed to be descended from the kings of Tula.

The Mixtecs of Oaxaca

The Mixtecs became the dominant people in Oaxaca in the Post-Classic period, eventually occupying such important Zapotec sites as Monte Albán and Mitla. They were among the first peoples of Mesoamerica to master the art of metallurgy, crafting exquisite gold jewelry. The Mixtecs also produced fine carvings in wood and bone and beautiful mosaics that adorned their buildings at Mitla, but they are best remembered for the brilliantly colored pictorial "books" they composed on deerskins, some of which record events as far back as 692 C.E. Eight of these codices have survived.

These sources chronicle the political history of various communities in Oaxaca and the genealogy of their rulers. We learn, for example, that between the years 963 and 979 a period of conflict known as the War of Heaven followed the decline of Monte Albán. The codices document the reign of a king that archaeologists call 8 Deer, lord of Tilantongo, located directly northwest of today's city of Oaxaca. His rise to prominence began in 1097. Eventually, he conquered at least 75 cities, including Monte Albán, and imposed his control over a wide area that included highland and coastal settlements. His reign ended with his assassination in 1115, but Tilantongo remained one of Oaxaca's most important kingdoms for more than two centuries thereafter. Toltec influences, including the adoption of the calendar used at Tula, have been attributed to links with the central Mexico established during 8 Deer's reign.

The Post-Classic Maya

During the Classic Period, as we have seen, Mayan civilization flourished in Central America, especially in Guatemala and the southern Mexican state of Chiapas. The Yucatán peninsula, though long inhabited by Mayan peoples, had comparatively few great population centers in Classic times. In the Post-Classic period, however, Yucatán flourished. Its most important city-state was Chichen Itza, but many others also rose to prominence.

The Yucatec Mayan cities had considerable contact with central Mexico in Post-Classic times. Many authorities believe that Chichen Itza and other sites were taken over by invading Toltecs following the fall of Tula, and that these conquerors joined the Itza (Mayan groups from outside Yucatán) in exercising political control over much of the peninsula. Other scholars suggest that central Mexican influences spread to Yucatán primarily through trade. In any event, there are many signs of Toltec cultural influence at Chichen Itza. The layout of the city itself resembles Tula's, and its great pyramid, known as the Castillo, was dedicated to Kulkulkan, the Mayan name for the feathered serpent of central Mexico. Warlike motifs reminiscent of Tula can also be found in its art and architecture.

Human sacrifice, though certainly not new in Mayan society, played an important role in Post-Classic ceremonial life. Skull racks similar to those of central Mexico can be found at Chichen Itza. The remains of sacrificial victims were thrown into *cenotes,* the deep sinkholes that mark the limestone surface of Yucatán, along with numerous objects made of gold and copper. There is substantial evidence that the huge cenote at Chichen Itza continued to be the site of sacrificial ceremonies down to the sixteenth century.

Like their forebears, the Post-Classic Maya were great astronomers. One of the few surviving pre-hispanic Mayan documents, the so-called Dresden Codex dating from the thirteenth century, contains an elaborate chart of the cycles of Venus. The traditional Mayan calendar and hieroglyphic writing also survived into the Post-Classic Period. Trade contacts with lowland Mayan regions as far south as Honduras also continued. Most of the gold ornaments found in great abundance in the cenote at Chichen Itza probably came from Central America.

After about 1200, Chichen Itza's dominance of its neighboring city-states ended. For the next 200 years, the city of Mayapán held sway over much of Yucatán. Although some of its architectural features resemble those found at Chichen Itza, everything was on a much smaller scale, and there is little evidence of any great artistic or technical breakthroughs during the late Post-Classic Period. By the time the Spaniards arrived in the early sixteenth century, Mayapán's control of the surrounding area had deteriorated, and no other town had succeeded in imposing political unity on the peninsula.

Peru After Tiwanaku and Wari

Like Post-Classic Mesoamerica, Peru experienced growing political instability and warfare from about 1000 to 1400, following the collapse of Tiwanaku and Wari. Throughout this period a series of regional states vied with one another for power, and the coast again surpassed the highlands in political sophistication and artistic creativity. Many archaeological sites dating from this period once

Slice of Life   THE CRAFT WORKERS
OF CHAN CHAN, 1400 C.E.

THE CHIMU KINGDOM OF COASTAL PERU was especially noted for its hand-icrafts, which included weaving, woodworking, and metalworking. At the capital city of Chan Chan and at numerous provincial centers, Chimu arti-sans wove carpets, wall hangings, and other textiles from cotton and alpaca wool. They also manufactured intricate wood carvings with copper inlays, as well as needles, tweezers, and other utilitarian goods made of copper. By the last century prior to the Inca conquest, Chimu leaders and bureaucrats supervised the mass production of these goods, which were then distributed throughout their dominions.

The artisans of Chan Chan may have numbered 20,000 or more by the year 1400 of the European calendar. Archaeologists speculate Chimu rulers forcibly recruited craftspeople from conquered provinces and sent them to Chan Chan. Metalworkers from the Lambeyeque River Valley in northern Peru, for example, were probably relocated following the Chimu conquest of the valley in the late 1300s. Wealth derived from the production of hand-icrafts supported most of Chan Chan's elite.

Excavations at Chan Chan have revealed something of the lifestyle of these highly skilled men and women who wore distinctive ear ornaments to denote their special standing in Chimu society. They were evidently full-time craft workers dependent on sources outside the city for their food. They specialized in a particular line of work. The artisans lived in their own sections of the city and their remains were buried at sites apart from those of the general populace. Each nuclear family had its own living quarters, complete with a kitchen, stor-age areas, and workspace. At home they did some of their work. Men proba-bly hammered sheet metal and women may have spun fiber into yarn. Other tasks were performed in workshops also located within the workers' com-pounds. Near the center of the city, archaeologists have unearthed structures that housed the transport workers who operated the llama caravans that car-ried goods to and from Chan Chan. These buildings could accommodate sev-eral hundred people and featured large communal kitchens. Huge storage facilities for raw materials and finished goods have also been excavated.

Craft production at Chan Chan ceased abruptly in 1465 when the Incas subjugated the Chimu. Many of the city's skilled workers were then taken to the Inca capital at Cuzco in the highlands. Evidently, they had no time to prepare for their journey. They left unfinished textiles, pots of food cooking on their hearths, and copper ingots on the floors of their workshops.

Questions for Discussion

What does the social status of these craft workers tell us about Chimu society? What can we learn about the everyday lives of the Chimu people from the kinds of goods these workers produced?

contained enormous caches of gold jewelry and precious stones, but they have been the targets of looters for several centuries.

One of the most important states to emerge along the coast was the Chimu kingdom, which began expanding from its base in northern Peru between 1150 and 1200. Eventually, its territory spanned some 625 miles from north to south. Like other Peruvian rulers both before and after them, the Chimu kings forced their subjects to perform labor for them and maintained satellite administrative centers throughout their sphere of dominance. They distributed luxury goods to local chieftains in an effort to secure and to keep their loyalty.

The people of Chimu were still around at the time of the Spanish conquest of Peru, and so our knowledge of them is based on observations of early conquistadors and missionaries as well as on the archaeological evidence. They displayed substantial cultural continuity with the Moche, who had occupied much of the same region centuries before. Elaborate irrigation works enabled them to flourish in the dry climate of the Peruvian coast. Their society was highly stratified, dominated by a hereditary nobility and kings who claimed to be divine. Theft and other offenses were harshly punished.

Chan Chan served as the capital of the Chimu kingdom. The city grew steadily as Chimu's power expanded. Each king evidently built himself a new palace complex at Chan Chan when he assumed the throne. By the year 1400, the city covered a territorial expanse of more than 24 square kilometers and boasted a population estimated at between 25,000 and 50,000. Chan Chan's glory days ended with its conquest by the Incas in 1465.

THE WORLD OF EARLY AMERICANS

For thousands of years after their ancestors unwittingly crossed the Bering Strait, the peoples of the Americas continually tested the potential of the many different physical environments they found as they migrated southward and eastward through North and South America. They hunted, fished, and gathered the fruits of the land, and in many places they domesticated plants and animals. They learned to make tools that lightened their labors and baskets and pottery to carry and store what they produced.

As these early Americans' ability to harness available natural resources grew, so too did the size and complexity of their communities. Some people could now devote a portion of their energies to pursuits other than providing for their own immediate subsistence. Leaders emerged who found ways to force or persuade others to work on construction projects requiring the coordinated labor of hundreds or thousands of people. Men and women also began to explore their creative potential, embellishing utilitarian objects like ceramics and textiles with designs and crafting jewelry to adorn their bodies. A select few spent their time probing the visible heavens and the worlds unseen that were the dwelling places of their gods.

Early Americans were open to new possibilities, willing to learn from people they encountered as they migrated from place to place. They readily exchanged material goods, subsistence techniques, strategies of warfare and governance, and philosophical ideas with one another. But they were also careful to conserve what their forebears had taught them about the best ways to meet the specific challenges of their local environment. This selective process of innovation and preservation produced a tremendous variety of cultures throughout the hemisphere.

People and Their Environment

Americans in the year 1400 of the European calendar had gone far beyond the simple quest for food that had lured their hunter-gatherer ancestors from Siberia to North America. They came to know the uses of thousands of plants that grew wild in the hemisphere's many different ecological zones. By lucky trial and tragic error they learned that some plants could satisfy their hunger and alleviate their ailments while others could make them sick or even kill them. They discovered other plants with stimulant or hallucinogenic properties—coca in South America, peyote in Mexico and what is now the southwestern United States, for example.

Over the course of thousands of years, early Americans also domesticated many plants. Little by little, they learned which plants yielded the highest caloric values for the amount of land and labor invested in production—hence the popularity of maize throughout much of the hemisphere and potatoes in the Andes. They also devised ways of preparing and preserving their food to maximize its nutritional value. Mesoamericans soaked their maize in water rich in lime, which provided a source of calcium and facilitated the absorption of protein from the beans that were another vital component of their diet. Peruvians learned to freeze-dry potatoes and other foods. Early Americans experimented with ways of seasoning food and learned to make intoxicating beverages, from the *balche* (made from honey and bark) of the Maya to the *pulque* (cactus beer) of the Mesoamericans and the maize beer, or chicha, favored by Andeans.

The natural environment, so full of possibilities to support human life, also posed challenges to the survival of the earliest Americans. Earthquakes and volcanic eruptions were ever-present threats from Mesoamerica southward through the Andes, while island and coastal peoples continually felt the devastating effects of tropical storms. Droughts lasting a single season or an entire generation could turn fertile fields to wasteland, while too much rain produced ruinous floods and landslides. The atmospheric phenomenon that today we call El Niño wreaked havoc on the lives of ancient Peruvians, bringing torrential downpours to areas that were normally very dry. Archeologists have attributed the decline of the Moche civilization to the effects of El Niño.

Everywhere the ancient Americans went, they left their mark on the physical landscape. Even the simple choice to domesticate certain plants at the expense of others altered the biosphere forever. In the forests of Brazil, they felled stands of virgin trees and cleared fields using slash and burn techniques in order to plant their crops. People living in more complex societies diverted streams for irrigation, terraced mountainsides to bring more land under cultivation, created artificial islands and lakes, and moved huge stones to build their palaces and pyramids.

Early Americans and Their Beliefs

The belief systems of ancient Americans focused heavily on survival—not so much that of the individual but definitely that of the community and the species. Success in hunting and gathering, agricultural abundance, pregnancy, and birth were all recurrent motifs in the ritual life of these societies. Human reproduction depended on the union of male and female, while soil and seed had to come together before plants would grow. Many societies attributed the origins of the world and the human species to some kind of union of opposing forces. Female deities figured heavily in the early American interpretations of the cosmos, as important as male gods and often even more so. Recent research has uncovered evidence of a state-sponsored cult to a goddess at Teotihuacan, for example.

As agricultural peoples, early Americans took careful note of the changing seasons and the movements of the celestial bodies that marked the passage of time. They devised increasingly sophisticated calendars and tracked constellations with growing precision. Many of their temples were carefully positioned to catch sunlight at a particular angle at a specific point in the solar year. Precisely at the moment of the spring and fall equinoxes, the sun strikes the edge of the principal pyramid at Chichen Itza in such a way that the light resembles a serpent running from the top of the pyramid to the bottom.

The Sun and the Moon became deities for many societies. The Moon was often female, probably because its monthly phases suggested a parallel with women's menstrual cycles, while the Sun was usually male. Gods associated with thunder, rain, and lightning were also typically male, while the Earth and particular crops, especially the all-important maize, were more often viewed as female. Many people associated mountains with clouds and rain, and some have speculated that ancient pyramids were meant to resemble mountains. For the fishing people along the Peruvian coast, the sea was a divine force, and fish and other forms of marine life figured prominently in their ritual art. Many societies believed that animals also possessed special powers, and motifs such as serpents and jaguars can be found at many archaeological sites.

Ancient Americans evidently saw themselves at the mercy of powerful supernatural forces that had to be appeased, often with sacrifices of human blood, in order to ward off droughts, plagues, earthquakes, and other calamities. Men and women who could communicate with and satisfy those powers occupied special places in their societies, and locations considered sacred to the gods and goddesses became ceremonial centers that often attracted pilgrims from great distances. Monuments constructed at these centers were designed to accommodate huge crowds. For example, a site on the Peruvian coast, built between 1100 and 850 B.C.E., featured a courtyard big enough for a standing-room audience of 65,000.

Early Americans were also concerned with what lay beyond the present, visible world. Rulers and other elites were buried in elaborate tombs, full of provisions for the journey to the afterlife and often the remains of servants specially sacrificed to accompany them. Concern for those who had gone before them can also be seen in the special care that many societies showed for the remains of their ancestors. In the Andes, people developed the practice of artificially mummifying their dead as early as 5000 B.C.E.

Communities, States, and War

The communities that early Americans formed varied in size and complexity, from small hunting bands with no fixed residence to huge, planned urban centers like Teotihuacan. Some people considered themselves part of communities that were not even comprised of contiguous spaces. In Peru, kinship groups secured access to land at a variety of different elevations in order to obtain food and other resources from many different microclimates. As communities grew in size, so too did the degree of social stratification—the differences in status, wealth, and power among people in the community. The cooperative, kin-based sharing of labor and resources characteristic of hunting bands and small villages gave way to coercive systems that allowed some people to command others to do their bidding.

Some ancient American communities were large and powerful enough that anthropologists have classified them as states, meaning that rulers emerged who were able to appropriate labor and goods from many people over wide geographical areas, sometimes so large that we can justifiably call them empires. This process began in selected places between about 1000 B.C.E. and 1 C.E. and accelerated in the millennium that followed. State formation almost invariably led to an increase in warfare, as rulers tried to gain access to vital resources—obsidian, for example—and to build their own power at the expense of rival states. Many states also enhanced their power and extended their cultural influence through long-distance trade.

None of ancient America's great states lasted forever. Teotihuacan, Monte Albán, Tiwanaku, and countless others all "fell," often after hundreds of years of political ascendancy and stunning cultural advance, just as the ancient Mediterranean cities of Athens, Carthage, and Rome all had their own days of glory and retreat. We have virtually no written sources that might help us document the reasons why so many cities of America declined so precipitously, but the archaeological evidence suggests that the causes were complex, ranging from climatic changes to rebellion on the part of subject populations.

CONCLUSION

All available evidence suggests that once the ice bridge linking North America and Siberia melted some 14,000 years ago, the societies we have examined in this chapter developed on their own, without significant contact with people from across the Atlantic or the Pacific. Ever since the voyages of Christopher Columbus revealed the existence of this "new world" to Europeans, many theories to the contrary have been advanced. Sixteenth-century European theologians thought that the natives of the Americas were descended from the lost tribes of Israel and that one of Christ's original twelve apostles must have brought the Gospel to the Americas. More recently, observers have noted that Olmec sculptures often have Negroid features, suggesting links with Africa. The propensity of early Americans to build mounds and pyramids has led many people to believe that there must have been some connection to Egypt.

A few early Americans may have had incidental contacts with the "old world" during the thousands of years following the migration of their ancestors to the hemisphere. Polynesians may have occasionally crossed the Pacific, and the twentieth-century Norwegian archaeologist Thor Heyerdahl theorized that ancient Peruvians could have traveled in the opposite direction. There is evidence too that northern Europeans might have made their way across Greenland to North America from time to time. We know for sure that Viking navigators set up an abortive colony in northeastern Canada around the year 1000 c.e.

For all practical purposes, however, the Americas developed independently, without "help" or interference from Europe, Africa, or Asia. While archaeologists can cite abundant evidence to show how the ancestors of the first Americans migrated from Siberia to North America, the traditions of Native American peoples offer another kind of truth. They place the origins of human life within their own ancestral homelands and stress the sacred ties of peoples to places. Indeed, it is in the thousands of years of people learning to survive and thrive in tropical lowlands, deserts, grasslands, and mountains that we find the cultural origins of the first peoples of the Americas.

LEARNING MORE ABOUT LATIN AMERICANS

Bawden, Garth. *The Moche* (Oxford, U.K.: Blackwell, 1999). A well-illustrated overview of Moche life and art, incorporating recent archaeological discoveries; one of the series *The Peoples of America.*

Fagan, Brian M. *The Great Journey: The Peopling of Ancient America* (London: Thames and Hudson, 1987). A noted archaeologist traces the migration of people from Siberia to America thousands of years before Columbus.

Joyce, Rosemary A. *Gender and Power in Prehispanic Mesoamerica* (Austin, TX: University of Texas Press, 2000). An anthropologist's exploration of gender roles among the Olmecs, the Maya, and the Aztecs.

Kolata, Alan L. *The Tiwanaku: Portrait of an Andean Civilization* (Oxford, U.K.: Blackwell, 1993). Another volume in the series *The Peoples of America;* shows how the Tiwanaku developed over the course of many centuries.

Lavellée, Danièle. *The First South Americans: The Peopling of a Continent from the Earliest Evidence to High Culture* (Salt Lake City, UT: University of Utah Press, 2000). Shows how the earliest peoples of South America interacted with the natural environment.

Silverman, Helaine, and Donald Proulx, *The Nasca* (Oxford, U.K.: Blackwell, 2002). Another volume in *The Peoples of America* series by two archaeologists who have done extensive fieldwork in the region; provides an up-to-date explanation of the famous Nazca lines.

2

AMERICANS AND IBERIANS ON THE EVE OF CONTACT

IN CHAPTER 1, WE SAW HOW the first peoples of North and South America adapted to the varied environments they found as they dispersed across the continents following their migration from Asia. In some places, they adopted agriculture and built sophisticated irrigation works, while elsewhere they obtained their subsistence through hunting, fishing, and gathering plants. Everywhere they developed systems of belief to explain their world and rituals to propitiate the supernatural forces controlling that world. Ceremonial centers, cities, and states appeared in particularly favored spots.

The fifteenth century in the European calendar witnessed the rise of two great empires in the Americas. The people we call the Aztecs came to dominate much of Mesoamerica, and the Incas controlled the Andean highlands of South America. Both of them drew upon cultural and religious traditions that had developed over many centuries, but they achieved a degree of political organization previously unknown in the Americas. At the same time, a similar process was occurring on Europe's Iberian Peninsula as the monarchies of Spain and Portugal took shape. In 1492, these parallel worlds would meet, with momentous consequences for human history.

MESOAMERICA IN THE FIFTEENTH CENTURY

Mesoamerica was home to many different political and linguistic groups in the year 1400. Most numerous were the Nahuas, so named because they spoke

Nahuatl, which was presumably the tongue spoken by the Toltecs. They inhabited many city-states in and around the Valley of Mexico (today's greater Mexico City) and included groups who had long resided in the area and later arrivals who had adopted the languages and cultures of those already there. The Tarascans lived to the northwest, in what is now the Mexican state of Michoacán, while Mixtecs and Zapotecs could be found in Oaxaca to the South. In Central America and Yucatán were the many city-states of the Post-Classic Maya.

Despite their linguistic differences, the peoples of Mesoamerica shared many cultural traits. They lived in sedentary communities that were usually headed by hereditary rulers. Most of their subsistence came from agriculture, and they shared a common diet based on maize, beans, squashes, and peppers. Their religion revolved largely around the agricultural cycle and typically involved human sacrifice and rituals to guarantee successful harvests. These cultural similarities did not lead Mesoamericans of the fifteenth century to view themselves as one people, any more than their contemporaries in Europe saw themselves as such. Warfare consumed increasing measures of human energies and resources in Mesoamerica as rival city-states vied with one another for territorial supremacy.

Mesoamericans also looked down upon neighbors whom they regarded as less culturally sophisticated than themselves. Particularly despised were groups who had only recently migrated to the region and still had far too much in common with the Chichimecas, the nomadic and "uncivilized" people who "lived like dogs" in the arid central plateau of northern Mexico. One such group was the Mexica, who had entered the Valley of Mexico a scant two centuries earlier. Today they are popularly known as the Aztecs, after their mythical homeland of Aztlán, somewhere to the north and west. From their inauspicious beginnings, they became the most powerful state in Mesoamerica by the early sixteenth century.

The Rise of the Mexica

As newcomers, the Mexica had no fixed residence in the valley. Only by attaching themselves to powerful city-states in the region could they secure a place for themselves. First, they served as mercenaries for Culhuacan, at the southern edge of Lake Texcoco, whose kings claimed descent from the mighty Toltecs. By the early 1300s, they had settled on a small island in the middle of the lake, at the heart of what is today Mexico City. Little by little, they expanded the size of their island by dredging soil from the bottom of the lake, and what would become the great city of Tenochtitlan ("Place Next to the Prickly Pear Cactus") took shape. In the 1370s, they established a dynasty that would endure until the arrival of the Spanish conquistadors a century and a half later. Their first king, Acamapichtli, was the son of a woman from the ruling lineage of Culhuacan,

TIMELINE

700–800
Muslims take over much of Spain and Portugal

c. 1200
Collapse of Tiwanaku in the Andes

1249–1250
Christian reconquest of Portugal and most of Spain

c. 1300
Mexica arrive in the Valley of Mexico

Late 1340s
Black Death in Spain and Portugual

1370s
Mexica ruling dynasty established

1385–1433
King João I establishes Aviz dynasty and political independence of Portugal

1415
Portuguese take Ceuta in North Africa

1418–1472
Rule of Nezahualcoyotl in Texcoco

1428
Triple Alliance defeats Azcapotzalco and gains control of the Valley of Mexico

1438–1471
Rule of Pachacuti Inca Yupanqui

1440–1468
Rule of Moctezuma I in Tenochtitlan

1450s
Droughts and food shortages in central Mexico

1469
Marriage of Isabella of Castile and Ferdinand of Aragón

1478
Spanish Inquisition established

1487
Dedication of the new temple of Huitzilopochtli in Tenochtitlan

1492
Voyage of Columbus; defeat of Granada

1492–1497
Expulsion and forced conversions of Spanish and Portuguese Jews

1493–1525
Rule of Huayna Capac

1498
Portuguese navigator Vasco da Gama reaches India

1502
Expulsion of Muslims from Spain

1516
Charles I becomes first monarch of a united Spain

and his successors formed marriage alliances with other important powers in the valley. The lowly Mexica had earned a measure of respectability at last.

By the beginning of the fifteenth century, Azcapotzalco to the west of Lake Texcoco had surpassed Culhuacan as the foremost city-state in central Mexico. In 1428, however, the Mexica king Ixcoatl formed an alliance (known as the Triple Alliance) with two other states, Texcoco and Tlacopan, and together they defeated Azcapotzalco. That victory was a major turning point in Mesoamerican history. Tenochtitlan soon became the dominant power within the Triple Alliance, with Texcoco a close second and Tlacopan a distant third.

The alliance's domain expanded dramatically over the next several decades. Particularly notable were the conquests achieved by the King Moctezuma I, who ruled at Tenochtitlan from 1440 to 1468, and his contemporary Nezahualcoyotl,

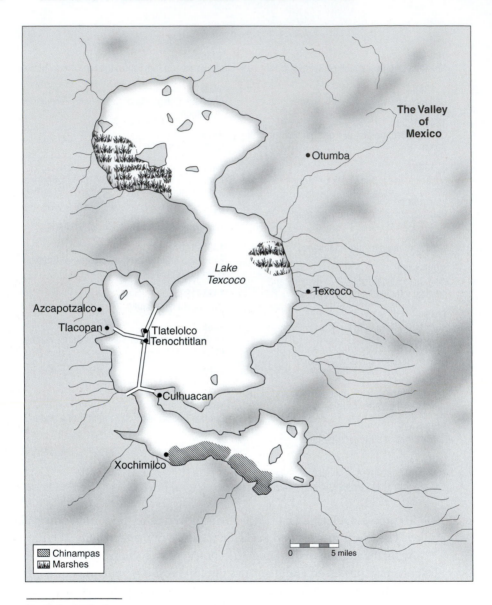

The Valley of Mexico

lord of Texcoco from 1418 to 1472. Together they extended their reach well beyond the Valley of Mexico, to Oaxaca in the south and to the Gulf Coast to the east. By 1500, the Triple Alliance controlled an area roughly the size of Italy. Subjugated territories paid their new rulers substantial quantities of goods in tribute, including cacao, gold dust, gemstones, cotton textiles, honey, featherwork, maize, and other staples. Provinces in the Gulf Coast region provided thousands of rubber balls used in the games played at Tenochtitlan and Texcoco. Local leaders in these conquered regions remained in place, enjoying considerable autonomy as long as they remained loyal to the alliance and handed over the tribute on a regular basis.

There were limits to what the Mexica and their allies could achieve, however. On numerous occasions, conquered provinces rose in revolt and had to be suppressed. Then too, there were enemies too fierce for the Aztecs ever to defeat. In 1479, the emperor Axayacatl launched a campaign against the highly militarized Tarascans of Michoacán that ended in a humiliating rout. Tenochtitlan's armies lost some 20,000 men who either died in battle or were taken prisoner by the enemy. The Mexica also failed to subdue the province of Tlaxcala to the east.

Mexica Statecraft

In theory, Tenochtitlan and Texcoco were equal partners ruling central Mexico. Each took a 40 percent share of the tribute provided by subject states, while Tlacopan received 20 percent. Texcoco continued to undertake conquests in its own name, even after joining the Triple Alliance. In practice, however, Tenochtitlan gradually eclipsed Texcoco and undermined the position of its ruling class, especially after King Nezahuacoyotl died in 1472.

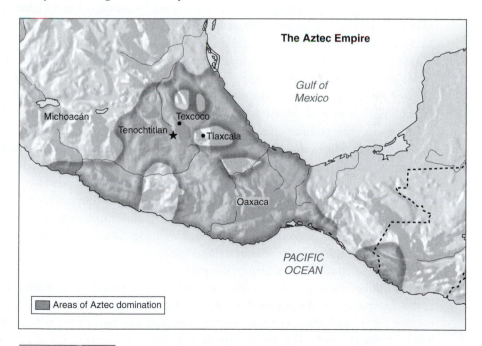

The Aztec Empire in 1519

The Mexica recognized the value of ideology and propaganda as they set about consolidating their ascendancy over rivals and allies alike. They fabricated a glorious history for themselves, deliberately exaggerating their own role in the victories of the Triple Alliance and downplaying the parts played by Texcoco and Tlacopan. Their official account emphasized the importance of their special god, Huitzilopochtli ("Hummingbird on the Left"), who had supposedly guided them safely from Aztlán to the Valley of Mexico. The Mexica were his chosen people, and any evidence that might betray their ignoble origins was carefully suppressed. Thousands of prisoners were sacrificed when a new temple honoring Huitzilopochtli was dedicated in 1487 (see Plate 6).

An Aztec noble named Tlacaelel Cihuacoatl evidently masterminded the rewriting of Mexica history and commanded some of the empire's most important military victories, including the great triumph over Azcapotzalco. He also served as a key power behind the throne for most of the fifteenth century, from the time of Ixcoatl until his death in 1496. Some authorities also suggest that in 1486 he arranged the assassination of the emperor Tizoc, whose 5-year reign was one of the least distinguished in the Mexica line.

Mexica Religion

Aztec religion drew heavily on the centuries-old traditions of central Mexico. Some of their gods, including the feathered serpent Quetzalcoatl and Tlaloc, god of rain, dated back to the time of Teotihuacan. Huitzilopochtli, however, was the Mexicas' most important deity, and a shrine dedicated to him stood alongside Tlaloc's atop the huge pyramid that stood in the center of Tenochtitlan. The Aztec symbol for conquest featured a burning temple, but in fact the Mexica allowed subject populations to keep their customary gods as long as they adopted Huitzilopochtli as well. Meanwhile, the Mexica readily adopted gods and rituals of people they conquered.

Dozens of deities therefore populated the Mesoamerican pantheon in the fifteenth century. The creator Ometeotl ("Two-god") was both mother and father to all the other gods, and Tezcatlipoca ("Smoking Mirror") held power over all. Several deities helped assure agricultural and human fertility. The goddess Xochiquetzal represented sexuality, pregnancy, and childbirth, as well as the traditional female occupations of spinning and weaving. Still other gods watched over the masculine pursuits of warfare and hunting.

Religious ritual was an important part of everyday life. The Mesoamerican calendar divided the year into 18 months of 20 days each, with a special 5-day interlude at the end. Each month had ceremonies that were closely related to the agricultural cycle. During the hot, dry period from May 4 to May 23, for example, the Mexica made sacrifices to Tezcatlipoca to guarantee a prompt start of the rainy season and bountiful harvests thereafter. Hundreds of priests presided over the many public observances held in the temples of Tenochtitlan.

Almost all Aztec rites included some sort of sacrifice to the gods. Mesoamerican theology held that the gods had given of themselves in creating the Sun, the Universe, and people, and the debt had to be repaid. The world might end if the gods failed to receive their due. Offerings included food, animals, seashells, and incense, but the most precious gift of all was human blood. Men and women of all social classes pierced their earlobes and other body parts at least occasionally in an effort to please the gods, while priests bled themselves daily.

But these sacrifices were not enough–the gods also demanded human lives. The most common ritual, one that particularly horrified the early Spanish conquistadors, involved carrying a person to the top of a temple, excising the heart, and displaying the skull in a rack along with those of previous victims. In ceremonies honoring Xipe Totec, a god of agricultural fertility, priests donned the flayed skins of their victims. Sacrifices also frequently included the ritual eating of small portions of the victim's flesh. Most of those offered to the gods were adult males captured in warfare, but some gods, such as Tlaloc, preferred young children. Women were sometimes sacrificed as well, especially to female deities.

Human sacrifice had a long history in Mesoamerica, and in many other world civilizations as well, but most authorities believe that these rituals increased in number and importance under Aztec domination. Human sacrifice not only pleased the gods but it served the Mexicas' political agenda as well. Priests were closely linked to the ruling class, and highly visible blood rituals impressed everyone–slaves, commoners, nobles, allies, and enemies alike–with the awesome power of the state.

Everyday Life in the Time of the Mexica

Most Mesoamericans in the fifteenth century were peasants who devoted the bulk of their time to producing their own food and the many goods they furnished in tribute to local rulers and imperial overlords. Even some residents of Tenochtitlan and other great cities farmed at least on a part-time basis. The basic unit of peasant society was the household, typically consisting of a married couple and their children, with many duties allocated along gender lines. From May to November, men spent most of their time working in the fields, while during the rest of the year they might serve as warriors or perform compulsory labor for their rulers. Women performed most domestic chores–such as food preparation, housekeeping, and childcare–marketed any surplus produce, and presided over religious rituals within the home. They also wove cloth required for the family's use and for tribute quotas.

Artisans formed another important segment of Aztec society, especially in urban areas. People who farmed for a living often made sandals, pottery, baskets, and other mundane commodities in their spare time, while luxury goods and obsidian weapons and tools usually came from the workshops of full-time craft workers. The Spanish conquistadors of the sixteenth century marveled at the skill of Aztec goldsmiths, sculptors, and featherwork artists. Recent archaeological investigations have shown that the town of Otumba in the Teotihuacan Valley was an important manufacturing center, specializing in the production of basalt metates and *manos* used for grinding maize, obsidian tools, and the stone ear ornaments and lip plugs worn by nobles throughout Mesoamerica.

Together the peasants and artisans made up the commoner class, the *macehualtin.* A dozen or more households formed a *calpulli.* In theory, the calpulli owned the land that member households farmed and a governing council controlled land allocation, but in practice, families passed their plots from one generation to another as if they owned them privately.

At the opposite end of Mexica society were the nobles, who comprised somewhere between 5 and 10 percent of the population. Tribute and labor supplied to them by the commoners supported their lavish lifestyles. Nobles had special perquisites, including the right to build homes of more than one story and to wear cotton clothing rather than the rough garments of maguey fiber used by commoners. Men of the noble class could also have more than one wife. For a time in the early fifteenth century, it had been possible for male commoners to rise to the ranks of the nobility by distinguishing themselves on the battlefield, but by late Aztec times this avenue to upward social mobility had narrowed considerably. Nobility became almost exclusively hereditary, and nobles generally married within their own class.

The *pochteca,* or long-distance merchants, comprised another important hereditary group in Mexica society. These men lived in a separate quarter of Tenochtitlan, had their own special gods, and settled disputes among themselves in their own courts. They carried on a rapidly growing trade within the Triple Alliance domains and beyond, as far south as Central America. When traveling in enemy territory, they often served as spies for the Mexica emperors. They made fortunes marketing jewelry, featherwork, stone sculptures, and other luxuries so avidly craved by nobles, but as commoners, they were not allowed to display their wealth in public. Sixteenth-century sources tell us that when returning to Tenochtitlan laden with the profits of a trading expedition, the pochteca snuck into town at night so that no one would see them.

Occupying the lowest ranks of society were slaves, though slavery in Mesoamerica differed markedly from the type of bondage that Europeans would introduce into the Americas when they imported thousands of Africans to perform heavy labor in their colonies. In Mexica society, people were not born into slavery. They became slaves as punishment for crimes or because they could not pay their debts or their tributes. In times of economic hardship, such as the great famine that struck central Mexico in the 1450s, many people sold themselves or their children into slavery. Many pochteca traded slaves along with other merchandise. Most slaves worked as servants in the households of nobles.

Mesoamerica on the Eve of the Spanish Invasion

For several decades, the size of the Mesoamerican population in the year 1500 has been the subject of heated debate among historians and archaeologists. Some estimates for the whole of Mesoamerica run as high as 25 million, but most experts now favor much more conservative numbers. The most reliable recent studies suggest a population of between one and two million for the Valley of Mexico (today's greater Mexico City) and several million more in the area subject to direct Aztec control. The city of Tenochtitlan alone had over 200,000 inhabitants. As we shall see in Chapter 3, the indigenous population fell precipitously following the Spanish conquest, and did not regain pre-conquest levels until the twentieth century.

Whatever the specific numbers, scholars agree that the population of central Mexico grew substantially during the period of Aztec supremacy. Only through an intensification of agriculture could all these people be fed. New lands were opened to cultivation, and irrigation systems were improved to increase the yield of fields already in use. Around the lakes, especially at Xochimilco in the south, people employed a centuries-old technique to turn swampland into productive farmland, building up artificial islands, or *chinampas*. The lakes themselves were another source of food, including fish, insect larvae, turtles, and an algae that Mexica warriors carried in dried form when they set out on their campaigns.

There were signs, however, that by late Aztec times population growth had begun to exceed the limits of available agricultural technology. Severe droughts struck in the 1450s, and food shortages loomed again after 1500. Political unrest mounted as well, even in Tenochtitlan's partner city of Texcoco, where Moctezuma II forcibly imposed his own nephew as ruler following a succession dispute in 1515. But the Mexica state had weathered many crises in the preceding century and may well have proven equal to these new challenges as well. When the Spanish conquistadors first gazed upon Tenochtitlan in November of 1519, they saw a thriving city that was the capital of one of their world's great empires and little to suggest that the power of the Mexica would crumble easily.

How Historians Understand   COUNTING PEOPLE IN PAST SOCIETIES

Even with state-of-the-art computers and a huge cadre of census takers, the governments of the United States and other countries today have difficulty determining the exact size of their populations. Historians face far greater challenges when they try to estimate how many people lived in a given place hundreds of years in the past. This is especially true when it comes to figuring the population of the Americas in 1492.

Many pre-Columbian societies left no written records. Even the Aztecs, long accustomed to putting ideas on paper, were not so much concerned with exact numbers of people as they were with preserving and embellishing their own historical memory and making sure that subject communities paid their tribute. The Incas kept their records on quipus, but few of these artifacts have survived, and scholars have not been able to interpret them all. Nor can population estimates made by early European observers be taken at face value. When they said they saw 10,000 natives at a particular place, they may well have meant just that they saw a lot of people, more than they could easily count. Early explorers and conquistadors hoping

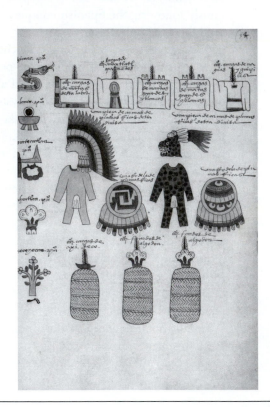

A page from the Mendoza Codex. The symbols in the column on the left stand for five different towns; each town's tribute consisted of 2000 woven cotton mantles, with each symbol representing 400 garments (top row), suits and headdresses worn by Aztec warriors (middle row), 400 loads of chili peppers and 800 bales of cotton (bottom row).

to gain favor with their monarchs or to encourage other Europeans to invest in colonization ventures also had compelling personal reasons to exaggerate the magnitude of their findings.

Historical demographers working on pre-Columbian societies have had to devise various techniques to circumvent the absence of reliable written evidence. Estimates of the population of central Mexico have used documents generated after the arrival of the Spanish that show how much tribute various communities rendered to the Aztecs. One such source is the Codex Mendoza, commissioned by the first Spanish viceroy so that he could better inform the king of Spain about this new dominion. Native artists painted the customary symbols for more than 300 towns that had paid tribute to the lords of Tenochtitlan, and next to them the items and quantities supplied every 80 days. Annotations in Spanish accompanied the pictographic text. Historians have then calculated how many people it would have taken to produce those amounts of goods while also providing for their own subsistence needs.

Historical geographers have also figured how many people a given environment could support, taking into account soil, climate, and available technology. Aerial photography has revealed important evidence of ancient irrigation systems and terraces—signs of intensive agriculture and therefore of high population density. Archaeological remains have yielded further clues, such as the number of houses in a settlement or the amount of labor that might have been required to build a particular structure or manufacture a given quantity of pottery or other artifacts found at a particular site. Still other researchers have used statistical models, working from more accurate data from the 1600s or 1700s to project back to earlier times.

No matter how sophisticated their techniques, however, historical demographers must accept that the results of their studies can only be educated guesses. For this reason, estimates of the total population of the Americas in 1492 vary widely, from as few as 10 million to as many as 100 million or more. For the island of Hispaniola, creditable demographic studies published in the late twentieth century have calculated a precontact population at somewhere between 60,000 and 7 million. What we do know for sure is that the indigenous population of the hemisphere declined drastically following the arrival of Europeans.

Questions for Discussion

Can you think of other types of evidence that might be used in estimating the population of particular localities? What are the connections between population size and cultural achievement in a society?

THE ANDES IN THE FIFTEENTH CENTURY

While the Mexica were establishing their hegemony in central Mexico, an even larger empire was taking shape in the Andes in South America. The Incas ruled this kingdom, which they called Tawantinsuyu ("The Land of the Four Quarters") from their magnificent capital at Cuzco, 11,000 feet above sea level in southern Peru. Like their Mesoamerican counterparts, they borrowed and built upon the achievements of the great civilizations that had gone before them. They derived their subsistence from exploiting many different ecological niches of the Andes and practiced centuries-old religious rituals. From art and architecture to strategies of governance, the Incas carried on the cultural traditions of earlier societies.

The Incas, however, attained a level of political consolidation previously unknown in the Andes and even greater than that of the Aztecs or the emerging monarchs of Western Europe in the fifteenth century. On the eve of the Spanish conquest, their dominions extended 2500 miles from the present-day boundary of Ecuador and Colombia in the north, southeast to Bolivia, as far as northern Argentina and central Chile in the south, and eastward beyond the slopes of the Andes, a territorial expanse larger than the Ottoman Empire or Ming China. Some authorities believe that by the early sixteenth century as many as 12 million people lived under Inca domination, but others place the figure closer to 3 million. In the early 1530s, at least 60,000, and perhaps as many as 150,000 men, women, and children resided in Cuzco.

The Rise of the Incas

Following the collapse of Tiwanaku in about 1200, the Andean region had many small chiefdoms, a situation roughly comparable to central Mexico in the same period. The Quechua-speaking Incas of Cuzco were one such group. In the thirteenth century, they began extending their control to neighboring areas. By the time of Pachacuti Inca Yupanqui, their ruler from 1438 to 1471, the Incas had emerged as the premier power in the Andes. Their conquests extended to include Aymara speakers in the region around Lake Titicaca in Bolivia. Pachacuti's successors, Topa Inca Yupanqui (1471–1493) and Huayna Capac (1493–1525), expanded Inca hegemony even further, achieving the definitive subjugation of Ecuador and conducting campaigns southward to Chile as well.

The Incas usually attempted first to persuade regional chieftains to submit voluntarily, offering them incentives including women, gifts, and the promise of retaining their positions. If these tactics failed, they waged war and took the recalcitrant leaders to Cuzco to be executed. The Incas achieved their conquests not through any superiority in weapons or tactics, but rather by drafting warriors from previously subjugated provinces into their service. They also exploited the long-standing and bitter divisions among the Andean peoples.

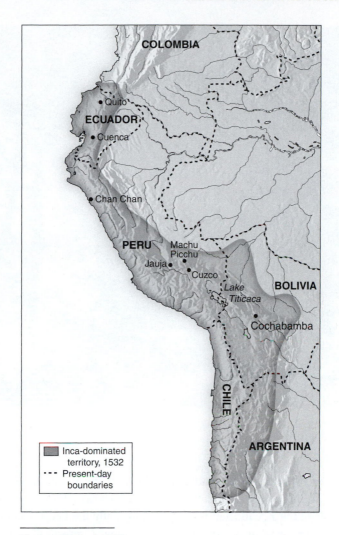

The Inca Empire in 1532

In addition to military service, the people of the empire were forced to perform many other tasks for the lords of Cuzco. They built roads, palaces, temples, and other buildings as dictated by their new rulers. They also cultivated lands, herded llamas and alpacas, and worked gold and silver mines that belonged to the Inca state or to Inca deities. Conquered peoples gave lands to the Incas and provided various commodities in tribute, although apparently not on as great a scale as subjects of the Mexica in Mesoamerica.

Just as the Aztecs found that they could not expand indefinitely, so too did the Incas. They had little luck in subduing people who were not sedentary peasants,

Silver drinking vessels used in Peru.

such as the inhabitants of southern Chile and the plains of eastern Bolivia. Repeated forays into the tropical forests of eastern Ecuador also ended in failure. The people of the Ecuadorian highlands, especially the fierce Cañaris who lived in the region near what is today the city of Cuenca, repeatedly rose in revolt as well. When Huayna Capac died in 1525, a power struggle between his two sons Huascar and Atahualpa divided the empire just as Spaniards were already approaching the coast of Peru.

Inca Statecraft

In many respects, the Incas were more intrusive in the lives of their subjects than the Mexica. Although colonies of conquered peoples could be found at Tenochtitlan, and representatives of the Aztec state fanned out across Mesoamerica, the Incas systematically relocated large populations in an effort to consolidate their hold throughout the Andes. They forcibly moved large numbers of Cañaris from southern Ecuador to Cuzco, along with many other recently conquered or notoriously restive peoples. Other groups, including many from Chan Chan on the coast of Peru, were resettled in Cuzco because they possessed specialized craft skills. Some groups originally from Quito were transferred all the way to the environs of Lake Titicaca, while Aymara from the highlands of southern Peru and Bolivia were sent at least temporarily to the lower-lying valley of Cochabamba to the east. At the same time, the Inca rulers dispatched Quechua-speaking *mitmaq,* or colonists, from the heart of the empire to outlying areas. Despite all of these movements, the Incas never succeeded in imposing any kind of cultural homogeneity on the peoples they conquered. Although the use of Quechua certainly spread as a lingua franca, many other languages could be heard throughout the Andes.

To communicate with their far-flung dominions, the Incas constructed 20,000 miles of paved roads, tunnels, causeways, and bridges, a land transportation network far superior to anything in Europe at the time. A series of east-west roads crossed the rugged terrain of the Andes to connect two north-south routes, one on the coast and the other in the highlands. Portions of the roads are still visible today. *Tambos,* or inns, provided shelter along the way.

Using these roads, specially trained relay runners carried messages to provincial governors stationed throughout the empire, covering the distance from Cuzco to the coast in about 3 days' time. They carried knotted, multi-colored cords known as quipus, which took the place of written documents in the Andes. The quipus contained census information, details about the labor obligations owed by each community, and other information vital to a highly centralized state. Writing in the early 1600s, the Indian historian Felipe Guaman Poma de Ayala noted, "With these cords the entire kingdom is governed."

A sense of reciprocal obligation between rulers and the ruled was deeply ingrained in Andean society and essential to Inca administration. The Inca state commandeered men for labor and military service and women to perform special ceremonial roles and to become weavers and brewers of chicha, an intoxicating beverage made from maize. The rulers at Cuzco required most subjects to provide various items in tribute as well. In return, the emperor was expected to take care of his people when they were in need. To this end, the state maintained an elaborate system of warehouses situated in provincial capitals and other strategic points all along its road network. There they stored large quantities of food produced on imperial lands and cloth gathered in tribute. Archaeologists have calculated that the storage capacity of the warehouses at Jauja, for example, exceeded 50,000 cubic meters. These supplies enabled the Incas to play the role of benevolent rulers in times of crisis and to provision their armies throughout the empire. State-ordered systems of distribution, rather than market forces, governed the movement and exchange of commodities.

Like the Aztecs, the Incas augmented their hegemony with the use of history. They portrayed themselves as a special people, apart from the rest of humanity, who had brought civilization and order to the land after a long period of darkness and chaos. Cuzco witnessed elaborate ceremonies, including special homage at the tombs of former Inca rulers, all designed to impress everyone with the power and splendor of the state.

Andean Religion in the Time of the Incas

The Incas also sponsored an official state religion that served their political purposes. Their principal deity was Inti, the Sun god, who took on increasing importance as their conquests spread, eventually surpassing the traditional Andean creator god Viracocha. Inca rulers claimed direct descent from Inti, and the walls of his magnificent temple at Cuzco were lined with sheets of gold. They required conquered peoples to incorporate the Sun god and other features of Inca state religion into their worship.

However much the Incas depicted themselves as special, they in fact shared with other Andeans religious beliefs and observances that dated back many centuries and did little to alter the traditional worship practices of their subjects. Few temples to the Sun god or other Inca deities appeared in conquered provinces. Local religious objects from throughout the empire were taken to Cuzco, where they received special attention. Under Inca domination, Andeans continued, as they had for centuries, to venerate the mummified remains of their ancestors as well as hundreds of *huacas,* or spirits attached to a particular place, to whom they offered sacrifices of guinea pigs and coca leaves.

Meanwhile, the ancient cult to the god Pachacamac, centered on the coast, continued to thrive. Much as their ancestors had flocked to Chavín de Huántar hundreds of years earlier, pilgrims speaking many different languages from throughout Peru, Bolivia, and Ecuador came to consult the oracle at Pachacamac's shrine and brought coca leaves, food, and textiles in tribute to the god and his ministers. Branch shrines supervised by priests from the central site were set up around the highlands and along the coast.

Fifteenth-century Andeans included human sacrifice in their religious rituals, as their ancestors had done for hundreds of years. In contrast to their counterparts in Mesoamerica, the Incas had no system of pictorial writing, and there are no eyewitness Spanish accounts of human sacrifice in Peru, so we have fewer details about the specific rituals they practiced. We do know that human sacrifice was evidently reserved for special occasions. Children were sacrificed whenever a king died and his successor took over. The sacrifice of enemy warriors taken in battle marked the celebration of important military victories. Young women, considered brides and priestesses of the Sun god, were also strangled and offered to him. At the shrine of Pachacamac, archaeologists have also found the mummified remains of sacrificial victims dating from Inca times.

Human sacrifice was part of the reciprocal relationship that Andeans maintained with their deities. Just as they provided labor and tribute to their rulers in return for help in time of need, they offered gifts to the gods, who in turn gave them protection and special favors. Sacrifices of human beings, animals, textiles,

auatesa   mamacona

mon jas   las

Chosen women who made textiles and chicha for the Incas, as depicted by the native historian Guaman Poma de Ayala.

and coca leaves restored harmony between people and the gods. Without such tradeoffs, earthquakes, crop failures, and other calamities inevitably resulted.

Everyday Life in the Time of the Incas

Borrowing from their ancestors, the people of the Inca Empire supported themselves by farming the steep slopes of the Andes, which they fashioned into terraces to prevent water runoff and soil erosion. The basic unit of Andean society,

LATIN AMERICAN LIVES

TANTA CARHUA, BRIDE OF THE SUN

AMONG THE MANY MARVELS that caught the attention of the Spanish conquistadors when they arrived in the Inca capital of Cuzco in the 1530s were the large dwellings set aside for specially chosen women. Some Spaniards likened these magnificently arrayed structures to convents, while others compared the women who resided in them to the vestal virgins of ancient Rome or the harems of Muslim potentates. Actually, these women were *acllas,* young virgins appropriated by the state who spent the remainder of their lives serving the Incas in various capacities.

The selection of local women to be acllas and the construction of a building to house them usually accompanied the Inca conquest of a region. They severed their ties with their ayllus, and all of them were taken at least temporarily to Cuzco. Many returned to their native provinces to be concubines of men who had rendered distinguished services to the state or to perform assigned duties in local religious observances. Others stayed on in Cuzco to be wives of the emperor or to weave textiles and manufacture chicha used in ritual celebrations.

A select few acllas were declared brides of the Sun god himself. Tanta Carhua was 10 years old when she was selected for this highest of "honors" during the final years of Inca rule. Her father, a provincial chieftain named Caque Poma, saw the political advantages to be gained from having his only daughter in the service of the Sun god. His role as a crucial intermediary between the empire and his home community was solidified, and he was able to pass that position on to his male heirs.

As for Tanta Carhua, her days were numbered, for she was to be sacrificed to the Sun god. First, she participated in a festival known as *capacocha* ("festival of the sacrificed"), held in Cuzco in the presence of the emperor. She then returned to her home province where she was buried alive on a mountaintop. At the emperor's orders, she was later revered as a special protector spirit, with lands and llama herds designated to support a cult in her honor and her relatives serving as its priests. A hundred years after her death, much to the consternation of Spanish Catholic missionaries, the people of her community continued to offer sacrifices of llamas and guinea pigs at her tomb and to invoke her help in times of trouble.

Questions for Discussion

How did the Incas use Andean gender ideologies to build their own imperial power? How might other young women from Tanta Carhua's province have viewed her experiences?

also dating back long before the Incas, was the *ayllu,* a group of people who claimed descent from a single ancestor, worked lands in common, and venerated their own special deities. Here too the notion of reciprocity was important. Everyone shared access to the ayllu's resources and claims on one another's labor. Those who were away from home on military duty or other service could expect other members of the ayllu to fill in for them back home.

The ayllus were not compact, nucleated settlements. Instead, they resembled archipelagos that controlled parcels of land at different elevations, assuring the community's access to a variety of ecological niches, including high areas for pasture and warmer, moister lowlands needed for coca production. This strategy of exploiting the sharply varied terrain of the Andes had been developed over the course of many centuries, and Inca domination did relatively little to disrupt such arrangements. The Inca policy of relocating various groups of people might have helped some ayllus gain access to an even wider range of environmental niches.

Inca fortress of Machu Picchu. Note the agricultural terraces in the background.

Like the people of Mesoamerica, Andeans divided chores along gender lines. Men worked the fields and waged war. Along with childcare and domestic tasks, women's work included spinning yarn and weaving textiles (see Plate 4). To a greater degree than in Mexico and Central America, however, traditional Andean society stressed complementarity between the sexes, with the contributions of men and women valued more equally. Everyone, regardless of sex, had a comparable claim on the resources of the ayllu. Men passed personal property on to their sons, women to their daughters; men traced their ancestry through the male line, women through the female. A woman's performance of household duties was considered a service to the community, not to her husband. Andeans incorporated a similar parallelism into their religious practices. Women presided over local rituals in honor of female deities and passed knowledge of these rites on to their daughters, while men performed rites dedicated to male gods and taught their sons to do likewise. During the final century before the Europeans' arrival in Peru, this complementarity of gender roles deteriorated. The Incas' emphasis on warfare valued men's roles more highly than women's, and women became objects of exchange used to cement bonds between conquered territories and the Inca state.

Reciprocity and theoretically equal access to resources were fundamental principles of Andean life, but this did not mean that there were no social distinctions. Some people, known as *yanaconas,* lived outside the ayllu structure and therefore did not enjoy the privileges that ayllu membership conveyed. They served as personal retainers of nobles or servants of the state or the gods, and their numbers were growing during the years of Inca ascendancy. Also on the rise were the ranks of the nobles who had earned special perquisites for their service to the empire. Social stratification was becoming more noticeable in the Andes as the fifteenth century progressed, just as it was in Mesoamerica under the Mexica.

The Aztecs and Incas Compared

There were many similarities between the Mexica and the Incas. Both rose to political supremacy a scant 100 years before the arrival of the first Spanish conquistadors. They extended their dominions through military conquest but could only rule these vast territories by co-opting local rulers and leaving them in place. As the empires grew, so too did class distinctions that separated nobles from commoners. Both empires demanded that their subjects provide soldiers for their armies and workers who built the great temples and palaces at Tenochtitlan and Cuzco. Aztecs and Incas alike promulgated versions of history that cast themselves in the most favorable of lights, chosen by their special gods to rule over others. Andean and Mesoamerican deities were similarly appeased through human sacrifice.

Neither the Aztecs nor the Incas were great cultural innovators, for both drew heavily on preexisting traditions and did relatively little to alter basic patterns of subsistence and belief among their subjects. People in the Andes had domesticated llamas, alpacas, and vicuñas, and they made greater use of metal for utilitarian purposes, but both societies showed great ingenuity in exploiting the natural environment to feed their growing populations, and humans provided virtually all of the muscle power in agriculture. Nowhere in North, Central, or South America did indigenous peoples use wheeled vehicles for transport.

Differences between the Aztecs and the Incas were mostly ones of degree. The Incas achieved significantly greater political centralization through their policies of relocating subject populations and dispatching emissaries throughout the empire over their impressive system of roads. Andeans had traditionally accorded women a greater role in religious observances and community affairs, but in both empires men were considered the heads of households for the purposes of state record-keeping, and the increasing militarization of society placed a premium on males as warriors.

Model of the marketplace of Tlaltelolco.

Slice of Life   THE MARKETPLACE AT TLATELOLCO

IF TENOCHTITLAN WAS THE RITUAL CENTER of the Aztec empire, its commercial heart could be found at Tlatelolco, an adjacent city annexed by the Mexica in 1473. Its huge market operated daily and attracted as many as 60,000 people, according to sixteenth-century Spanish observers. Its stalls held a dazzling variety of goods, everything from basic staples brought in from the surrounding valley by canoes and human carriers, to exotic luxuries that were the stock in trade of the pochteca, the professional long-distance merchants. There were fruits, vegetables, and herbs, as well as maize, tortillas, salt, fish, pottery, baskets, brooms, and tools made of copper and bronze. Precious stones, ornaments made from gold and silver, cotton thread in a multitude of hues, and brilliantly colored parrot feathers were available to those able to afford them.

Other commodities for sale included live animals—rabbits, deer, and small dogs that were all used as sources of protein in the Mesoamerican diet. Male and female slaves were also bought and sold. Indeed, the Tlatelolco market offered many of the services of a twenty-first–century shopping mall. One could stop and eat at the many booths that sold prepared food and drink. Barbers washed and cut people's hair, and porters could be hired to carry customers' purchases home. A trip to the market was also a chance to socialize.

Trade was carefully regulated at Tlatelolco, with cacao beans used as a kind of currency. Vendors were arranged according to the products or services they sold. At the center of the marketplace stood an imposing building where a dozen judges, all of them members of the guild of pochteca, stood ready to adjudicate disputes, while other officials patrolled the stalls, checking for inaccurate measures and other signs of fraud.

The Tlatelolco market was the primary one for the Mexica capital, but there were numerous smaller markets around the city and in smaller towns throughout central Mexico, especially in late Aztec times. Most of them were open only once every 5 days and sold basic commodities, but a few specialized in particular wares—dogs at the town of Acolman near the site of the ancient city of Teotihuacan, for example. When the Spaniards introduced a cash economy in the sixteenth century, the people of central Mexico adapted quickly, for they already had long-established habits of buying and selling.

Questions for Discussion

When Spaniards arrived in Mexico in 1519, the Tlatelolco market was one of the first sights they saw. What would they have thought as they observed it? What, if anything, would have appeared strange to them, and what would have seemed very familiar?

One of the most pronounced differences between these two great civilizations was the way in which commodities were circulated and exchanged. Among the Incas, the state largely controlled the flow of food, cloth, and other supplies necessary for survival, storing these goods in their strategically placed warehouses, ready for distribution in time of calamity. The Aztecs likewise maintained reserves of the many items they received in tribute, but Mesoamericans had a much more fully developed market economy, and merchants comprised an important social group with special privileges.

Whatever their differences, in many ways the Aztecs and the Incas each had more in common with the Europeans of their time than they did with the simpler societies of the Caribbean and coastal South America who would be the first to encounter the European invaders in 1492. When Spanish conquistadors arrived in Tenochtitlan and Cuzco, they were awestruck by the size and splendor of these two great cities, as dazzling as anything they had known in Europe. Once they got over their initial shock at human sacrifice and other rituals they considered grotesque and diabolical, they found much that made sense to them. They could easily relate to temples comparable in grandeur to the cathedrals and mosques they had seen back home, kings who claimed their position by virtue of divine approval, and governments capable of taxing many millions of people and mustering their young men for military service and forced labor.

THE DIVERSITY OF AMERICAN PEOPLES

The systems of social organization of the interior highlands of Mesoamerica and South America ranked among the world's most complex in the fifteenth century of the Christian calendar. But to focus exclusively on the great empires of the Aztecs and the Incas would be to minimize the cultural achievements of people who made their homes in areas where the natural environment was less favorable to population growth. We would also miss the tremendous diversity of indigenous societies on the eve of European contact.

Native peoples of the Americas found ingenious ways to eke out a living in many climate zones of the hemisphere. Some provided for virtually all of their own material needs themselves, while others carried on a certain amount of trade. Their types of social and political organization varied from small bands that roamed from place to place in search of wild game and plants for gathering to kingdoms that nearly rivaled the Andeans and Mesoamericans in their level of political sophistication. Some were extremely warlike, while others were more peaceful. Every indigenous society had its shamans or other specialists who communicated with the unseen forces that controlled or influenced the lives of humans. Some practiced human sacrifice and ritual cannibalism, and most maintained elaborate oral traditions that explained the origins of the world and the nature of the gods.

The diversity of native society was readily apparent to Europeans who arrived after 1492. The first peoples they encountered, the Tainos and Caribs of the Caribbean and the Tupi speakers of coastal Brazil, lived far more simply than those they would later encounter in Mesoamerica and the Andes. The people they called the Pueblos of northern New Mexico developed a highly sophisticated society in a challenging physical environment, but the Spaniards who first saw them in the early 1540s found them primitive in comparison with what they had seen at Tenochtitlan and Cuzco.

The Tainos and Caribs

According to some experts, the islands of the Caribbean together contained an estimated 750,000 inhabitants in 1492, but other scholars believe that the population was much larger, perhaps as many as 2 or 3 million. The island of Hispaniola—today's Haiti and the Dominican Republic—was the most densely populated, with perhaps as many as half a million people. Cuba and Puerto Rico, by contrast, each had about 50,000 people at most. By far, the most numerous of the Caribbean peoples were the Tainos, whose settlements were located in the Bahamas, Hispaniola, Cuba, Puerto Rico, and Jamaica.

The Tainos were agricultural people with techniques appropriate to their environment. They minimized soil erosion and improved drainage by planting their crops in earthen mounds 3 feet high and 9 feet in diameter. Their most important staple was cassava, also known as manioc, a root that could be ground into calorie-rich flour or mashed and fermented to yield intoxicating beverages, but they also cultivated sweet potatoes, maize, peanuts, peppers, beans, tobacco, and cotton. Abundantly available fish, sea turtles, shellfish, lizards, manatees, and small game provided protein in their diet. Their settlements were located in the places best suited for agriculture and ranged in size from a few hundred to as many as 5000 people.

Men (and a few women) known as *caciques* ruled over one or more villages. Hispaniola had six such chiefs in 1500, while in Puerto Rico 18 caciques headed a much smaller total population. Succession to the chieftainships was reckoned along matrilineal lines. When a cacique died, his oldest sister's oldest son usually took his place. Taino caciques presided over local religious rituals and enjoyed certain perquisites attached to their positions. They lived in larger houses than their neighbors and wore ornaments made from gold mined in the interior mountains of Cuba, Puerto Rico, and Hispaniola, but they received no tribute or labor service from their people.

Indeed, the ever-increasing social distinctions that characterized life in Mesoamerica and the Andes were unknown among the Tainos. Everyone lived so simply that Christopher Columbus called them "a people short of everything." In the warm climate of the Caribbean there was little need for protective clothing or shelter, and in a region prone to tropical storms it made little sense to build anything more elaborate than mud huts and ceremonial ball courts. But the Tainos had mastered such crafts as woodcarving, weaving of cotton, and pottery, and they carried on trade with neighboring islands. Like their contemporaries in Mesoamerica, they were fond of a kind of ball game.

One of the most peaceful people of the Americas, the Tainos had a hard time defending themselves against their more warlike neighbors or the Spanish intruders after 1492. Smallpox and other European diseases left them all but extinct by the mid-sixteenth century, although liaisons between Spanish men and Taino women assured their contribution to the gene pool of post-conquest Caribbean society. Their enduring cultural legacy can be seen in the many Taino words that passed into Spanish and then into English and other European languages. "Cacique" became the generic term used by Spaniards throughout their American colonies to describe indigenous rulers and still is used to describe local political bosses. Other words of Taino origin are *canoa* (canoe), *hamaca* (hammock), *barbacoa* (grill, hence the English word barbecue), and *maíz* (maize). Scholars have surmised that had there been no European invasion, the Tainos might have continued their cultural development and established close contact with the great mainland civilizations of Mesoamerica.

People called Caribs could be found in the islands known as the Lesser Antilles, from Guadeloupe south to Martinique and Grenada, and in northern South America. Their religious customs and political organization were evidently less well developed than those of the Tainos, but they were much more warlike. War canoes carrying up to 100 men raided Taino settlements and took away women and children as slaves. Male enemies taken in battle were sacrificed and eaten in a form of ritual cannibalism, although sensationalized accounts penned by early Spanish explorers tended to exaggerate the importance of this practice among the Caribs.

In many other ways, the Caribs' lifestyle resembled that of their less violent neighbors. They drew their subsistence from agriculture just as other Caribbean peoples did. When Taino women taken as slaves bore the children of Carib men, they spread Taino cultural traits throughout the region. Meanwhile, the Tainos were becoming more like the Caribs at the beginning of the sixteenth century, fighting back against their aggressors using similar weapons and battle tactics.

The Tupi of Coastal Brazil

The natives of coastal Brazil had much in common with the people of the Caribbean. They too based their subsistence on slash-and-burn agriculture as well as hunting, fishing, and gathering fruits and nuts. Manioc was their principal crop, but they also produced maize, beans, peanuts, and cotton. The importance of shellfish in their diet can be seen in the huge mounds of shells they left behind. The Tupi also possessed a detailed knowledge of the many resources that could be found in the forests that surrounded their settlements. From the tree that the Portuguese would later called brazilwood, the Tupi produced a red dye used to color their cotton garments.

Like the Arawaks, they lived very simply, and each village was largely self-sufficient. Their lack of interest in accumulating personal possessions mystified the sixteenth-century Europeans who first encountered them. One observer noted that among the Tupi "what belongs to one belongs to all." But they did take great pride in adorning themselves with red and black body paint, necklaces and bracelets made from stones and shells, and lip plugs fashioned from polished jadeite. Brilliantly colored feathers were also used to make headdresses and other garments worn by shamans and other important people.

Tupi settlements usually had from 400 to 800 inhabitants. Groups of up to 60 interrelated nuclear families lived together in large houses. Leadership at the family level and higher was patrilineal. Councils of male elders made decisions for their tribes and preserved the collective memory. Labor was divided by gender. Men felled trees, hunted, and fished, while women planted and harvested crops. Certain crafts, such as the making of baskets and hammocks, were performed by both men and women. Females as well as males also served as shamans or healers in Tupi society.

The Tupi were aggressive people who often fought among themselves. Young men had to distinguish themselves in battle before they were allowed to marry, and men of all ages earned prestige by taking enemy captives. Prisoners were then sacrificed and eaten, but not before they had been carried back to their captor's home and subjected to public humiliation by the women of the village.

The "Pueblo" Peoples of New Mexico

The people who lived in what is now the northern part of the state of New Mexico received their first foreign "visitors" when Francisco Vázquez de Coronado and his entourage arrived in the early 1540s. The Spanish admired their large apartment-like adobe dwellings, calling them *pueblos*, the Spanish word for town. In time, the name came to be applied to the people as well, even though they were in fact made up of several different groups who spoke mutually unintelligible languages.

The dry climate and cold winters of New Mexico forced the Pueblo peoples to work hard to provide for their basic needs. They developed elaborate irrigation systems to water their fields of maize, squash, cotton, and tobacco. They also obtained buffalo hides and other goods by trading with the hunter-gatherer Apaches who inhabited the plains east of Pueblo territory.

Pueblo society stressed social conformity and subordination of the individual to the group. Younger adults were expected always to defer to their elders in matters of leadership and service. Gender roles were also carefully prescribed. Men were hunters and warriors and performed heavy labor in the fields, while women cooked, cared for children, and made pottery and baskets. Women also constructed and maintained the adobe dwellings. Although people traced their lineage through the female line and observed a gender complementarity somewhat comparable to that of Andean peoples, males dominated Pueblo religion. At least until after menopause, women were not permitted to enter the *kivas,* the circular buildings where sacred objects were kept and important rituals performed.

The Pueblos developed a highly sophisticated culture in a challenging environment, but nothing on the order of what the Aztecs and Incas achieved. In the 1530s, Spaniards in Mexico heard rumors about them and concluded that *otro México*–another Mexico–lay deep in the interior of the continent. Immediately, they organized an expedition to the far north. What they found there was a bitter disappointment–adobe buildings that scarcely compared with the temples and palaces of the lords of Tenochtitlan and rulers whose political control reached only to the limits of a single "town." The Pueblos provided sixteenth-century Europeans with yet another example to show that the people they lumped together as "Indians" in fact were even more diverse than the societies they had known back in the "old world."

THE SPANISH AND THE PORTUGUESE

Just as the Inca and Aztec rulers were building their power, half a world away a similar process was taking place on the Iberian Peninsula at the southwestern tip of Europe as the emerging national monarchies of Spain and Portugal asserted their control over their political rivals. Like their counterparts in Mesoamerica and the Andes, the new monarchs of Iberia achieved greater political centralization than their predecessors and used history, religion, and ideology to buttress their positions. To a much greater degree than the Aztecs or the Incas, however, they insisted that their subjects conform fully to the officially sanctioned religion and eventually expelled religious deviants from their dominions.

Also in sharp contrast to the lords of Cuzco and Tenochtitlan, the Iberian monarchs showed an interest in what might lie beyond the ocean. Members of Portugal's royal family took the lead, experimenting with new navigation techniques and sponsoring expeditions along the coast of Africa from the early fifteenth century onward. By the time that King Ferdinand and Queen Isabella assumed their thrones in the 1470s, Spain was ready for overseas exploration as well. The Iberians' curiosity would have fateful consequences for the peoples of the Americas.

Centuries of Conquest

Iberia's position at the western end of the Mediterranean meant that for hundreds of years it was exposed to outsiders that indelibly shaped its culture. The Phoenicians, from the eastern Mediterranean, were among the first to exert such influence. Beginning between 800 and 1100 B.C.E., they established colonies at Cádiz and other points along the southern coast. The Phoenicians were well known as merchants throughout the Mediterranean, and they sold oil, wine, jewelry, and ivory to Iberians in exchange for gold, silver, copper, and tin. They also brought new techniques of metalworking, new architectural styles, and a form of writing that archaeologists have found on tombstones in what is now southern Portugal. Greek traders appeared in Iberia by about 600 B.C.E., followed in turn by the Carthaginians, who conquered the central and southern parts of the peninsula in the third century B.C.E. and set up a naval base at the present-day Spanish port of Cartagena.

Next came the Romans. They began their conquest of Iberia in 218 B.C.E. and drove out the Carthaginians, but met stiff resistance from indigenous Iberians that lasted more than a century. Dozens of Roman settler colonies appeared throughout Hispania, the Roman name for the Iberian Peninsula. The Romans' cultural impact was enormous, ranging from law and architecture to language and religion. Latin evolved on the peninsula into modern Spanish, Portuguese, and Catalan. Christianity entered Iberia in the Roman period, by the middle of the third century C.E. Under Roman rule, the peninsula carried on a thriving trade with the rest of the Mediterranean, exporting olive oil, horses, wine, wool, and metals. Roman domination ended in the fifth century, as the empire itself crumbled. Vandals, Visigoths, and other Germanic peoples crossed the Pyrenees Mountains and set up kingdoms in what are now Spain and Portugal.

In the early eighth century, Iberia witnessed yet another conquest, as Muslims crossed the Strait of Gibraltar from North Africa, took over most of the peninsula, and eventually set up the Umayyad Caliphate that ruled from their magnificent capital at Córdoba. Only the Basque country and the tiny kingdom of Asturias in the north remained under the control of Christian kings who claimed descent from the Visigoths. The Muslims extended religious toleration to Jews and Christians living in conquered territory, but many of the latter chose to convert to Islam.

Intellectual, artistic, and practical pursuits flourished in Muslim Iberia. The newcomers brought with them Arabic translations of texts on astronomy, mathematics, geography, and medicine from Persia, India, and Greece, including the work of the philosopher Aristotle. Christian scholars later rendered these texts into Latin, and subsequently circulated them to the rest of Europe. The Muslims also enhanced the productivity of agriculture in Spain and Portugal, introducing better irrigation techniques and new crops such as sugar cane and rice. They taught Iberians new craft specialties such as silk weaving and leatherworking. Spain's famous steel industry at Toledo also dates from the Muslim occupation. Arabic became the mostly widely spoken language in Iberia, not only among Muslims but among Christians and Jews as well. Christians even celebrated the mass and other rites in Arabic, and hundreds of Arabic words made their way into the Spanish and Portuguese languages.

Medieval Iberia and the Reconquista

By the mid-eighth century, Christians of the northern kingdoms began the *Reconquista,* a centuries-long process by which they wrested control of the

Spain and Portugal in 1492

Iberian Peninsula from the Muslims. Religion supplied a powerful driving force, but hunger for land to support a growing population also figured heavily in motivating the Christians' advance. As they gradually expanded their domains, the kingdoms of Castile (so named for the many castles, or *castillos,* built along the enemy frontier)—as well as León, Aragón, and Portugal took shape. But medieval Iberia also witnessed long periods of relatively peaceful coexistence between Christian and Muslim states. Often divided among themselves, Christian kingdoms sometimes struck alliances with Muslims against other Christian kingdoms.

The balance of power began shifting in the Christians' favor with the fragmentation of Muslim political unity after 1031. By the mid-thirteenth century the Reconquista was nearly complete. The capture of the southern region known as the Algarve in 1249 eliminated the last Muslim power in Portugal. Meanwhile King Fernando III of Castile, later canonized as a saint by the Catholic church, conquered Andalusia in the south, including the great cities of Córdoba and Seville. At Córdoba, the victorious Christians reconsecrated the city's splendid mosque as a Catholic church. In the east, Aragón took Valencia in 1238. Only the kingdom of Granada in southern Spain remained under Muslim control, and its rulers were forced to pay regular sums of money in tribute to the monarchs of Castile (see Plate 5).

The centuries of intermittent war with the Muslims left important marks on Iberian society and culture. Knights who led the southward thrust were rewarded with vast tracts of land, and other Christians willing to settle in the newly conquered territories received grants as well, thereby setting a precedent that would later be followed in the Americas. The Reconquista also reinforced traditional gender roles and a double standard of sexual conduct. Men were valued for their fighting abilities, and local authorities tolerated their sexual transgressions. Women, on the other hand, contributed to the Reconquista by recreating Christian family life in the new settlements within the seclusion of their homes and under the patriarchal sway of husbands and fathers.

The apostle St. James, known in Spanish as Santiago Matamoros, "killer of Moors" (Muslims), was believed to have aided in the Christian victories. His reputed burial place at Compostela in Galicia became a popular pilgrimage site by the tenth century. Mock battles between Christians and Moors became a part of Spanish folklore that would later be transported to America. Spain's national epic, *El Cid,* also dates from the Reconquista. It tells the story of Rodrigo Díaz, known as "the master," or *al-sayyid* in Arabic, who died in Valencia in 1099. He fought at various times as a mercenary for both Muslim and Christian kings, but legend subsequently made him a great champion of the Christian cause.

Iberian Monarchies in the Fifteenth Century

The defeat of the major Muslim principalities in the thirteenth century failed to bring immediate peace and prosperity to the Iberian Peninsula. Civil wars among the victorious Christian kingdoms continued over the next 200 years. Famines and epidemics added to the misery, especially when the infamous Black Death plague reached Iberia in the late 1340s. Portugal achieved a measure of political stability first. In 1385, King João I of the Aviz dynasty defeated a Castilian rival and assured the political independence of his kingdom, even though intermittent wars with Castile continued. João reigned until 1433, permitting him to trim the power of nobles who had sided with Castile and to consolidate his position further with the enthusiastic backing of a cadre of university-trained bureaucrats.

For Spain, the decisive turning point came in 1469 with the marriage of Isabella, a claimant to the thrones of Castile and León, and Ferdinand, heir to the crowns of Aragón, Catalonia, and Valencia. In 1474, Isabella's partisans defeated those of a rival contender and she became queen. Five years later, Ferdinand came into his legacy as well. The road to the nation's political consolidation lay open, and in 1516 their grandson Charles I became the first monarch of a united Spain.

Like the kings of the house of Aviz in Portugal, Ferdinand and Isabella curbed the political power of the feudal nobility and created a professional bureaucracy that would later play a crucial role in administering Spain's overseas colonies. They also reorganized the royal armies and dispatched a cadre of *corregidores,* who asserted crown authority over local municipal councils. Meanwhile, Ferdinand and Isabella became the champions of a militant Catholicism, with dire consequences for the many Jews and Muslims of Iberia.

The Breakdown of Iberian "Convivencia"

Despite the intermittent battles of the Reconquista, medieval Iberia enjoyed a fair degree of peaceful coexistence, or *convivencia,* among Christians, Jews, and Muslims. Jews often occupied positions of trust, serving as tax collectors and physicians to Christian kings and as administrators to Muslim potentates. Jews also figured among the peninsula's most prominent merchants and bankers. Although religious leaders of all three faiths exhorted their followers to refrain from participating in the rituals of "infidels," Christians sometimes visited mosques and synagogues with their Muslim and Jewish friends, and Muslims occasionally shared in Christian religious festivities. Muslim rulers officially forbade Christians living in their kingdoms to build new houses of worship, but as early as the ninth century there were various churches under construction not far from Córdoba.

Mutual toleration had its limits, however. In Christian and Muslim states alike, bloody purges periodically took the lives of many Jews, and Christians were sometimes sold as slaves to Muslims in Morocco. Discrimination against Jews grew noticeably in the fourteenth and fifteenth centuries. In Iberia and just about everywhere in medieval Europe, Jews living in Christian kingdoms had to wear special identifying badges and paid higher taxes than others. Many towns confined them to specific residential enclaves and restricted their economic activities. All Jews were banished from Aragón in the fourteenth century. In the face of rising persecution, many Spanish and Portuguese Jews nominally converted to Catholicism but often continued to practice their ancestral faith in secret. These "New Christians" became targets of popular prejudice and of restrictive laws barring them from certain occupations.

Ferdinand and Isabella thus assumed their respective thrones in a time of mounting religious intolerance. Known in Spanish history as the "Catholic Kings," they did not hesitate to use the power of the crown to enforce conformity. In 1478, they received the pope's permission to establish the Holy Office of the Inquisition to discipline New Christians who persisted in the practice of Judaism, as well as other Catholics who entertained ideas that ran counter to the teachings of the Church. Some 2000 New Christians were reportedly executed under Inquisition auspices in the 1480s, while many others were banished from their hometowns. In 1492, the monarchs ordered all remaining Jews to convert to Catholicism or leave Spanish territory. As a result, the number of superficial converts grew. Many Jews fled to Portugal, only to be faced with the same choice of forced conversion or permanent exile just a few years later. Portuguese authorities proved much more lax than their Spanish counterparts in enforcing these provisions, and those who did convert to Christianity fared somewhat better in Portugal because until 1536 there was no Inquisition to scrutinize their behavior.

The growing concern for religious purity brought fateful consequences for Muslims as well. Castile embarked upon a campaign to capture Granada in the 1480s and succeeded in 1492. Zealous clergy, with support from Queen Isabella, then set about converting Granada's Muslims to Catholicism and ordered the burning of thousands of Islamic books. In 1502, all Muslims living in Spain were told to become Catholics or leave. The Portuguese crown had issued a similar decree a few years before. Many Muslims followed the example of the Jews, converting superficially while continuing to practice Islam in secret.

A key figure in Spain's growing religious militancy was Francisco Jiménez de Cisneros, Archbishop of Toledo and head of the Inquisition. While working to eradicate all traces of Islam and Judaism, he also turned his attention to reforming the Spanish Catholic Church from within, exhorting his fellow clergy and the faithful to return to the doctrinal purity and behavioral austerity of the early Christians. The Spanish Church thus purged itself without breaking from Rome, and stood ready to defend Catholicism against the Protestant Reformation and to undertake ambitious missionary efforts in the American colonies.

Iberian Society in the Fifteenth Century

Population estimates for Spain and Portugal in the fifteenth century are nearly as uncertain as those for the Americas. The best available figures are about four million for the dominions of Castile and another one million apiece for Aragón and Portugal. Lisbon, Seville, Barcelona, and Valencia, each with fewer than 50,000 inhabitants, were the only real cities. Most Iberians were farmers, with wheat, wine, and olive oil the most important products. In the southern part of the peninsula, the warm climate favored the production of citrus fruits and sugar cane. The high and dry central plateau of Castile was best suited for cattle and sheep ranching.

Even though they had seen some of their political power undermined by the emerging monarchies of Spain and Portugal, the titled nobility–dukes, counts, marquises, and the like–still stood at the apex of Iberian society. Many of them purported to be descended from the early Visigoth kings, and most asserted that they or their ancestors had distinguished themselves fighting infidels during the Reconquista. They usually had large landholdings and many vassals who owed them tribute and allegiance. Much more numerous, especially in the north, were the untitled nobles, called *hidalgos* (or *hijos de algo,* "sons of something") in Spain and *fidalgos* in Portugal. These people were often of humble economic status but nonetheless boasted a distinguished lineage. They enjoyed exemption from certain taxes and freedom from arrest by anyone but the monarch's direct representative. Titled or not, all nobles cited their *limpieza de sangre*–literally, purity of blood, which meant that neither they nor their ancestors had ever been Jews, Muslims, or heretics prosecuted and convicted by the Inquisition.

The percentage of titled nobles and hidalgos in the total population varied considerably, from as many as 75 percent, most of them fairly humble hidalgos, in some parts of the north, to as few as 2 percent in the south. At most, they comprised about 10 percent of Castile's total population. The rest were commoners, the most prosperous of whom generally resided in the peninsula's many cities and towns. They exercised a variety of trades and professions. They were physicians, teachers, lawyers, merchants, and master craftsmen. Other commoners were peasant farmers or day laborers. Africans, both enslaved and free, constituted a small but growing segment of Iberia's population after Portuguese merchants began trading along the coast of Africa in the fifteenth century. Many were domestic servants in the wealthiest households of Seville, Lisbon, Valencia, and other towns, but some worked as stevedores and artisans. In sixteenth-century Seville, crown officials appointed free blacks to help govern the city's rapidly growing African community, and black Catholics created their own religious organizations. Resident colonies of foreign merchants, many of them from the Italian city of Genoa, could be found in the most important ports.

Queen Isabella, as we have seen, was a dynamic leader who brought considerable change to Castile during her long reign. But Isabella became queen only because there were no suitable male heirs in line for the throne of Castile. She was an exception to the long-entrenched rule of patriarchy, a system of social relations that vested virtually all authority from the household to the highest levels of church and state in male father-figures. Priests and judges exhorted wives to obey their husbands and live modestly within the seclusion of their homes. Denied access to the priesthood, women had no formal roles in official religious ritual comparable to those of their counterparts in Andean society. Even nuns were subject to the discipline of their bishops.

Not all women lived within the rules dictated by patriarchy, however. Lower class women simply could not remain secluded within their homes; they had to seek whatever work they could find in order to support themselves and their families. More and more women headed their own households, especially as growing numbers of men headed off on the overseas expeditions that began when Portuguese navigators first began probing southward along the African coast in the fifteenth century. Women also resisted the forced orthodoxy that Catholic authorities tried to impose. It was often mothers who kept Jewish beliefs and rites alive within the privacy of New Christian households, and the Inquisition prosecuted numerous women, old Christians and new alike, for heretical beliefs.

Iberia and the Beginnings of Overseas Expansion

The Mediterranean Sea bustled with commerce in the fifteenth century. At its eastern end, merchants exchanged woolen textiles and other European goods for Asian merchandise transported by caravans along the famous Silk Road of Central Asia or on ships up the Red Sea from the Indian Ocean. Cinnamon, pepper, ginger, cloves, and other spices from India and points eastward had become highly coveted additives to the Western European diet. Asian silks, cotton textiles, sugar, slaves, and precious stones found ready markets in Europe as well. Italians from Genoa and Venice dominated this trade, and they had pioneered sophisticated systems of credit, accounting, contract law and maritime insurance.

Meanwhile, Europeans were making significant advances in navigation science, including the use of the magnetic compass and new ships that could take better advantage of winds on the open sea. By the fifteenth century, Portugal had taken the lead in these developments, thanks in large part to the initiative of King João I's son Prince Henry (dubbed "the Navigator" by nineteenth-century historians). He gathered experts in navigation and geography and sponsored voyages along the coast of Africa and out into the Atlantic, voyages that would launch his nation as a world power.

Portugal's overseas empire officially began with the seizure of the Muslim stronghold of Ceuta on the Moroccan coast opposite Gibraltar in 1415. Over the next several decades, Portuguese merchants and sailors pushed farther south along the coast of Africa, establishing trading posts where they obtained gold, ivory, and slaves from local rulers in exchange for European horses, saddles, clothing, and tools. By 1482, they reached the mouth of the Congo River, and 6 years later Bartolomeu Dias had rounded the Cape of Good Hope at the southern tip of Africa. In 1498, another Portuguese expedition led by Vasco da Gama sailed around Africa and on to India, and over the next few decades his countrymen established trading posts at Goa on the west coast of India, in present-day Malaysia and Indonesia, and at Macao on the coast of China.

Portuguese merchants no longer needed Italian or Muslim intermediaries to access the wealth of what fifteenth-century Europeans called the "Indies," a term that included not only India but all of Asia and, by extension, any far-off land that might yield exotic merchandise and handsome profits. By no means did they believe that sailing around the tip of Africa was the only way to the lucrative markets of Asia, however. Most knowledgeable people understood that the world was round and that one could therefore sail westward and eventually reach the Orient.

In fact, Iberian navigators had already begun to venture out into the uncharted waters of the Atlantic. During the course of the fifteenth century, Portugal settled the previously uninhabited Azores and Madeira. Both Spain and Portugal fought over the rights to the Canary Islands until the dispute was settled in favor of Castile in 1479. The Guanches, native to the Canaries, were all but destroyed in the process, sharing the fate that would later befall Native Americans. Spanish and Portuguese sugar plantations in the Atlantic islands also foreshadowed the ones they would later set up in Brazil and the Caribbean.

CONCLUSION

The fifteenth and early sixteenth centuries of the Christian calendar witnessed the rise of four great monarchies—the Aztecs and the Incas in the Americas and Spain and Portugal on the southwestern fringe of Europe. As neighbors, Spain and Portugal of course were well aware of one another. Portugal had fought many battles to avoid being absorbed by Castile. The lords of Tenochtitlan and Cuzco may have heard sketchy rumors of one another's existence, but devoted their attention entirely to people closer to home that might become new subjects for their expanding dominions.

No one in Iberia or America knew what lay across the Atlantic. The Portuguese and the Spanish, however, were open to the possibility that venturing out to sea might yield great wealth and untold adventure. For many generations, they had heard the tales of China brought back by the thirteenth-century Italian traveler, Marco Polo, and they were familiar with exotic merchandise to be had from Asia, even if it had to pass through the hands of many middlemen before they were able to acquire it. Their religious traditions taught them something of far-off lands as well. Many believed that the apostle Thomas had carried the teachings of Jesus to India, and legends of Christian kingdoms in the east circulated throughout medieval Europe. Their knowledge of distant lands, both real and fictional, spread even more quickly following the invention of the printing press in the mid-fifteenth century.

In matters of geography, the people of Mesoamerica and the Andes had narrower horizons than their contemporaries on the other side of the Atlantic. Many of Europe's greatest cities in the fifteenth century—Genoa, Venice, Barcelona, Seville, Lisbon—lay close to the sea, while the most imposing settlements of North and South America were located inland. The Aztecs and the Incas accumulated vast riches from distant places, but these goods came to them chiefly by land, on the backs of llamas and other camelids in the Andes, and of human carriers in Mesoamerica. Waterborne transport was limited to canoes that plied the coast of Central America and the great inland lakes, such as Texcoco in Mexico and Titicaca in Peru.

It was not that the priests and rulers of Cuzco and Tenochtitlan lacked curiosity about distant worlds or kingdoms unseen. Like their forebears, they possessed detailed knowledge of the movements of the stars and the planets, in many ways superior to what Europeans of their time could boast. They maintained, elaborated, and passed on stories that explained the origins of the world they knew and the demise of worlds that had gone before. The underworld, the afterlife, and the realms of their many gods all occupied the attention of the best minds of the ancient Americas.

Nezahualcoyotl, ruler of Texcoco in the mid-fifteenth century, was a philosopher and poet as well as a king. Inside his 300-room palace compound were a library and archive, as well as special quarters for poets, philosophers, and historians. Many of his verses speculated on what awaited humans' discovery in the afterlife. It was not for want of intellectual prowess or curiosity, then, that the existence of flesh-and-blood human beings across the ocean caught the peoples of the Americas by surprise.

LEARNING MORE ABOUT LATIN AMERICANS

Carrasco, David, and Scott Sessions. *Daily Life of the Aztecs: People of the Sun and Earth* (Westport, CT: Greenwood Press, 1998). Places special emphasis on the importance of religion to the Aztec people.

D'Altroy, Terence N. *The Incas* (Oxford, U.K.: Blackwell, 2002). Another volume in *The Peoples of America* series; the best recent survey of Inca society, with information on the outlying fringes of the Inca Empire in Ecuador and Chile.

Menocal, María Rosa. *The Ornament of the World: How Muslims, Jews, and Christians Created a Culture of Tolerance in Medieval Spain* (New York: Little, Brown, 2002). A highly readable overview of the extraordinary cultural complexity of Spain from the eighth century to the early seventeenth century.

Perry, Mary Elizabeth. *Gender and Disorder in Early Modern Seville* (Princeton, NJ: Princeton University Press, 1990). An excellent social history of the Spanish city that became the chief port for trade with the Americas.

Silverblatt, Irene. *Moon, Sun, and Witches: Gender Ideologies and Class in Inca and Colonial Peru* (Princeton, NJ: Princeton University Press, 1987). A well-known feminist anthropologist shows how the Incas and the Spanish conquerors used ideologies of gender in consolidating their rule.

Smith, Michael E. *The Aztecs* (Oxford, U.K.: Blackwell, 1996). One of the leading authorities on pre-hispanic Mexico writes this volume for *The Peoples of America* series, with special emphasis on the technical achievements of the Aztecs.

3

THE EUROPEAN CONQUEST
OF AMERICA

WHEN CHRISTOPHER COLUMBUS first stepped ashore on the tiny island of Guanahaní in the Bahamas on October 12, 1492, he believed that the great continent of Asia could not be far off. Sailing along the north coast of Cuba a few weeks later, he was convinced he had reached Cipango (Japan). His dream of shipping valuable cargoes of silks and spices to the eager markets of Europe now lay at hand, and he would be Queen Isabella's viceroy, her personal representative, there in what he called "the Indies."

Over the next several decades, it became clear that Columbus had not reached Asia but instead had found a "new world," especially once intrepid conquistadors fell upon the magnificent empires of the Aztecs and the Incas. Isabella and Ferdinand and their grandson King Charles I accordingly expanded their ambitions far beyond the handful of trading posts envisioned in 1492. They now saw the Indies as new kingdoms to enhance the power, wealth, and prestige of Spain, and the natives of these lands—the "Indians"—as dutiful, tax-paying subjects. To administer this vast empire they dispatched a cadre of loyal bureaucrats to supplant the unruly explorers and conquistadors. Meanwhile, the monarchs' militant Catholicism drove them to sponsor a vigorous campaign to convert the natives of this new world to Christianity. By the mid-sixteenth century, the Portuguese crown had set up a colonial government in Brazil and Catholic missionaries had begun working there as well.

Isolated from Europe, Africa, and Asia for thousands of years, the natives of the Americas now became part of emerging empires that spanned the globe.

They not only had to swear allegiance to new sovereigns and accept a new religion; they also had to contend with the grandiose plans of thousands of Spaniards and Portuguese who followed Columbus westward across the Atlantic. These settlers saw the "Indians" as a source of labor to help them build their colony and exploit the natural resources of the new continent to serve the needs and desires of the newcomers. When Indians resisted their political, religious, or economic demands, the Europeans resorted to war, killing thousands and enslaving many more. Countless others died of smallpox, measles, and other "old world" diseases to which they had no previous exposure.

The natives who encountered Columbus and his crew on Guanahaní could not have known it, but these travel-weary sailors constituted the advance guard of a massive and brutal occupation of the Americas. The people of this hemisphere did not simply become passive victims of Spanish and Portuguese conquest, however. Some persistently fought back or retreated to remote deserts, mountains, and jungles beyond the intruders' reach. Others forged tactical alliances with the invaders in hope of gaining an advantage over long-standing enemies or to assure their personal survival and advancement under the new regime. The result was a colonial society built on indigenous accommodation and resistance as well as on European greed, military prowess, political drive, and religious fervor.

THE EUROPEANS ARRIVE

The people of the Caribbean and coastal Brazil were the first to experience the European invasion. Their settlements, their material culture, and their political organization bore little resemblance to Columbus's hometown of Genoa or the highly sophisticated societies of Asia that the European sailors knew at least by reputation. But ambitious Spanish and Portuguese colonists quickly found other ways to turn a profit from their accidental landfall—gold in the interior of Hispaniola, Cuba, and Puerto Rico, and valuable dyewoods in Brazil. Their pursuit of these valuable commodities inaugurated a chain of events that would have profound consequences for the native Caribbeans and Brazilians.

Columbus and the First Encounters

Queen Isabella of Castile was a busy monarch in the early months of 1492. In January, she accepted the surrender of the last Muslim ruler of Granada, and three months later she signed a contract with an Italian navigator named Christopher Columbus, who had finally persuaded her to sponsor a voyage to the west, across the "Ocean Sea." Both the queen and Columbus had high expectations for what the voyage might yield. Isabella accordingly named him admiral, viceroy, and governor of whatever lands he might encounter, and guaranteed

TIMELINE

1492
Columbus's first voyage

1500
Cabral's expedition lands in Brazil

1502
Nicolás de Ovando arrives as governor of Hispaniola, with 2500 colonists

1508–1511
Spanish settlement of Puerto Rico, Jamaica, and Cuba

1516
Charles I becomes first monarch of a united Spain

1518
First recorded outbreak of smallpox in the Americas; first direct slave imports from Africa to Spanish America

1519–1521
Conquest of Mexico

1532
Pizarro and Atahualpa meet

1536
Revolt of Manco Inca

1537–1548
Civil wars in Peru

1539–1542
Expeditions of Francisco Vásquez de Coronado and Hernando De Soto

1542–1543
New Laws issued in an attempt to curb abuses of natives in Spanish America

1549
Tomé Sousa arrives as governor of Brazil

1556
Philip II becomes king of Spain

1559–1562
Smallpox epidemic in coastal Brazil

1560s
Taqui Onkoy rebellion in Peru

1572
Defeat of the neo-Inca state at Vilcabamba in Peru

1580
Philip II of Spain becomes king of Portugal

1607–1608
Permanent English and French colonization of North America begins

1610s
Portuguese authorities defeat santidade movement in Brazil

1630–1654
Dutch control northeastern Brazil

1640
Portugal declares independence from Spain

him "one-tenth of all merchandise, whether pearls, gems, gold, silver, spices, or goods of any kind, that may be acquired by purchase, barter or any other means, within the boundaries of said Admiralty jurisdiction."

Columbus then proceeded to outfit three ships and a crew of 90 men for his voyage. The crew set sail in early August of 1492. Arriving at Guanahaní on October 12, he planted the royal standards of Ferdinand and Isabella on the island before heading on to the north coast of Cuba, where he concluded that he had found Cipango (Japan), and then proceeded eastward to Hispaniola. Embarking for Spain in January of 1493, a triumphant Columbus arrived in early March. With him sailed several Tainos he had taken into custody.

Eager to persuade the monarchs to finance a return voyage, Columbus gave a glowing report on his discoveries. "I found very many islands, inhabited by numberless people," he proclaimed. Cuba and Hispaniola constituted nothing short of a tropical paradise, with fertile soil, fine harbors, lush vegetation, fresh water, succulent fruits, and exotic birds. He described the people of the islands in equally enthusiastic terms. They were "exceedingly straightforward and trustworthy and most liberal with all that they have." The natives of Hispaniola, he noted in particular, willingly traded gold for whatever trinkets his crewmen offered. Columbus also found the islanders timid, "readily submissive," and not given to idolatry. He therefore concluded that they would make ideal candidates for conversion to Catholicism.

Columbus's account convinced the queen to outfit 17 ships that set out for the islands in late 1493. Some 1500 men (and apparently no women) were aboard, along with domestic animals, sugarcane and other plants, seeds, and tools needed to establish a permanent colony on Hispaniola. Meanwhile, word of the new lands spread quickly in Europe, and others hastened to join in the adventure and profits to be had. Columbus and others traveling under Spanish auspices soon reconnoitered the coasts of Puerto Rico, Jamaica, Central America, and Venezuela, while Portuguese navigators landed on the northeast tip of Brazil in 1500. Within a quarter century of Columbus's first voyage, European explorers and cartographers had sketched a remarkably complete outline of the Caribbean, as well as the eastern coasts of North, Central, and South America, and had crossed the Isthmus of Panamá to the Pacific Ocean. The Italian Amerigo Vespucci's accounts of his journeys circulated so widely in Europe that a form of his first name, "America," began appearing on maps of the new continent.

The Caribbean Colonies

Only Spain and Portugal were at this point ready to follow up the discoveries by attempting to form permanent colonies in the Americas. Spanish settlement remained confined to the island of Hispaniola for nearly two decades following Columbus's voyage. The city of Santo Domingo, founded in 1496, became the capital of the new colony. Queen Isabella soon reneged on the broad concessions she had made to Columbus, as the potential riches of Hispaniola became more evident and he proved incapable of establishing order there. In 1500, Francisco de Bobadilla arrived as governor and promptly had Columbus arrested. Two years later, Governor Nicolás de Ovando brought more than 2500 new colonists, men and women, and took definitive control of the colony. Between 1508 and 1511, other Spaniards began the permanent occupation of Puerto Rico, Jamaica, and Cuba.

Early settlers in the Caribbean supported themselves by panning for gold in the islands' interior highlands. Adapting practices employed during the reconquest of Iberia from the Muslims, they commandeered local natives to work and raided outlying islands and the southeastern mainland of North America for slaves. Popular legend holds that Juan Ponce de León, a veteran of Columbus's second voyage and conqueror of Puerto Rico, was looking for a "fountain of youth" when he landed in Florida in 1513. In truth, he sought gold and slaves. He never found the former, but native peoples from Florida were forcibly taken off to work for Spaniards in the Caribbean islands. Spaniards who engaged in slave raids assuaged their consciences by arguing that these Indians had resisted Christianity and thus had been legitimately captured.

The indigenous population of the Caribbean region declined dramatically during the first two decades after 1492. Some natives died in battles with the Spaniards, while others succumbed to the exploitive new labor regime. The demands of the European colonists disrupted native agriculture. Sickness, aggravated by malnutrition, also played a significant part. Although the first recorded outbreak of smallpox did not come until 1518, influenza and bacterial infections afflicted Spaniards and natives alike from the 1490s onward.

A few Spaniards rallied to the natives' defense. Foremost among them were a handful of Dominican friars newly arrived in Hispaniola. On the Sunday before Christmas in 1511, Antonio de Montesinos delivered a fiery sermon to the leading Spanish settlers in Santo Domingo, warning that they faced eternal damnation if they continued in their ways. Later, another Dominican, Bartolomé de Las Casas, took up the cause. In response to pressure from the Dominicans and other clerics, King Ferdinand issued laws codifying the *encomienda,* as the practice of distributing Indian workers to individual Spaniards had become known, and stipulated that the holders of these grants, called *encomenderos,* were to protect and Christianize the natives allotted to them.

The Portuguese in Brazil

Like Columbus in the Caribbean, Portuguese navigators were on their way to Asia when they first made landfall in Brazil. Pedro Alvares Cabral's fleet of 13 vessels set sail in 1500 intending to follow up on Vasco da Gama's successful voyage around the southern tip of Africa to India two years earlier. By design or by accident, Cabral pursued a more westward course and landed on the coast of Brazil. He and his crew spent eight days ashore before heading on to their original destination, while one ship hastened back to Portugal to inform the king of the discovery.

In 1501, the Portuguese returned, this time with the express purpose of reconnoitering the land. Early Portuguese impressions of the Brazilian natives were as glowing as Columbus's reports from the Caribbean: "In every house they all live together in harmony, with no dissension between them. They are so friendly that what belongs to one belongs to all." The only commodity of any value the Portuguese found was brazilwood, a dyewood long used by the Tupi

BARTOLOMÉ DE LAS CASAS, 1474–1566

THE EARLY LIFE of Bartolomé de Las Casas differed little from that of countless other Spaniards who made their way to the Americas in the sixteenth century. Born the same year that Queen Isabella claimed the throne of Castile, he was the son of Pedro de Las Casas, a merchant in Seville who accompanied Columbus to the Caribbean on his second voyage. In 1502, Bartolomé joined Nicolás de Ovando's colonizing expedition to Hispaniola. There he received an encomienda grant and assisted his father in outfitting the military campaigns that were so characteristic of early Spanish activity in the Caribbean. At the same time, he began learning indigenous languages and developed a sensitivity toward the natives not often found among his compatriots.

Within a short time, Bartolomé returned to Spain to resume his studies for the priesthood, a vocation he had abandoned when he shipped out to the Indies. He was ordained in Rome in 1507. Three years later, he was back in Hispaniola, and shortly thereafter he accompanied Diego de Velázquez to Cuba, baptizing natives as the conquest of the island proceeded. In Cuba, Las Casas received another encomienda as well as a land grant.

Soon, however, Las Casas had renounced his encomiendas and embarked upon a struggle to protect the natives of the Americas from Spanish exploitation, an effort that would claim his undivided attention for the rest of his long life. He made little headway in trying to convince other colonists to mend their ways, so he decided to take his case directly to the young King Charles. Arguing in favor of peaceful colonization and conversion rather than military conquest, he persuaded the king to abolish the encomienda. The simultaneous victory of Cortés in Mexico made that decree a dead letter, however.

Undaunted, Las Casas returned to the Indies and tried to put his ideas on peaceful colonization into practice. On the coast of Venezuela, he established what he hoped would be a model settlement, but local encomenderos soon sabotaged his plans. In Guatemala, he tried another experimental community, again with little success. Meanwhile, he became a member of the Dominican order, joining forces with the outspoken Antonio de Montesinos and other well-known critics of military conquest.

In 1544, his appointment as Bishop of Chiapas in southern Mexico gave him an opportunity to exercise spiritual leverage over Spaniards who exploited natives. He told priests in his diocese to deny the last rites of the Church to dying encomenderos who refused to liberate their Indians. With growing fervor, he argued that all Spanish wealth in the Indies was ill-gotten. In the eyes of authorities on both sides of the Atlantic, his increasingly militant stance veered perilously close to treason, questioning as it did the very presence of Spain in the Americas. Viceroy Antonio de Mendoza

(continued on next page)

BARTOLOMÉ DE LAS CASAS *(continued from previous page)*

openly reprimanded him, the Council of the Indies ordered him to return to Spain, and he resigned his post as bishop.

Las Casas was not to be silenced, however. He continued to press his case before King Charles and the Council of the Indies, arguing that the natives of the Americas, even if they were not baptized, were rational beings equal to Europeans in the eyes of God and that they possessed natural rights to their lands and a certain amount of political freedom. He even suggested that human sacrifice and ritual cannibalism were manifestations of native peoples' innate if mistaken yearnings to serve the one true God. Las Casas locked horns with the famous Spanish humanist Juan Ginés de Sepúlveda, who believed the philosopher Aristotle's idea that some people were slaves by nature and that military conquest was justified. The influence of Las Casas's views can be seen in the crown's continued initiatives to curb the power of encomenderos and protect the Indians from other abuses. It should be noted, however, that never did he suggest that the indigenous peoples of the Americas be allowed to reject Christianity in favor of their traditional religions.

During his long career, Las Casas wrote numerous treatises on the sufferings of the native peoples of the Americas under Spanish domination. His works were immediately translated into many languages and circulated throughout Europe. England and other rival powers, anxious to discredit Spain and claim a piece of the Indies for themselves, used his writings to rationalize their own colonial ventures in the Western Hemisphere. The wide circulation of Las Casas's ideas contributed heavily to the formation of the so-called Black Legend, a highly negative view of Spain and its empire that persists to the present, especially in the English-speaking world.

Questions for Discussion

Can Bartolomé de Las Casas be considered a man ahead of his time? Why or why not? Are there people in our own time who resemble Las Casas in their ideas and tactics? Are they more successful in getting their ideas across than he was? Why or why not?

to color their cotton fabrics. For the next two decades, the European presence in Brazil consisted of simple trading posts, permanently staffed by just a few individuals, similar to those they had set up in Africa. Natives cut the dyewoods and traded them for European tools, and Portuguese merchants were far more interested in the lucrative new opportunities for trade with India and the Far East that lay open for them at the dawn of the sixteenth century. A few Portuguese men, however, settled in native communities, married local women, and served as cultural intermediaries between Europeans and native Brazilians.

The crown's attention focused on its developing commercial empire in Asia, and there was little reason to spend precious resources setting up an elaborate government for a colony that yielded only dyewoods. Kings Manuel I (1495–1521) and João III (1521–1557) relied instead on private enterprise to explore and defend their American claims, awarding monopoly contracts to dyewood merchants willing to take on these added responsibilities. Such initiatives proved ineffective at keeping French interlopers from cutting into the brazilwood trade and setting up fortified posts along the coast. After a series of naval expeditions failed to dislodge the French, King João sent a large fleet under Captain Martim Afonso de Sousa to establish a more permanent Portuguese presence. In 1532, de Sousa founded the town of São Vicente on the southern coast of Brazil, about 300 miles southwest of today's city of Rio de Janeiro.

Meanwhile, King João attempted to promote the colonization along the entire length of Brazil's coastline while continuing to delegate substantial authority to private individuals. He divided the coast into 15 captaincies, and granted them to proprietors known as *donatários*, who had proven their loyalty to the crown through government service or participation in the establishment of Portugal's settlements in India. The donatário could recruit colonists, make land grants, found cities, administer justice, collect taxes, and receive a percentage of the profits from the trade in native slaves and dyewoods within his jurisdiction. Most of the captaincies failed for reasons that included hostility from local Indians, poor administration, and internal dissension among the colonists, many of whom resented the lordly pretensions of the proprietors. Four of the captaincies were never even settled at all.

A few of the proprietary colonies prospered, however. As donatário at São Vicente, Martim Afonso de Sousa fostered the development of sugar mills, partially financed by northern European investors. A short distance inland from São Vicente, the new town of São Paulo became a base to provide food and other supplies needed for the sugar industry. The captaincy of Pernambuco in the north also succeeded in solidifying the Portuguese presence in Brazil. Proprietor Duarte Coelho Pereira, a former soldier and diplomat in India, recruited a sizeable contingent of settlers and expanded the region's economic base, previously centered on dyewoods, to include sugar production. He also cultivated good relations with Indians in Pernambuco. His brother-in-law married the daughter of a local chief, and the proprietor encouraged other colonists to do likewise.

In other respects, however, the development of these captaincies proved disastrous for the indigenous peoples of Brazil. During the first 30 years after Cabral's arrival, when Portuguese settlers were few in number, the natives retained substantial control over the terms of their interaction with the foreigners. They cut dyewood when and where they pleased and exchanged the logs for knives and other useful tools brought from Europe. The successful donatários and their accompanying entourages disrupted this simple barter economy, as aspiring sugar planters enslaved the natives and appropriated their lands.

THE SPANISH IN MESOAMERICA AND THE ANDES

Meanwhile, the Spanish were steadily modifying their colonial agendas as they learned more about the new discoveries overseas. Abandoning their plans for the trading posts Columbus had envisioned, they established sizable permanent colonies, well stocked with familiar plants and domestic animals, and forced indigenous peoples to extract gold from the islands' interior highlands. Almost overnight, the natives of the Caribbean went from trading partners to slaves. At the same time, explorations along the coast of Mesoamerica yielded tantalizing rumors of fabulous kingdoms on the mainland. In 1517 and 1518, two separate expeditions landed in Yucatán. Even in decline, the Mayan city-states were far more impressive than anything Europeans had seen thus far in the Americas. Then in 1519, Hernán Cortés led several hundred of his countrymen over the mountains to the great city of Tenochtitlan. The discovery of the Inca empire followed 13 years later.

Given the formidable military prowess and imperial grandeur of the Aztecs and the Incas, conflict with the invaders was all but inevitable. Victory in battle, usually with the help of native allies, transformed the Spanish colonial project once again. The mainland held riches far greater than the islands of the Caribbean. The large and highly disciplined populations of Mexico and Peru looked like ideal candidates to become tribute-paying subjects of the Spanish crown, converts to Christianity, workers in the colonists' new enterprises, and active collaborators in building a new society in the Americas.

Cortés and the Aztecs

By 1518, Cuba had become the center of Spanish operations in the Caribbean, and it was from there that the expeditions to Mesoamerica were launched. With word of promising discoveries in Yucatán, Cuba's governor, Diego Velázquez, commissioned a local encomendero, Hernán Cortés, to lead an expedition to the mainland. Cortés prepared energetically for his new assignment, so much so that the governor began to see him as a rival and rescinded his commission. Ambitious and headstrong, Cortés set sail anyway, with 11 ships and about 500 men under his command.

The expedition headed first for Yucatán. There they met Jerónimo de Aguilar, a Spaniard who had shipwrecked there eight years before and was now fluent in the local Mayan dialect. Aguilar joined Cortés, and they proceeded along the coast to Tabasco, where native chiefs made a conciliatory offering of twenty young women to the Spaniards. As the expedition headed north along the Gulf Coast, Spaniards noticed that one of these women, known to history as Malinche, could converse with Nahuatl-speakers they encountered. She could also speak Mayan with Aguilar, who then translated her words into Spanish. Through these two interpreters, Cortés communicated with couriers dispatched by the Aztec emperor Moctezuma to investigate rumors of strange-looking intruders on the coast.

The messengers begged Cortés not to venture on toward Tenochtitlan, but he and his men were not to be deterred. Early in the march inland, they learned of unrest within the Mexica empire, as one disgruntled chief offered them several hundred porters to help carry weapons and supplies on their journey. Hearing next of Tlaxcala's long-standing enmity toward the Aztecs, Cortés proposed an alliance. The Tlaxcalans initially rejected his overtures, but they sued for peace after a few days' battle. Cortés next set his sights on Cholula, a nearby town only recently under Aztec control. There the Spaniards and their native

A map of Tenochtitlan–Mexico City designed by Cortés. In the sixteenth century, the custom of placing north at the top of maps had not yet become standard. In this map, the southern part of the valley of Mexico, with its fresh water lake, is at the top.

How Historians Understand	MALINCHE AND THE USES OF HISTORICAL MEMORY

Some historical figures capture the popular imagination, becoming the subjects of myth, fiction, and film. Sometimes too, they come to symbolize the preoccupations of later generations, even becoming scapegoats for collective anger and frustration. In the process, the real person and the historical context in which he or she lived are lost in emotionally charged debate. Such is the case of the Mexican woman baptized as Marina and more commonly known as Malinche.

As Cortés's interpreter, Malinche played a pivotal role in the Spanish conquest of Mexico, but we know very few details about her life. She was born about 1500, somewhere on the frontier between the Nahua and Maya regions of Mexico, and evidently was sold into slavery as a child. She was initially "given" to one of Cortés's lieutenants, Alonso Hernández de Puertocarrero. Only when her facility in Nahuatl became apparent did Cortés appropriate her for himself. In 1521 or thereabouts, she gave birth to Cortés's son Martín, and a short time later she married the Spaniard Juan Jaramillo in a Catholic ceremony. When Cortés departed Mexico City for Honduras, she and her husband went along, as did the deposed, captive emperor Cuauhtemoc. Along the way, Cortés charged that Cuauhtemoc was plotting rebellion and ordered him tried and executed. Malinche reportedly translated as Francis-

The massacre at Cholula, by an Indian artist of the sixteenth century. Malinche is shown on the right.

can friars heard the young king's confession. Meanwhile, she and Juan Jaramillo had a daughter, and shortly thereafter she died.

These are all the verifiable biographical details we have about Malinche. From her own time forward many conflicting images of her have appeared. The conquistador Bernal Díaz del Castillo made her the heroine of his lengthy narrative on the conquest of New Spain, describing occasions on which she reportedly saved the Spaniards from ambush and certain death. Sixteenth-century native pictorial representations of Malinche, with notations in Nahuatl, show her as a powerful figure much honored by her people. Later accounts present a highly romanticized story, full of patently false embellishments. Some, for example, have her traveling to Spain and being presented at the court of King Charles. Indians in Mexico down to today have appropriated her in folk dramas that depict the coming of Christianity.

Other portrayals of Malinche have not been so kind. Nationalistic Mexicans of the nineteenth and twentieth centuries vilified her for having "sold out" her own people to serve her own interests, and the term "malinchista" came to mean "traitor." Because she bore the children of Spaniards, Malinche has been cast as the archetypal mother of the Mexican nation, raped or seduced by the invaders. The Mexican philosopher Octavio Paz called her *la chingada,* a vulgar and highly pejorative term suggesting both rape and personal dishonor. Still other depictions trivialize her, presenting her as the love slave of Cortés.

What all of these accounts lack is an understanding of Malinche in the context of her situation. As feminist writers have pointed out, she and countless other native women were sexual objects in the eyes of native and Spanish men alike. What distinguished Malinche was her linguistic capability. Her childhood experiences gave her knowledge of two languages, but the historical record suggests that she possessed an exceptional ability to understand various dialects in both Maya and Nahuatl. She also apparently learned Spanish readily.

Malinche did what human beings in most other times and places have done. She used her special talents to make the best of a difficult situation, one in which women served as sexual objects and as pawns in the political intrigues of men. Those who blame her for betraying "her people" forget that the natives of the Americas saw themselves as many separate peoples of different languages, cultures, and political loyalties, with no more in common than sixteenth-century Spaniards thought they had with Germans or Swedes. Their common fate as colonial subjects transformed them into "Indians," first in the eyes of Europeans, and only much later in the eyes of native peoples themselves.

(continued on next page)

MALINCHE AND THE USES OF HISTORICAL MEMORY *(continued from previous page)*

The task of historians is to place Malinche and other historical figures within the context of the times in which they lived, with all of the possibilities and limitations that context provided. To cast her as a love-struck girl mesmerized by Cortés or as a duplicitous traitor is to make her something less than human.

Questions for Discussion

If a man had served as Cortés's principal interpreter, would the events of the conquest have been any different? Why or why not? Would the historical memory of a male interpreter have been different? If so, how? If not, why not?

---

consorts massacred several thousand warriors in a deliberate attempt to warn any others who might stand in their way. Meanwhile, Moctezuma could not halt the Spaniards' advance to Tenochtitlan.

On November 19, 1519, Moctezuma and Cortés met on the causeway at the southern entrance to the Mexica capital. Moctezuma allowed the Spaniards to enter the city and offered them lodging in the palace built by the emperor Axayacatl (1469–1481) at the center of town. For most members of the expedition, it was the largest city they had ever seen, with a population at least triple that of Seville. But Cortés felt vulnerable surrounded by potential enemies, and having no scruples about betraying Moctezuma's trust, he took him captive. An uneasy calm settled over the Valley of Mexico for the next several months, as leaders of surrounding city-states grew increasingly suspicious of the strangers' motives.

In the spring of 1520, Cortés learned that Governor Velázquez had sent an expedition from Cuba to oust him from the mainland. Leaving 80 Spanish soldiers in charge at Tenochtitlan, he headed to the coast, where he defeated his rival and added several hundred men to his own forces. The Spaniards' position at Tenochtitlan deteriorated badly in his absence when Cortés's lieutenant, Pedro de Alvarado, ordered an attack on a large gathering of Aztec nobles and the Mexica revolted.

Arriving back in Tenochtitlan, Cortés attempted to restore peace. He brought Moctezuma out on a rooftop to see if he could calm the populace. Instead Moctezuma was killed—by his own people, according to Spanish accounts; by the Spaniards, according to indigenous sources. Cortés and his forces then beat a hasty and undignified retreat, sustaining heavy losses as they fled on the night of June 30, 1520, the so-called *Noche Triste* ("sad night"). They did not abandon hope of taking Tenochtitlan, however. At Tlaxcala, they began preparing for a new assault. In December of 1520, some 550 Spaniards and 10,000 Tlaxcalans set out for the Valley of Mexico once again.

The attack on Tenochtitlan began in May, 1521. Swords, pikes, and armor made of steel, as well as crossbows, arquebuses, and cannons gave the invaders a clear advantage over adversaries armed only with wooden and obsidian weapons. Entering the city, however, they encountered fierce resistance. Block by block they advanced, destroying buildings and engaging defenders in hand-to-hand combat. On August 13, 1521, the battle for Tenochtitlan ended as the Spaniards captured the young king Cuauhtemoc. Cortés then subdued the surrounding valley, and the mighty empire of the Mexica collapsed. Tenochtitlan became the city of Mexico, capital of the colony that Cortés called "New Spain."

The Search for "Otro México"

Once they had seen the splendors of Tenochtitlan, the Spaniards reasoned that the new continent must hold other magnificent kingdoms. During the 20 years following Cortés's victory, a flood of new immigrants joined veteran conquistadors in a frantic search for "another Mexico." In so doing, they reconnoitered a vast expanse of territory reaching across what is now the United States from the Carolinas to California, southward to Central America, Peru, and Chile, and the entire length of the Amazon River.

Mexico and the Caribbean in the sixteenth century

- - - Present-day political boundaries

Cortés himself spearheaded the quest for new worlds to conquer. He ventured first to Central America, reaching Honduras by 1524, and later sponsored expeditions in the Gulf of California. His key lieutenant, Pedro de Alvarado, founded Guatemala City in 1524. Nuño de Guzmán, a bitter rival of Cortés and a brutal conquistador, headed north from Tenochtitlan, conquering of the Tarascan kingdom of Michoacán and founding the city of Guadalajara, while Francisco de Montejo set his sights on Yucatán.

In the 1520s, an abortive Spanish colony was established in present-day South Carolina, and numerous expeditions sought fortunes in Florida without success. Alvar Núñez Cabeza de Vaca was a survivor of one such venture. Fleeing hostile natives, he and many others attempted to return by sea from Florida to Mexico but shipwrecked on the coast of Texas instead. Most of his companions died, but Cabeza de Vaca and three other men spent the next several years wandering across Texas and northern Mexico, where they heard of great kingdoms somewhere to the north. In 1539, Francisco Vázquez de Coronado set off from Guadalajara to check on these reports. His travels took him to the people who became known as the Pueblo in present-day New Mexico and east to Kansas. One of his lieutenants even sighted the Grand Canyon. Meanwhile, Hernando De Soto reconnoitered over a wide area from the Appalachians to the Mississippi River, but neither of these expeditions found anything comparable to Tenochtitlan.

The Pizarros and the Incas

In the South American Andes, however, the Spaniards did find "another Mexico." As early as 1523, word circulated in Panama that a large empire lay somewhere to the south. Among those eager to follow up these leads was Francisco Pizarro, a Spaniard who had resided on the isthmus for several years. In 1531, Pizarro sailed with 180 men from Panama to the coast of Ecuador and Peru, gathering information on the Incas as he went. Learning that Atahualpa had defeated his rival and half-brother Huascar, Pizarro hastened to the mountains near Cajamarca, where the new emperor and his army were headquartered.

Pizarro and Atahualpa met at Cajamarca on November 16, 1532. The Spaniards had a familiar routine for such encounters. Native rulers were summarily informed that the invaders represented the true God and a great sovereign from across the sea and were "invited" to become Christians and subjects of the king of Spain. Atahualpa was not particularly impressed, even though the priest Vicente de Valverde presented him with a Bible and explained the intricacies of the Catholic faith. The emperor's scornful response provided the Spaniards an excuse to attack his troops and take the emperor into custody. Atahualpa then offered his captors a room full of gold and two of silver in exchange for his freedom, and arranged to have more than 13,000 pounds of gold and 26,000 pounds of silver brought to Cajamarca. Pizarro and his associates, however, decided that the emperor was a threat to their safety. In a mock trial, they convicted him of plotting against them and executed him in July of 1533. In the meantime, native warriors loyal to Atahualpa had killed Huascar.

Meanwhile, Pizarro seized Cuzco with the help of Indians hostile to the Incas and installed Atahualpa's half-brother Manco Inca as emperor, naively expecting him to cooperate fully with the Spaniards. In contrast to Cortés, Pizarro declined to make Cuzco the capital of the new colony of Peru, choosing instead the city of Lima on the coast, the "city of the kings," which he founded in 1535. Lima was well situated for Peru's integration in the emerging Spanish maritime empire, but it left Cuzco as a power base for his enemies, both Spanish and Indian. Other Spaniards marched northward into present-day Ecuador and Colombia.

Early in 1536, Manco Inca led a revolt, attacking Lima and besieging the Spanish settlers at Cuzco for nearly eight months. Unable to dislodge the Spaniards from either locale, Manco Inca and his forces retreated to the remote mountain fortress of Vilcabamba north of Cuzco, where they maintained a rebel neo-Inca state for more than 30 years. Meanwhile, civil war brewed among the conquistadors themselves. A key player was Diego de Almagro, a former sup-porter of Pizarro who felt he had not been suitably rewarded for his role in the conquest of Peru. In 1535, Almagro led an expedition to Chile, hoping to find there an alternative kingdom for himself. The venture yielded little, and two years later these frustrated would-be conquistadors straggled back to Cuzco to find the city in ruins and governed by Pizarro's brothers Hernando and Gon-zalo. Almagro felt that the right to control Cuzco was rightfully his, and he launched a revolt against the Pizarros.

The civil war lasted over a decade. Both Almagro and Francisco Pizarro died, and Hernando Pizarro spent 20 years in a Spanish prison for his role in the disturbances. In 1546 Gonzalo Pizarro and his supporters assassinated Peru's first viceroy, Blasco Núñez Vela, sent by King Charles to impose order and to enforce laws requiring that the colonists cease exploiting the Indians. Unrest continued until 1548, when a new governor arrived, defeated Gonzalo's forces, and had him beheaded. Although rivalry among the conquistadors continued, Spanish control of Peru now rested a more stable base, and by the early 1570s they defeated the native rebels at Vilcabamba.

Military Conquest or Strategic Alliance?

Historians have long debated how just a few hundred Spaniards, far from home and often divided among themselves, succeeded in toppling the mighty Aztec and Inca empires. Without question, European technology—steel swords, gunpowder, Spanish crossbows, the ships that Cortés constructed for his marine assault on Tenochtitlan via Lake Texcoco—gave them certain tactical advantages. Their weapons enabled them to kill at greater distances than their

Cartagena

COLOMBIA

Quito
ECUADOR

Cajamarca

PERU
Lima   Vilcabamba
      Cuzco

BOLIVIA

Pernambuco

Salvador
Da Bahia
De Todos
os Santos

BRAZIL

CHILE

São Paulo
Rio de Janeiro

Santiago   Buenos Aires   Montevideo

Strait of
Magellan

**South America in the sixteenth
century**

    - - - Present-day political boundaries

enemies could. Steel armor provided better protection than the quilted cotton
gear of native warriors. Spanish horses gave them superior mobility, at least in
open areas. Mastiffs, the huge dogs who accompanied the Spanish forces in Mexico, also inflicted casualties.

European technological superiority did not guarantee victory, however. By August of 1521, Cortés's forces had only 80 horses and 16 artillery pieces. Pizarro set off for Peru in 1531 with only 30 horses. Guns proved useless when powder supplies ran short, horses could not maneuver well in the narrow mountain passes of the Andes or on the causeways leading to Tenochtitlan, and native warriors readily seized swords from fallen conquistadors.

Infectious diseases also played a role in the Spanish conquests of Mexico and Peru. Smallpox struck Hispaniola in 1518 and apparently reached Mexico in 1520. It then spread to Peru well in advance of the conquistadors themselves. The disease disrupted native leadership, claiming the lives of the Mexica emperor Cuitlahuac, who succeeded Moctezuma, and the Inca Huayna Capac, father of the rivals Huascar and Atahualpa. The smallpox virus undermined the natives' will to resist the invaders, but it killed many native allies of the Spaniards as well.

Some historians and many popular writers have stressed psychological factors in explaining the victories of Cortés and Pizarro. They have portrayed Moctezuma as a fatalistic mystic incapable of decisive action as the bearded strangers drew near his capital. These writers have made much of later Spanish and indigenous reports, compiled a generation after the fact, that the Nahuas viewed Cortés and his men as gods, but there is no evidence that these claims are anything more than justifications crafted long after the fact. Cortés's own account shows no sign that the people of Mexico took him for a god.

A decisive factor in the "Spanish conquest" of Mexico and Peru was the assistance of thousands of indigenous people who fought alongside them. Historians have estimated that as many as 200,000 natives assisted Cortés as warriors and porters. Shrewd native chiefs looked to enhance their own political positions by ordering their soldiers to battle, not so much as allies of the Spanish, but as enemies of the Aztec and Inca states that had imposed so many demands upon them. These leaders understood the invaders had a significant technological edge, one that might well tip the balance and bring the downfall of Tenochtitlan and Cuzco. They could not have foreseen the consequences of this tactical maneuver—the creation of a colonial society in which Spaniards claimed the upper hand.

BUILDING A COLONIAL SOCIETY

For the native peoples of the Americas, the brutal slave raids and the defeat of the Aztec and Inca empires constituted just the first phase of the European occupation. Far more deadly were the diseases the intruders unwittingly brought with them. Their burdens mounted as conquistadors looked to translate what they had won on the battlefield into positions of power and wealth for themselves and commandeered native workers to help them build their colonies. Meanwhile, a new society was taking shape, as thousands of European immigrants and African slaves crossed the Atlantic during the course of the sixteenth century.

The Ecological Conquest

Humans were not the only living things that participated in the European invasion. Plants and animals brought by the incoming colonists and the unseen microbes that stowed away aboard ships crossing the Atlantic brought about a transformation of the natural environment unprecedented in human history. Smallpox struck some people even before they saw their first European, and it took many victims even as people of Tenochtitlan waged war on Cortés's forces. But these outbreaks were just the beginning of a long cycle of disease that repeatedly ravaged native peoples for many generations to come. Periodic episodes of smallpox, measles, influenza, plague, and typhus took thousands of lives and severely disrupted native society.

Even those who survived an epidemic might become its victims. Young children might be left with no one to care for them. When illness struck at a crucial point in the agricultural cycle, few hands were available to plant or harvest crops,

Engraving by the sixteenth-century Flemish artist Theodor de Bry, based on a woodcut published in 1557 by Hans Staden, a German soldier held captive by Tupis for several years. Images such as this circulated widely in Europe, helping fuel the Black Legend, the idea that the Spanish and the Portuguese were exceptionally brutal conquerors.

and famine loomed. Malnourished and weakened by the invaders' excessive labor demands, native people were in turn left more vulnerable to the next outbreak of disease. Because the epidemics took so many adults in the prime of their reproductive years, birth rates plummeted in native societies.

The new diseases and their indirect consequences brought demographic disaster for the indigenous peoples of the Americas. In the Caribbean, the native population all but disappeared within a couple of generations. Fifty years after Columbus's landfall, fewer than 2000 Indians remained on the island of Hispaniola. Coastal Brazil lost an estimated 95 percent of its aboriginal population during the sixteenth century, so that by 1600 only about 5000 Tupi survived. Estimates of the pre-contact population of the highland empires of Mexico and Peru vary widely, but there is no doubt that the population declined precipitously, perhaps by as much as 90 percent, over the first century following the Spanish invasion. Central Mexico had at least 10 million inhabitants when Cortés arrived, and perhaps as many as 25 million, while a century later the native population stood at just over 1 million. Only after the mid-seventeenth century, as native peoples began to acquire some resistance to the new diseases, did their numbers begin slowly to climb.

Diseases were just one element in the ecological conquest of the Americas. The Europeans brought many animals previously unknown to the native peoples. Although in time the Indians adopted horses, cattle, oxen, sheep, donkeys, goats, pigs, and chickens for their own uses, the immediate impact of these animals was severe damage to the ecosystem. Animals spread disease, trampled newly planted crops and polluted water supplies, while their grazing denuded the landscape and led to soil erosion, a problem further exacerbated by the Europeans' insatiable demands for timber and firewood. In coastal Brazil, on the other hand, the forest gained a reprieve with fewer natives to exploit its resources, but with the disappearance of the indigenous population, vital knowledge of the many uses of those resources was lost.

Not all effects of the ecological conquest were negative. Imported animals provided new sources of protein for the indigenous peoples. The natives also supplemented their diets with many new fruits and vegetables introduced by the Europeans. By the end of the sixteenth century, one could find apples, pears, and plums in many places, along with citrus fruits wherever the climate was warm enough. But even when the effects were beneficial, there is no question that the European invasion radically transformed the landscape of the Americas and the daily lives of native peoples.

Conquistadors, Encomenderos, and Native Peoples

Even before they set foot on the mainland of North and South America, the Spaniards had come to expect that they would tap the native labor supply to help them build their colony. In the Caribbean, they distributed encomiendas, which

Transporting horses
to America.

permitted individual colonists to compel groups of natives to work for them, and raided outlying areas for slaves. When they learned of the customary arrangements used by the Aztecs and the Incas to compel their subjects to work, they immediately began devising ways to redirect this vast labor supply to their own purposes.

Cortés, Pizarro, and other conquistadors gave encomiendas to their favored associates almost immediately following their military victories. Each of the 168 men who accompanied Pizarro at Cajamarca got encomiendas, and by 1542 Peru had 467 grantees, while in Mexico and Central America their numbers topped 600. Again following pre-hispanic custom, encomenderos in Mesoamerica and the Andes also received tribute in the form of various commodities from "their" Indians, and they claimed the right to bequeath their encomiendas to their sons and daughters.

Authorities in Spain were not happy with this development. Reformers such as the outspoken Dominican priest Bartolomé de Las Casas had convinced King Charles to abolish the encomienda just as the conquest of Mexico was taking place. When he heard of Cortés's victory, the king reluctantly changed his mind, accepting the argument that the incentive of encomiendas that could be passed on to their heirs would persuade restless conquistadors to settle down and build Spanish colonies. King Charles also feared that a powerful, hereditary encomendero class might threaten his own control over his new dominions, and over the next three decades he did what he could to prevent them from consolidating their position. He found excuses to confiscate encomiendas from those who flagrantly exploited their Indians and to prevent encomenderos from bequeathing their grants to succeeding generations. According to the "New Laws" of 1542–1543, encomenderos could only demand tribute, and not labor, from natives allotted to them, while other royal orders supposedly forbade the further enslavement of native peoples. Meanwhile, the steady decline in the native population greatly reduced the amount of tribute that encomenderos could expect.

Measures designed to trim the power of the encomenderos found enthusiastic support from Las Casas and other defenders of the Indians but met stiff resistance from Spaniards residing in the colonies. Prudent royal officials frequently suspended laws emanating from Spain. Those who headed new colonization expeditions to outlying areas got royal permission to grant encomiendas, and settlers in frontier regions from New Mexico to Chile continued outright enslavement of native peoples as well. Even when an encomendero's rights were in fact revoked, the natives got no reprieve. They now just delivered their tribute to the king's treasury and were subjected to forced labor drafts mandated by colonial officials.

A Multiracial Society in Formation

Encomenderos and other veterans of the early expeditions of exploration and conquest were the founders of civil society in the Spanish colonies. It was they who established many of Latin America's most distinguished cities, from Guadalajara and Durango in northern Mexico to Santiago in Chile. Soon, however, growing numbers of people who had not participated in the conquest appeared. A cadre of bureaucrats loyal to the crown arrived to take the reins of political power from the conquistadors just as they had supplanted Columbus in the Caribbean. And as word spread in Spain that riches could be had in the new lands, thousands of people ventured out to the Indies, especially after rich silver deposits were discovered in Mexico and Peru in the 1540s. A substantial merchant class developed in Lima even during the tumultuous years of civil war. Indeed, some merchants profited handsomely from selling provisions to the rival armies. Meanwhile, by the early 1540s hundreds of Spanish artisans plied their trades in Mexico City and Peru—tailors, shoemakers, hatters, barbers, carpenters, silk weavers, and blacksmiths, to name a few.

The vast majority—90 percent or more—of the early immigrants to Spanish America and Brazil were male, and most were relatively young, in their 20s and 30s. This preponderance of males, together with a conquest mentality that encouraged both forcible and consensual sex with Indian women, resulted in the birth of racially mixed children called *mestizos* in the Spanish colonies and *mamelucos* in Brazil. A male was called a mestizo or a mameluco; a female was a mestiza or a mameluca. The words "mestizos" and "mamelucos" could denote a group of males or a group composed of both males and females.

Some Spanish conquistadors married newly baptized Indian women in Catholic ceremonies. In fact, the crown encouraged unions between encomenderos and daughters of the Indian nobility as a way of consolidating control over the native ruling class. Children of these marriages grew up as virtual Spaniards in their fathers' households and often stood to inherit considerable wealth and social status. Some mestizos born out of wedlock were recognized and cared for by their fathers as well. Martín Cortés, son of Hernán Cortés and Malinche, went to Spain with his father and became a page to King Philip II, while Pedro de Alvarado's mestiza daughter married into the Spanish nobility.

Many other mestizos born out of wedlock remained with their mothers in Indian communities or were left abandoned in the streets of the new cities of Spanish America. In the eyes of the Catholic Church, they bore the stigma of illegitimacy. Civil authorities saw mestizo boys as a threat to the stability of the colony, although they harbored some hope that girls, if properly educated, could become good wives to future Spanish immigrants.

People of African descent formed another important component of early colonial society. Free blacks from Seville and other Iberian towns joined some of the earliest expeditions to the Americas. Enslaved Africans first appeared during the Caribbean phase of settlement and increased in importance as Spaniards set up households and farms on the mainland. Africans shared the Europeans' acquired immunity to the diseases that so devastated the native communities, and Spaniards and Portuguese settlers generally believed that Africans were physically stronger than Indians. At first, King Charles allowed only Christianized slaves who had lived in Spain to enter the colonies, but in 1518 he authorized direct imports from Africa. By the end of the sixteenth century, between 75,000 and 90,000 enslaved Africans had entered the Spanish colonies. Blacks outnumbered Europeans throughout the Latin American colonies, sometimes overwhelmingly. In Hispaniola, for example, there were reportedly 30,000 Africans and only 2000 Spaniards in 1567.

Spanish and Portuguese law provided various ways for slaves to gain their freedom. Some masters freed at least a few slaves in their wills, and a slave could accumulate money to buy his or her freedom. Still others simply ran away, fleeing to outlying frontiers where they could reinvent themselves as free men and women. Some runaways formed communities where they defied colonial authorities and resisted all efforts to re-enslave them. Children born to free women were automatically free, regardless of their racial identity or the status of their fathers. Africans both enslaved and free coupled with whites and natives. Offspring of these unions were often called *mulattos* in both the Spanish and Portuguese colonies. Males were mulattos; females were mulattas. By the end of the sixteenth century, a multiracial colonial society was rapidly taking shape throughout Latin America.

Slice of Life THE CUZCO CABILDO FOUNDS A CONVENT, 1551

THE DUST had barely settled from Peru's civil wars and the neo-Incas were still holding forth at Vilcabamba when the cabildo members convened on the morning of April 17, 1551. At the top of their agenda that day were their concerns about the city's growing population of mestizos, the offspring of Spaniards and Indian women. The oldest of these were now in their teens, and the boys among them especially were nothing but troublemakers in the councilmen's view. For young women of mixed ancestry (mestizas), however, the city's founders saw a potentially positive role in building Spanish society in the Andes. As the leading Spanish citizens of Cuzco saw it, if these young women were removed from the baneful influence of their Indian mothers and properly instructed in the ways of Christian womanhood, they might become the wives of Spaniards and the mothers of the next generation of the city's growing hispanicized community.

Not incidentally, these women could also help the encomenderos to consolidate their position. King Charles had recently reaffirmed his determination to confiscate encomiendas of unmarried men in an effort to get unruly conquistadors to settle down into proper domesticity. As Spanish women were still in short supply, these acculturated mestizas could become an attractive alternative. Although at this point apparently all of Cuzco's encomenderos had Spanish wives, perhaps they were looking ahead to arranging acceptable marriages for the sons who would, they hoped, inherit their encomiendas. Moreover, some of the town's leading Spanish citizens had no surviving children other than ones they had fathered by Indian women. Especially if their mestiza daughters stood to inherit substantial estates, even encomiendas, it was important that they receive a suitable upbringing.

The council therefore voted that April morning to establish a convent where these young women might receive the education and indoctrination they needed while preserving their virginity, a prerequisite for a proper Catholic marriage. Over the next few weeks, the cabildo purchased property from the executor of Hernando Pizarro's estate, using funds donated by one of their number, the wealthy conquistador and encomendero Diego Maldonado. Like most of his fellow councilmen, he had fathered mestizo children, a son and a daughter, out of wedlock. They were his sole heirs, for he and his Spanish wife had no offspring. Their mother was a sister of the Inca emperor Atalhualpa "given" to him by Francisco Pizarro at Cajamarca.

A Spanish widow named Francisca Ortiz de Ayala, later known as Francisca de Jesús, agreed to serve as the convent's first abbess. Over the next 10 years, dozens of girls, most of them mestizas, entered the Convent of Santa Clara. Some were "orphans," meaning that at least their Spanish fathers were dead or unknown, even if their Indian mothers were still living. A greater number, however, were the daughters of living Spaniards who had personally placed

(continued on next page)

THE CUZCO CABILDO FOUNDS A CONVENT, 1551   *(continued from previous page)*

them in the convent and provided stipends for their support. A few of the women and girls housed there were Indians, like Beatriz Clara Coya, daughter of one of Vilcabamba's neo-Inca emperors, Inca Sayri Tupac, who in the early 1560s abandoned the rebel cause, made peace with the Spaniards, and placed the six-year-old Beatriz in the convent of Santa Clara.

Eighteen of the convent's first cohort became nuns and remained within its walls, but nearly twice as many left, and at least ten of them married Spaniards, fulfilling one of the founders' most compelling objectives. Meanwhile, the convent began accumulating real estate. As early as 1565, its assets included several houses in the city itself and a store on its central plaza, as well as various rural properties and even an encomienda.

In time, the role of the Convent of Santa Clara changed, reflecting the transformations underway in colonial society at large. Growing numbers of Spanish women entered the convent and dominated its internal governance, while mestiza nuns found themselves relegated to second-class status. The crucial role of mestizas as builders of a new empire had passed, as colonial elites found more and more women of Spanish extraction available as wives.

Questions for Discussion

Compare the role of women in the building of the Spanish Empire with that of women in the Inca Empire. What does the history of the Convent of Santa Clara tell us about the position of mestizas in Spanish colonial society?

THE "SPIRITUAL CONQUEST" OF LATIN AMERICA

Even as they coped with the effects of biological conquest and the formation of a colonial society, the indigenous peoples of the Americas faced a challenge to their religious beliefs and practices. To the European mind, the moral justification for Spanish and Portuguese occupation of this new world rested on their commitment to convert the natives to Roman Catholicism. This conversion had to be a total one. Natives were not to be allowed to choose which elements of Christianity they adopted and which elements of their old religions they retained. Missionary efforts made little headway in the early phases of settlement in the Caribbean, but the chance to baptize thousands at a time in Mexico and Peru prompted what some historians have called the "spiritual conquest" of America. In fact, as the missionaries would soon discover to their dismay, they failed to secure the natives' absolute acceptance of Christianity to the exclusion of all other faiths.

Early Evangelization

The Spanish Church experienced a major revitalization just as the age of overseas colonization was beginning. Members of monastic orders such as the Franciscans and Dominicans eagerly participated in this attempt to rid the church of corruption and return the observance of Catholicism to a purity and simplicity closer to the teachings of Jesus. The new colonies across the Atlantic offered a prime site to build a new church that would more faithfully embody these ideals.

Although two priests accompanied Cortés, baptizing the nobles of Tlaxcala even before the defeat of Tenochtitlan, the spiritual conquest of the mainland empires began in earnest when 12 Franciscan friars arrived in Mexico in 1524. These men believed that the end of the world and the second coming of Christ were imminent, and they saw themselves engaged in a struggle with the devil himself for the hearts and minds of the natives. The early Franciscans felt that, once freed from the clutches of Satan, the Indians could become good Christians.

As natives submitted to baptism, the Franciscans' optimism grew. They even envisioned the eventual creation of a native priesthood, and they identified promising candidates for ordination, often the sons of local rulers. In 1536, they established the College of Santa Cruz de Tlatelolco in Mexico City, where these young men studied Catholic theology and Latin while also learning to write Nahuatl in the European alphabet. Indian girls were ineligible for the priesthood, but the Franciscans did emphasize the importance of preparing them to be good Christian wives and mothers. Missionaries established ten schools for daughters of the native Mexican elite in the 1520s. A Spanish woman directed one such school in the town of Texcoco. Along with their catechism lessons and training in practical skills such as embroidery, pupils learned about Catholic ideals of feminine behavior.

Augustinians, Dominicans, and other orders soon joined the Franciscans. By 1559, some 800 missionaries were at work in Mexico. With the help of thousands of native laborers, they built 160 churches and monasteries, frequently on the sites of pre-hispanic temples. Evangelization in Peru got a later start and proceeded more slowly due to the civil wars among the Spaniards, but Franciscans, Dominicans, Mercedarians, and Jesuits were all active in former Inca domains by the 1570s. Meanwhile, Jesuits and other missionaries began work among the Tupi in Brazil.

Missionaries faced the daunting challenge of communicating with their potential converts. They used pictures, pantomimes, and native interpreters, but many priests became convinced of the need to learn indigenous languages in order to proceed with their work. Dozens of grammar books, dictionaries, confession manuals, and sermons soon appeared in many different native tongues. The first book printed in the Americas was a Nahuatl catechism produced in Mexico City in 1539.

In fact, however, missionaries were often hard pressed to learn more than one new language, and they usually concentrated on Nahuatl in Mexico and Quechua in Peru. As the Aztec and Inca empires had extended their dominions

Church of Santo Domingo, Cuzco, Peru, built on the foundations of an Inca temple.

in the fifteenth century, each of these two languages had become a lingua franca, a means of communication among native speakers of many other indigenous tongues in Mesoamerica and the Andes. In the sixteenth century, universities established in Mexico City and Lima began offering courses in Nahuatl and Quechua for men training to become priests, who then used them in their missionary work. The spiritual conquest thereby contributed to the continued spread of Nahuatl and Quechua in Mesoamerica and the Andes respectively.

The Impact of Evangelization

For the native peoples of the Americas, conversion to Christianity meant much more than the substitution of Christian ritual and dogma for their traditional ways of ceremony and belief. Family and community life changed dramatically under missionary rule. Priests often forced them to move their homes. In many parts of Mesoamerica and the Andes, priests and civil authorities tried to consolidate widely dispersed communities into more compact units, closer to the monasteries, where they could receive more regular indoctrination and where their behavior might be more closely monitored.

Franciscans and Jesuits working in Brazil rounded up Tupis in raids that differed little from slave-gathering expeditions. They then resettled the natives in compact mission villages called *aldeias* in hopes of transforming them into Portuguese-style peasants. Concentration of the native population helped spread disease among the Tupi. A smallpox epidemic swept coastal Brazil between 1559 and 1562, claiming the lives of one-third of the Indians living in the Jesuit aldeias and forcing missionaries and surviving natives to abandon many of the villages. The missions that remained served as tempting targets for slave raiders, and the Jesuits became outspoken critics of the enslavement of the Brazilian natives. At the same time, however, the missionaries frequently rented Indians out to Portuguese settlers in need of laborers.

Conversion to Catholicism brought many other changes as well. Native peoples received saints' names at baptism. The Christian calendar with its 7-day week and cycle of holy days replaced old ways of reckoning the passage of time and regulated activities such as market days. Evangelization also altered customary gender roles, especially in Peru, where women had played an important part in traditional religious life by maintaining cults of female deities. Catholic ritual recognized no comparable roles for women.

Catholic missionaries' reach extended to the most intimate spheres of native life. They tried without a great deal of success to suppress what they viewed as indigenous societies' excessive tolerance for premarital sex and divorce. They exhorted couples to marry in Christian ceremonies and expected those living in polygamous relationships to settle down with one spouse. Europeans also believed that the nuclear family consisting of husband, wife, and children was the building block of a civilized society. Franciscan missionaries in Yucatán thus broke up extended family households at a time when smallpox and other diseases were already disrupting native kinship networks.

Resistance to Christianity

The native peoples' responses to the missionaries were ambivalent at best. In many places, they had long been accustomed to accepting the gods and rituals of a conquering people without abandoning their traditional deities and practices. The friars' insistence that they reject their "pagan" beliefs entirely and embrace Christian dogma wholeheartedly proved more troubling, especially for those who had reached adulthood before the arrival of the Europeans. For this reason, missionaries in Mexico and Peru targeted young people for indoctrination, often consciously undermining parental authority in the process.

Natives' resistance to conversion dampened the friars' initial optimism about the possibility of turning them into model Catholics and training a native priesthood. Particularly disillusioning were the cases of their "star pupils" who slipped back into their old ways after having apparently accepted Catholicism, and the missionaries often reacted harshly. The early bishops in Mexico subjected Indians to the proceedings of the Inquisition. In one particularly notorious case, Bishop Juan de Zumárraga ordered the public execution of the young Indian

chief Carlos Ometochtzin of Texcoco, who had allegedly relapsed into pagan-
ism after having been considered a prime example of the missionaries' success.
Another famous episode occurred in Yucatán in 1562. The Franciscan Diego de
Landa became alarmed at reports that Mayas whom he had considered willing
converts were in fact continuing their customary rites, including human sacrifice. Thousands were taken into custody and interrogated under torture, and
Landa ordered the destruction of all pre-hispanic Mayan books. Only four manuscripts are known to have survived.

In some places, native resistance to Christianity took the form of militant
mass rebellions that aimed to overturn European domination and restore the
supremacy of ancient gods. One such movement, known as Taqui Onkoy, spread
throughout the Andes in the 1560s. Its adherents came from a broad spectrum
of native society, including a number of traditional rulers (*kurakas*) as well as hispanicized Indians who had lived in Spanish settlements. Over half its participants were female.

The Taqui Onkoy rebels exhorted Andean natives to set aside their ethnic
divisions to form a united front against the Spaniards. They rejected all Christian religious symbols while promoting pre-Inca regional gods. Rebel leaders
urged their followers to resist tribute and labor demands imposed by the Spanish. In place of an exploitive colonial society, they promised a new millennium
of abundance. The pan-Andean unity projected by the rebels proved difficult to
achieve, however, and the rebellion collapsed in the face of brutal repression
mounted by Spanish authorities.

Other sixteenth-century rebellions utilized Christian symbols in their rejec-
tion of European domination. A series of messianic revolts known collectively
as *santidade* swept northeastern Brazil, for example. Indians who had come into
close contact with Portuguese settlers, either as aldeia residents or slaves, along
with Africans who had escaped from their Portuguese captors, set up their own
communities. They envisioned a golden age that would follow the expulsion of
the invaders. The rebels fashioned idols that they believed would make them
less vulnerable to whites, but they also made free use of such Catholic religious
artifacts as the rosary, appointed their own "pope" and "bishops," and sent "missionaries" to spread the word. By 1610, an estimated 20,000 blacks and Indians
had fled to santidade communities. Portuguese authorities then ordered an all-
out military offensive to wipe them out.

In the face of the many calamities they suffered during the course of the sixteenth century, the natives of the Americas were often unsure which gods they
had offended. Were their familiar deities angry because they had submitted to
baptism and allowed the Catholic priests to destroy old idols and temples? Or,
as the missionaries repeatedly told them, was the Christian god upset because
they had not given themselves completely to the new faith? Most people
undoubtedly hedged their bets as best they could, electing to appease any and

all supernatural forces. They outwardly conformed to the missionaries' message while continuing to practice traditional rituals as well. In the eyes of the Church, they became *niños con barbas* or "children with beards," incapable of comprehending the full intricacies of Catholicism and in need of constant supervision and teaching by missionary priests.

THE CONSOLIDATION OF COLONIAL EMPIRES

The century following Columbus's voyage witnessed the creation of the first empires to span the entire globe. The Portuguese led the way, starting trading ventures along the coast of Brazil at the same time their countrymen were establishing similar posts at Goa in India and Macao in China, half a world away. Spain was not far behind. Just as Cortés was conquering Mexico, King Charles sponsored the first expedition to circumnavigate the globe, captained by the Portuguese navigator Ferdinand Magellan. Their route took them through what would soon become known as the Strait of Magellan at the southern tip of South America and then across the Pacific to the Philippine Islands, which became a Spanish colony following their definitive conquest in the 1560s.

Administration of these vast new empires required new institutions of government overseas to insure that European settlers and colonial subjects behaved themselves and maintained respect for royal authority. Especially in Spanish America, an elaborate bureaucracy appeared, charged with the task of overseeing the flow of revenue into the king's coffers. Equally important was the creation of a Church infrastructure to minister to colonists and carry on the work of converting "heathens" to Christianity.

The Viceroyalties of New Spain and Peru

The most powerful colonial officials in the sixteenth century were the viceroys, literally "vice-kings," who represented the king of Spain in Mexico City and Lima. These men supervised virtually every aspect of government, from administration of justice to finance and defense, as well as the operations of the Church. The jurisdiction of the viceroy of New Spain included all of what is now Mexico and adjacent portions of the southwestern United States, as well as the Caribbean, Central America, and the Philippines. The viceroy of Peru governed all of Spanish South America.

Those chosen for these positions had to be people the king could trust, not ambitious conquistadors likely to put their own interests first. Antonio de Mendoza, who in 1535 arrived in Mexico City to take command as the first viceroy of New Spain, was a particularly dedicated servant of the crown. A member of the Spanish nobility and a former ambassador to Rome, Mendoza successfully relegated Hernán Cortés to the sidelines. He enforced a royal order that forbade

Cortés to meddle in political affairs or even to enter Mexico City, but the king compensated the conqueror with an encomienda of over 100,000 Indians and the title of Marqués del Valle de Oaxaca. When rumors surfaced that a fabulous kingdom might lie somewhere in the far north of New Spain, Mendoza sent a trusted associate, Francisco Vázquez de Coronado, to investigate them, rather than let Cortés or anyone else be the one to discover "another Mexico."

Viceroy Mendoza supervised the activities of the Church in Mexico and personally established numerous schools, hospitals, and other social welfare institutions. He also contributed to the political stability of the colony by negotiating a workable compromise between the king and the encomenderos over the implementation of the New Laws of 1542–1543, a set of regulations aimed at ending the abuse of native peoples and trimming the power of the encomenderos. The effectiveness of royal control over New Spain became evident in the mid-1560s, when the king's representatives decisively suppressed an uprising of young encomenderos who had rallied around Martín Cortés, the only son born to the conquistador and his Spanish wife (not to be confused with Cortés's son by Malinche, also named Martín). Several of the ringleaders were beheaded, though not Cortés.

The consolidation of royal government in Peru proceeded less smoothly. Angry colonists assassinated the first viceroy, Blasco Núñez Vela, when he tried to quell civil unrest and enforce the New Laws. In 1550, the king dispatched Antonio de Mendoza to see if he could do in Lima what he had done in Mexico City, but Mendoza died shortly after assuming his post. It was not until 1569, with the arrival of Peru's decisive, heavy-handed fourth viceroy, Francisco de Toledo, that Spanish government became firmly established in the former Inca domains.

Toledo first spent five years traveling throughout the viceroyalty with an elaborate entourage and developing a plan of government. Defeat of the rebel neo-Inca state at Vilcabamba was a top priority, accomplished by 1572, when the viceroy personally ordered the execution of the native leader Tupac Amaru over the objections of leading churchmen. Meanwhile, he effectively curbed the power of the encomenderos and imposed massive changes on the native population of the Andean highlands. To supply workers for the developing silver mines of Peru, he instituted the labor draft known as the *mita,* modeled on pre-hispanic practices but far more onerous. He also ordered the resettlement of the surviving native population into more compact units, a process that seriously disrupted traditional ayllu networks and forced native peoples to abandon sites sacred in their traditional religious practice. By the 1570s, then, new rulers representing a distant monarch had decisively replaced the lords of Tenochtitlan and Cuzco.

The Spanish Colonial Bureaucracy

Many other individuals played key roles in Spain's rapidly developing machinery of empire. Some governed from the mother country itself. In 1503, Queen Isabella established the Casa de Contratación, or House of Trade, to regulate the flow of goods and people to and from the colonies. Following the conquest of Mexico, a more elaborate infrastructure was needed to supervise the growing overseas dominions. In 1524, King Charles created the Council of the Indies to formulate colonial polices.

Others performed important duties in the colonies. Major Spanish cities, beginning with Santo Domingo in 1511, became seats of *audiencias,* bodies comprised of three or more lawyers who acted as courts of appeal and carried out various kinds of administrative functions over fairly large districts. The audiencia of Mexico City, established in 1527, held jurisdiction over much of central Mexico, while a similar body headquartered at Lima assisted the viceroy in governing Peru. By 1560, additional audiencias had been set up at such cities as Guadalajara in Mexico, Quito in Ecuador, and Chuquisaca in Upper Peru (present-day Bolivia). Other audiencias followed, including one established at Santiago, Chile, in 1609.

As direct representatives of the viceroys, provincial governors wielded executive, judicial, and military authority in outlying areas. With the development of silver mining in Mexico and Peru came an elaborate bureaucracy to collect taxes that miners owed to the royal treasury. Town councils, known as *cabildos,* also appeared in the most important Spanish towns in the colonies. At first, the conquistadors played leading roles in the cabildos, but later merchants and other prominent townsmen replaced them. Among the cabildos' many responsibilities were the administration of justice, supervision of markets, and sponsorship of civic and religious festivals in the towns. Local officials, known as corregidores or *alcaldes mayores,* represented crown authority and exercised administrative and judicial functions throughout the colonies.

In areas with large indigenous populations, the corregidores and alcaldes mayores shared power with Indian elites. Some of these Indian officials were traditional rulers in their societies; others were opportunistic individuals willing to make deals with the new colonial authorities in order to advance their own positions. Throughout much of Mesoamerica and Peru, these native officers were responsible for maintaining order within their villages and delivering tribute from their communities to encomenderos and royal officials.

In theory, all colonial appointees were supposed to do the king's bidding to the letter of the law, but in practice they had considerable leeway to adjust edicts issued in Spain to suit the situation on the spot. Antonio de Mendoza knew that he depended on the encomenderos to defend New Spain against potential native uprisings, and he realized that he could push these powerful men only just so far, so he suspended what they viewed as the most objectionable features of the New Laws. Whenever colonial officials hesitated to carry out a royal directive, they invoked the phrase "*obedezco pero no cumplo,*" literally, "I obey but do not comply." These words signified that they acknowledged the king's authority to command all subjects but local conditions made enforcement of a particular law impossible or unwise. Many crown appointees no doubt used this formula simply to avoid performing their duties, but a certain amount of flexibility was necessary in order to govern such a huge empire, where an order issued in Spain took many months to reach local officials in the colonies.

Royal Government in Brazil

For the first several decades following Cabral's landfall, the kings of Portugal left Brazil in the hands of private entrepreneurs, who managed to settle and defend only a tiny portion of the eastern coastline of South America. By the late 1540s, the continued French challenge to Portuguese control and hopes that silver deposits similar to those recently found in Peru might lay somewhere inland in Brazil prompted João III to tighten his hold on the colony. He therefore appointed Tomé de Sousa to be royal governor-general of Brazil, charged with creating a centralized command that would gradually replace the proprietary captaincies in governing. The king further instructed the new governor to stop the enslavement of Brazilian natives–an impossible task, given the settlers' continued demands for labor.

Sousa arrived in 1549, accompanied by a royal treasurer, a chief justice, other bureaucrats, the first six Jesuit missionaries to serve in the Americas, and 1000 new colonists. He founded the city of Salvador da Bahia de Todos os Santos, located on the coast in a potentially rich sugar-producing area, to serve as capital of the colony. Later governors continued consolidating Portugal's hold on Brazil. With the help of Indian allies, Governor Mem de Sá (1557–1574) finally ousted the French, destroying a settlement they had established on Guanabara Bay and founding the city of São Sebastião do Rio de Janeiro in its place. Mem de Sá also subdued rebellious natives near Salvador and assisted the Jesuits in gathering pacified groups into mission villages. In the three decades following the establishment of royal government in Brazil, the colony's European-born population grew sizably. By the 1580s, Rio de Janeiro had 150 Portuguese households, while in the city of Salvador and its immediate environs more than 2000 Portuguese households could be found.

Never, however, did royal governors in Brazil achieve the power that the viceroys of Mexico and Peru enjoyed in Spanish America. Rather, municipal councils known as *senados da càmara* governed at the local level in Salvador, Rio de Janeiro, and other towns and wielded relatively more power than their counterparts in the Spanish colonies. Drawn from local elites, the councils were especially outspoken in their opposition to any restrictions imposed on their exploitation of native labor. The senados da càmara, along with royally appointed magistrates and a high court (*relação*) located in Salvador, shared responsibility for the administration of justice in colonial Brazil.

The Church in Spanish America and Brazil

The Spanish and Portuguese monarchs also paid careful attention to the development of the Catholic Church in their overseas domains. They justified their occupation of the Americas by arguing that they were bringing Christianity to the natives, and Pope Alexander VI granted them broad powers over the operations of the Church in the Americas. These concessions included the rights to nominate bishops, create new dioceses, issue licenses required for clergymen to travel to the colonies, and approve papal pronouncements before they could be published in the Indies. Although clergymen might dispute secular authorities on the treatment of natives and other issues, in many respects the ecclesiastical establishment served the interests of the colonial powers. In return, the Church received substantial state subsidies for its activities, and prominent clergymen often maintained close relationships with government officials.

Not all clergy were subject to the same degree of crown supervision. As we have seen, members of religious orders such as Franciscans and Dominicans played a very prominent role in early missionary efforts in Spanish America. Known collectively as regular clergy because they lived according to the rule (*regula* in Latin) set by their particular order's founder, these men operated more freely from royal authority than the secular clergy, who belonged to no order and answered directly to the bishop of their diocese, who in turn owed his appointment to the king. Royal policy envisioned that secular clergy would gradually replace the regular clergy once conversion of the Indians in a particular area was achieved, and the orders would advance to more remote frontier areas to continue the process of evangelization.

Secular clergy were also needed to minister to the growing number of non-Indian Catholics in the colonies' cities and towns. Naming of bishops to direct Church operations usually followed closely after the initial settlement of new territory. Within 20 years of Columbus's landfall, bishops had been appointed for Santo Domingo and Puerto Rico, and in 1513 the first bishop on the mainland took up residence on the Isthmus of Panamá. Between 1527 and 1561, seven separate dioceses were created in Mexico, and other bishoprics spanned South America from Cartagena on the Caribbean coast of Colombia in the north, to Santiago, Chile, in the south. Shortages of suitable secular clergymen led King Charles to appoint members of religious orders as some of the earliest bishops in Mexico and Peru. The Franciscan Juan de Zumárraga, for example, served as the first bishop of Mexico City.

Bishops had a wide range of duties. They personally presided over worship at the cathedral church and oversaw the work of the secular clergy throughout their dioceses. Church courts, with jurisdiction over most civil and criminal matters involving members of the clergy, formed another important component of the evolving ecclesiastical bureaucracy. Acting in concert with viceroys and other high-ranking government officials, bishops supervised the founding and operation of educational and social welfare institutions and the colonies' many convents for women.

Nowhere was the colonial church a monolithic organization. Competition between the regular and secular clergy and among the different religious orders often distracted clerics from their spiritual duties. In Spanish America, many religious orders were also divided within themselves as American-born members vied with those born in Europe for control of the organization's assets and activities. Although divided within itself, the Catholic Church was nevertheless a powerful institution that helped buttress Spanish and Portuguese rule in the colonies.

The Spanish and Portuguese Empires

With the consolidation of the Spanish kingdoms inherited from his grandparents Ferdinand and Isabella, the conquests of Mexico and Peru, and the establishment of Spanish settlements from northern Mexico to Chile, King Charles I was a powerful monarch indeed. His dominions extended well beyond the Iberian Peninsula and the Americas, however. His Spanish possessions came to him through his mother, Juana, daughter of Ferdinand and Isabella, and they included portions of Italy belonging to the crown of Aragón. His paternal inheritance not only brought him territories in northern Europe (Belgium, Luxembourg, and the Netherlands), but also the substantial holdings of the Hapsburg dynasty of Austria. In 1519, just three years after assuming the throne of Spain, he succeeded his Hapsburg grandfather Maximilian I as Holy Roman Emperor (Charles V), exercising authority over much of modern Germany and Austria.

In 1556, Charles abdicated the Spanish crown in favor of his son Philip II, leaving his Austrian possessions to brother Ferdinand. Philip nonetheless remained the world's first global monarch. In 1565, Spanish navigators established a permanent colony in the Philippine Islands, giving Philip's subjects access to the markets of Asia. Vast quantities of silver and other riches of the Indies, both east and west, poured into Spain during his reign. When the last representative of Portugal's Aviz dynasty died in 1580 without leaving a direct heir, Philip claimed that throne as well, and officially became king of Portugal in 1580. For the next 60 years, he and his successors, Philip III (1598–1621) and Philip IV (1621–1665), ruled over Portugal and all of its overseas dominions, from Brazil in the west to Goa and Macao in the east.

Students of literature often refer to the late sixteenth and early seventeenth centuries as Spain's *Siglo de Oro,* its golden age. This was the time of Miguel de Cervantes's great satiric novel *Don Quixote* and the great playwrights Lope de Vega, Tirso de Molina, and Pedro Calderón de la Barca. In other respects, however, these were troubled years for Spain. In 1566, the Netherlands revolted against Spanish rule, and for the next several decades a good portion of American silver went to outfit Spanish armies that tried unsuccessfully to subdue the Dutch. On more than one occasion, the royal treasury lay empty. Meanwhile, Philip continued King Charles's crusade to protect and advance the cause of Catholicism against its enemies, undertaking naval campaigns against the

Ottoman Turks and trying to stop the spread of the Protestant Reformation in Europe. His marriage to Mary Tudor, the Catholic daughter of King Henry VIII and the queen of England from 1553 to 1558, brought Spain into direct conflict with her Protestant successor, Elizabeth I. The English inflicted heavy losses on both sides of the Atlantic, most spectacularly in the defeat of Spain's famous Armada off the coast of Ireland in 1588.

Sixty years of Spanish rule drew Portugal into the international conflicts of the three Philips. The best ships of the "Spanish" Armada were in fact Portuguese vessels that Philip II had appropriated along with his throne. Spain's Dutch enemies attacked Portuguese trading posts in Asia, elbowed their way into the African slave trade, and seized the rich sugar-producing region of northeast Brazil in 1630. Ten years later, Portugal's nobles rallied around the Duke of Braganza, proclaiming him King João IV and successfully asserting their independence from Spain in a series of battles that lasted nearly three decades. Meanwhile, Brazilians expelled the Dutch from their territory in 1654. The damage to Portugal's empire had been done, however. During their time in Brazil, Dutch entrepreneurs had learned the business of sugar production, and they used that knowledge to set up rival sugar colonies in the Caribbean, thereby seriously undercutting Brazil's competitive position in European markets.

Iberia's exclusive territorial claims to the Americas were utterly shattered during the first half of the seventeenth century. The first permanent English colonists settled at Jamestown, Virginia, in 1607, followed by the Pilgrims and Puritans of Massachusetts in 1620 and 1630, respectively. A half-century later English colonies extended down the east coast of North America as far as South Carolina. The Frenchman Samuel de Champlain sailed up the St. Lawrence River in 1603 and founded the city of Quebec five years later. By the 1680s, French fur traders, missionaries, and explorers had penetrated westward across Canada to the headwaters of the Mississippi River and down the river to the Gulf of Mexico. British, French, and Dutch colonists all permanently occupied various Caribbean islands in the seventeenth century.

CONCLUSION

Columbus's voyage launched a military, biological, political, and ideological invasion of the Americas that resulted in the creation of the first two seaborne empires of the modern era, the Spanish and the Portuguese. By the early seventeenth century, Spanish settlements extended from Santa Fe, New Mexico, and St. Augustine, Florida, in what is now the United States, to Santiago, Buenos Aires, and Montevideo in South America. Meanwhile, Portuguese towns, missions, and sugar plantations dotted the coast of Brazil southward from Salvador to Rio de Janeiro and beyond. The English, French, and Dutch seaborne empires, based in part on the riches of the Americas, were taking shape as well.

Columbus's first voyage, then, ended several millennia of American isolation from contact with the Eastern Hemisphere. The human and natural resources of the Americas now came to serve the purposes of an emerging world economy and the dictates of European monarchs. To advance the political and military agendas of unseen monarchs thousands of miles away, the indigenous peoples of the Americas found themselves subject to increasingly heavy burdens of taxation and forced labor. Spanish and Portuguese immigrants and their American-born descendants also exploited Indians and the colonies' abundant natural resources for their personal benefit.

LEARNING MORE ABOUT LATIN AMERICANS

Burkhart, Louise. *The Slippery Earth: Nahua-Christian Moral Dialogue in Sixteenth-Century Mexico* (Tucson, AZ: University of Arizona Press, 1989). Explores the exchange of religious and philosophical concepts by Franciscan missionaries and indigenous people during the "spiritual conquest" of Mexico.

Cervantes, Fernando. *The Devil in the New World: The Impact of Diabolism in New Spain* (New Haven, CT: Yale University Press, 1994). A Mexican historian looks at indigenous responses to Christian moral and religious concepts.

Clendinnen, Inga. *Ambivalent Conquests: Maya and Spaniard in Yucatán, 1517–1570* (Cambridge, U.K.: Cambridge University Press, 1987). Traces the early years of the Spanish presence in Yucatán, with special emphasis on the Franciscans' attempts to impose Catholicism.

Cook, Noble David. *Born to Die: Disease and the New World Conquest, 1492–1650* (Cambridge, U.K.: Cambridge University Press, 1998). One of the leading historical demographers of Latin America explores the drastic population decline that followed the European conquest of the Americas.

Crosby, Alfred W. *The Columbian Exchange: Biological and Cultural Consequences of 1492* (Westport, CT: Praeger Publishers, 30th anniversary edition, 2003). Still the classic treatment of the ecological conquest.

Dor-Ner, Zvi. *Columbus and the Age of Discovery* (New York: Morrow, 1991). Lavishly illustrated companion volume to a Public Broadcasting System series aired at the time of the 500th anniversary of Columbus's voyage.

Hemming, John. *Red Gold: The Conquest of the Brazilian Indians, 1500–1760* (Cambridge, MA: Harvard University Press, 1978). The classic account of the impact of Portuguese settlement on the natives of Brazil.

León-Portilla, Miguel. *The Broken Spears: The Aztec Account of the Conquest of Mexico* (Boston: Beacon Press, Revised edition, 1992). Aztec sources translated from Nahuatl show how the native peoples of Mexico remembered the Spanish conquest.

Melville, Elinor G. K. *A Plague of Sheep: Environmental Consequences of the Conquest of Mexico* (Cambridge, U.K.: Cambridge University Press, 1994). This award-winning book is perhaps the best concise treatment of the ecological conquest of the Americas.

Restall, Matthew. *Seven Myths of the Spanish Conquest* (New York: Oxford University Press, 2003). Explodes various popular misconceptions about the Spanish conquest of America.

Viola, Herman J., and Carolyn Margolis. *Seeds of Change: Five Hundred Years since Columbus* (Washington, DC: Smithsonian Institution Press, 1991). Beautifully illustrated history of the long-term ecological consequences of the European discovery and conquest of the Americas.

4

THE IBERIANS' NEW WORLD

"WE CAME TO serve God, and to get rich." With these words the conquistador Bernal Díaz del Castillo described the motives that supposedly drove him and his fellow Iberians to the Americas. For those first on the scene, this new world offered quick and obvious avenues to wealth—outright plunder and the appropriation of tribute systems in the highly developed societies of Mesoamerica and the Andes, panning for gold in Hispaniola and Cuba, and the gathering of dyewoods in Brazil, to name a few.

As they became more familiar with this new environment, they saw that it teemed with additional possibilities for self-enrichment. Massive silver deposits lay beneath the Earth's surface in Bolivia and northern Mexico. The varied climate zones of the New World invited the commercial cultivation of wheat, grapes, and other staples of the Mediterranean diet, highly profitable Old World crops such as sugarcane, and even exotic new commodities like chocolate and *cochineal* (a red substance used to dye textiles) that could be exported back to Europe. Wealth derived from mining and commercial agriculture in turn generated lucrative opportunities for trade in everything from the finest lace and silks that dressed colonial elites to maize, potatoes, and dried beef consumed by the laboring populations. The transport of all these commodities provided fortunes for transatlantic shippers and more modest livelihoods for carters and muleteers.

Spanish and Portuguese colonists and their descendants included many talented and ambitious entrepreneurs eager to exploit the American environment for profit. Their plantations, mines, warehouses, and shipyards soon transformed

110

the landscape of Latin America, creating a world that was in many ways "new" for indigenous peoples and immigrants alike. They marshaled native peoples to work in their varied enterprises through outright enslavement or somewhat more subtle forms of political and economic coercion and imported Africans in chains to augment the labor force in the colonies.

Iberian Americas also craved the amenities of life as they had known it—or imagined it—back home. With profits from their many business ventures, they erected magnificent cities laid out according to European notions of grandeur and propriety. These cities became the seats of civil and ecclesiastical administration, centers of art and learning, and showcases for conspicuous consumption by successful mine owners, merchants, and commercial farmers.

THE LURE OF PRECIOUS METALS

The presence of gold and silver in their New World caught the attention of Spanish explorers and conquistadors within just a few years of Columbus's first landfall. As we saw in Chapter 3, they began mining gold on Hispaniola in the 1490s. Once on the mainland, they saw the magnificent treasure gathered for Atahualpa's ransom and heard persistent rumors of El Dorado—the man of gold—and other tantalizing hints that their New World held fabulous wealth indeed. For centuries, natives of the Americas had worked gold and silver to craft funerary objects, jewelry worn by ruling classes, and the elaborate images and vessels used in religious rituals. Renaissance Europeans likewise valued gold and silver, but for them these precious metals served purposes beyond the decorative and ceremonial purposes. International trade within Europe and with the great markets of Asia revolved around gold and silver coin.

Over time, some Spanish colonists found fortunes of gold in Colombia, southern Ecuador, and Chile, shipping more than 180 tons of it to Europe between 1500 and 1650. Even more substantial gold deposits fell to their Portuguese counterparts who ventured to the interior of Brazil in the late seventeenth and early eighteenth centuries. The real wealth of the Indies lay in silver, however—more than 16,000 tons were mined in the first century and a half following Columbus's voyage. For centuries to come, the silver bullion of Mexico, Peru, and Bolivia became the prime medium of exchange for global commerce, circulating freely from China and India to Europe and the Americas.

The Silver Boom

Already by the 1530s, ambitious Spaniards, including Fernando Cortés himself, had begun mining silver at scattered sites in central Mexico. Then in the mid-1540s, nearly simultaneous silver strikes at Zacatecas in northern Mexico and

Potosí in Upper Peru (present-day Bolivia) launched a mining boom that exceeded all expectations. Prospectors at Potosí found literally a mountain of silver and launched a rush to the new town they established at its base. The town had 14,000 residents within two years of the silver discoveries, and by 1610 its population reportedly topped 160,000. In the 1590s, there were more than 600 separate mine shafts at Potosí. Together they yielded upwards of 150,000 kilograms of silver ore per year, or about half the total output of the Spanish colonies.

Other bonanzas followed during the remainder of the sixteenth century, at such sites as Guanajuato, Sombrerete, Durango, and San Luis Potosí in Mexico and Castrovirreina in Peru. Even a faint rumor of silver lured thousands of men and women to distant and unlikely places, and boomtowns appeared wherever deposits were especially plentiful. The successive bonanzas in northern New Spain drew colonists deeper and deeper into the Gran Chichimeca, the arid and uninviting plateau whose indigenous inhabitants killed the intruders and raided their supply trains. Only after 50 years of warfare did Spanish authorities succeed in subduing them.

Production at many mines began to decline in the seventeenth century, as the most readily accessible ores were exhausted and mine owners faced shortages of labor, capital, and the mercury used in processing ore. Potosí's output fell more or less steadily after 1610, never to regain the preeminent position it had once enjoyed. Zacatecas and other Mexican mines experienced more gradual falloffs that were partially offset by periodic new discoveries, at Parral and Chihuahua, for example. After 1700, and especially after 1750, governmental subsidies and tax cuts, technical improvements, and more abundant supplies of mercury combined to boost overall silver production far beyond the levels reached earlier, most notably in Mexico.

Labor and Technology in Silver Mining

Mining silver required considerable inputs of capital and grueling labor. Miners cut tunnels and shafts that often extended hundreds of feet underground, and in the seventeenth century, some of the more ambitious entrepreneurs began using gunpowder to deepen and widen the shafts. Workers used picks to loosen silver-bearing rocks, while others shouldered 100-pound sacks of ore and hauled them to the surface.

Then commenced the difficult labor of extracting silver from the ore. Early miners in Peru borrowed smelting techniques that native Andeans had developed centuries before. Only the best quality ores could be smelted in this way, however, and the process required large amounts of firewood, a scarce commodity on the barren plateaus of northern Mexico and Upper Peru. In the 1550s, refiners in Mexico adopted a more efficient method, known as amalgamation, which involved crushing the ore to a consistency resembling sand, then mixing it with salt, copper pyrites, and mercury. In the resulting chemical reaction, the silver bonded with the mercury. When the silver-mercury amalgam was heated, the mercury vaporized, leaving more or less pure silver. In 1563, the fortuitous discovery of mercury mines at Huancavelica in Peru encouraged more refiners to use this technique.

Workers in mines and refineries worked long hours under extremely hazardous conditions. Those underground worked in dark, damp, and poorly ventilated quarters, and they often fell from the makeshift ladders that led to and from the surface. Shafts and tunnels frequently collapsed or flooded, killing many workers. Those who worked in the refineries were exposed to mercury and the consequent likelihood of a slow, excruciating death by poisoning. Workers in mines and refineries in the Andes routinely dulled their senses by chewing coca leaves or drinking chicha, a fermented beverage made from maize.

Procuring a Labor Supply

Securing a reliable and efficient labor supply posed a major challenge for operators of silver mines and refineries. African slaves were far too expensive for more than occasional use in such hazardous tasks. Mining entrepreneurs therefore preferred to rely on the "cheaper" and more readily available native population. During the 1520s and 1530s, Indians held as slaves and in encomienda worked the mines of central Mexico. By the 1540s, mine owners in areas with substantial concentrations of native population turned to the *repartimiento,* the forced labor draft adopted in New Spain following the formal abolition of Indian slavery and labor obligations for encomienda Indians. Under this system, each Indian community was required to supply a stipulated number of able-bodied men at regular intervals, and government officials allocated these workers to would-be employers.

Miners in Peru made extensive use of forced labor through the notorious mita organized by Viceroy Toledo in the 1570s. Each year, highland communities from as far away as Cuzco in the north and Tarija in the south sent one-seventh of their adult male populations to Potosí, where they worked a full year

LATIN AMERICAN LIVES

ANTONIO LÓPEZ DE QUIROGA, BOLIVIAN ENTREPRENEUR

IN THE EARLY 1640S, a Spaniard in his twenties named Antonio López de Quiroga (1620?–1699) arrived in Lima, one of many thousands of ambitious young men who emigrated to the Americas over three centuries of Spanish rule. There was little about him that suggested that he would end his days more than a half century later as one of the richest men in all the Indies. Born in the economically backward province of Galicia in the north of Spain, he was an untitled nobleman of modest means, though a distant relative of Pedro Fernández de Andrade, Count of Lemos, who would serve as viceroy of Peru from 1666 to 1672.

After a brief stint as a merchant in Lima, Antonio headed off for the fabled Potosí. There he established a shop on the *Calle de los Mercaderes* (Merchants' Street), most likely trading in silks and other fine textiles imported from Spain as well as coarser fabrics from the obrajes of Quito. Within a short time, he had also become a *mercader de plata* (silver trader) who bought silver in bulk from refiners, arranged for payment of the king's one-fifth, and then had the remainder minted into coins, all at a tidy profit to himself. He also supplied credit to miners and refiners who repaid the principal and interest in still more quantities of silver.

López de Quiroga's next step was to become a silver miner and refiner himself. He pioneered in the use of blasting to dig adits that provided access to silver deposits deep beneath the surface of the Earth. One such passageway cost more than 300,000 pesos and took ten years of labor and 30,000 pounds of gunpowder to cut. His willingness to reinvest his profits and to experiment with new techniques of extracting silver enabled him to make a fortune even though the best of Potosí's bonanza years had already long passed. Antonio produced 200,000 pounds of silver ore between 1661 and 1669, and his mines accounted for more than 10 percent of the silver produced in the district of Potosí during the last three decades of the seventeenth century.

By far the richest man in Potosí, Antonio López de Quiroga could afford to live well. He owned two lavish houses just off the central plaza. When his daughter Lorenza married in 1676, her dowry was worth 100,000 pesos, including 20 large sacks of silver coin that together weighed about 3000 pounds, as well as six black slaves, a gilded bed frame, a damask bedspread embroidered in gold, a sedan chair, a writing desk made of ebony and ivory, linens worth 6000 pesos, and numerous pieces of jewelry. He also made generous gifts to churches and charities in Potosí.

Like many other successful merchants and miners, Antonio also entered the ranks of the large landowners. In 1658, he paid 52,000 pesos for his first property, a hacienda in the province of Pilaya y Pazpaya, located southeast of Potosí. By the 1670s, he had expanded his holdings there to several hundred square miles. Scores of black slaves worked his properties, producing wine, brandy, beef jerky, tallow, maize, and *chuño* (freeze-dried potatoes) for sale in Potosí.

Antonio López de Quiroga was an astute and hard-headed businessman whose acumen and ingenuity clearly rivaled those of other entrepreneurs who would appear throughout the world in later centuries. But he had another side as well, one that bore greater resemblance to the conquistadors who had settled in Spanish America more than a century before his time. Indeed, he dreamed of being something of a conquistador himself. He spent more than 200,000 pesos outfitting an expedition of discovery and conquest, led by his nephew, to the legendary kingdom of the Gran Patití—another putative lost Inca state rumored to lie far to the northeast of Potosí where today Brazil, Paraguay, and Bolivia meet.

The excursion to Patití yielded nothing, but López de Quiroga still aspired to the power and social status that conquistadors of an earlier time had enjoyed. He longed for a title of nobility—he suggested "the Count of Pilaya and Pazpaya"—with seignorial jurisdiction reminiscent of what Fernando Cortés once had in Mexico. He certainly could have afforded the sizable purchase price of a title, but he never quite convinced authorities in Spain that he merited so lofty a rank. Nor did he ever hold office on the Potosí town council, except for the honorific military titles of captain and field marshal, which allowed him to play ceremonial roles in municipal rituals but carried no real power. His distant kinsman the viceroy paid little heed when López de Quiroga met him personally to ask for in increase in the allocation of mita workers for Potosí. Though he failed to achieve all he wanted, Antonio López de Quiroga attained a level of wealth that other Spanish immigrants could only dream about. His portrait hangs today in the Casa de la Moneda in Potosí, a lasting reminder of the town's grandeur in colonial times.

Questions for Discussion

Would someone like Antonio López de Quiroga feel at home in the business climate of our own time? Why or why not?

before being replaced by a new contingent. In the early seventeenth century, approximately 14,000 mita workers, or *mitayos,* were present at Potosí at any given time. Usually, they worked in the mines and refineries for one week and then had two weeks to rest, but they were often assigned other tasks during their "time off." Mita workers were paid for their labor, but their wages seldom covered the high cost of living in Potosí. Another 2200 mitayos went to the mercury mine at Huancavelica each year.

The precipitous decline in the native population made it increasingly difficult to muster the numbers of men required for the smooth operation of the repartimiento and mita systems. In the Andes, young men often fled their native ayllus to avoid mita service, further compounding the problem, and those who did submit to the draft sometimes were required to serve more often than every 7 years. Kurakas and caciques often appealed to Spanish courts to seek commensurate reductions in the quotas for their communities.

In the Andes, it was possible for Indians who could afford it to buy their way out of mita service by paying for a substitute, so that by 1620 many provinces were providing more than half their allotments in cash rather than labor. In effect, mine owners received direct cash subsidies, known as *indios de faltriquera* ("Indians in the pocket"), instead of actual workers. The miners then used these funds to hire *mingas,* or wage laborers. Sometimes these workers were simply mitayos moonlighting during their off-duty periods, but others were permanent wageworkers. Mingas became concentrated in the more skilled and less dangerous tasks and earned three to four times what a mitayo did—sufficient inducement to convince many Indians to stay on in Potosí following completion of their mita service, rather than return home only to be drafted again within a few years. As a result, the supply of men available for the mita declined further.

In 1603, the Indian labor force at Potosí numbered at least 30,000. Of these, about half were mitayos. Meanwhile, some 4000 mingas worked in refineries and only 600 in mining itself. Other wage earners sorted ore and hauled it to and from the mills, tended llamas, and transported other supplies used in mining and refining. More than 10,000 Indians delivered foodstuffs from surrounding areas to the markets in Potosí. Despite the steadily growing importance of wage labor at Potosí, the mita endured until the end of the colonial period. As late as 1789, a total of 3000 mitayos were in residence there.

Paid labor was even more prevalent in Zacatecas and other mining centers in northern Mexico, where sparse and often intractable resident Indian populations made forced labor drafts impractical. Mine workers commonly contracted to deliver to their employers a set quantity of ore each workday. Once they met their quotas, they were free to collect additional ore, which they sold directly to refiners. For most workers, these bonuses were far more important than the modest wages, rations, and housing their employers provided.

Goods supplied on credit by their employers constituted an added inducement for many workers in northern New Spain. In theory, indebted workers remained bound to their jobs until they worked off these loans, but many simply fled without paying or contracted with other employers who paid off their existing debts and then extended new credits to get them to sign on. In eighteenth-century Chihuahua, a worker's accumulated debt might easily exceed his nominal annual salary. Silk and linen cloth, fine stockings, and even lace from Flanders figured among the commodities offered to workers on credit during Chihuahua's silver boom in the 1730s. Not everyone fared this well, but throughout colonial

Silver mining and refining in Peru. Here the earlier refining techniques are being used.

Latin America the prospect of material gain continually drew workers to wherever fresh bonanzas might wait.

Gold Mining in Brazil

The case of colonial Brazil offers yet another example of how word of mineral wealth could put people in motion. For nearly two centuries following Cabral's landfall, persistent rumors circulated of gold in the interior, but for the most part, Portugal's American subjects found their treasure in such commodities as dyewood and sugar, and their settlements remained clustered close to the coast. The vast hinterland remained largely unexplored, except for expeditions led by slave-hunting *bandeirantes* from São Paulo. In the 1690s, however, the bandeirantes struck gold in the sparsely populated region that soon became known as Minas Gerais ("general mines").

A frantic gold rush ensued. Paulistas (people from the area around São Paulo) and northeastern Brazilians, as well as considerable numbers of recent immigrants from Portugal, all flocked to the mining region. A brief civil war ensued in 1708 and 1709 as the tough Paulista frontier people resisted the encroachments of the *emboabas* (sometimes defined as tenderfeet), as they derisively labeled the Brazilians and Europeans who encroached on territory they considered their own. The crown intervened to secure the outsiders' access to the gold fields and imposed stricter government control on the region, creating the captaincy of Minas Gerais. Meanwhile, the Paulistas continued their prospecting expeditions farther inland, yielding additional finds to the west in Goiás and Mato Grosso. From 1700 to 1799, Brazil produced more than 170,000 kilograms of gold. The discovery of diamonds in the 1720s further enhanced the attraction of the hitherto uninviting interior.

Most of the gold in Brazil was to be found in streambeds, where panning and other simple techniques were used. Although workers often suffered from pneumonia, malaria, and dysentery, they faced fewer risks to life and limb than their counterparts in the silver mines of Spanish America, and it made greater economic "sense" to use Afro-Brazilian slaves in the gold fields. Indeed, a mining code drafted in 1702 based the size of claims awarded to miners on the number of slaves they owned.

Other factors also abetted the growth of a slave labor force in the mining region of Brazil. Proximity to Africa and a well-established Portuguese slave trade made slaves relatively cheaper than in the Spanish colonies. Furthermore, the sugar industry of northeastern Brazil had entered a period of decline after 1650, and planters were often willing to sell slaves to would-be miners heading to the interior. Within 20 years of the first gold finds, there were already 30,000 slaves in Minas Gerais alone, and by 1775 the province had more than 150,000 slaves.

AGRICULTURE

Precious metals constituted only one of many avenues to wealth in colonial Latin America. Through a process of trial and error, many Spanish and Portuguese colonists found their livelihoods in the commercial production of crops both native to the Americas and introduced from overseas. In addition, those who had made fortunes through mining and trade often diversified their holdings and enhanced their prestige by investing in landed estates. These properties ranged from modest farms in well-watered areas, to extensive cattle ranches in the dry Brazilian interior and the northern plateau of Mexico, to sugar plantations that required substantial investments in slaves and equipment.

Sugar Plantations

Spaniards and Portuguese were already familiar with the production of sugarcane, a crop native to India, both at home and in the Atlantic islands they had settled in the fifteenth century. The tropical climate of the Caribbean immediately suggested that sugar could be cultivated in the Americas, and Columbus brought sugar plants with him when he returned to Hispaniola in 1493. Cortés and other enterprising Spaniards introduced sugarcane in Mexico, while others began planting it in coastal Peru. Sugar achieved its greatest prominence along the coast of Brazil, especially in the northeast around Pernambuco and Salvador da Bahia, where rich soil, abundant rainfall, and easy access to overseas shipping created ideal conditions for the development of plantations. By 1580, Brazil had become the world's leading producer of sugar, a distinction it continued to hold for the next century.

Like silver mining, sugar production required substantial inputs of hard labor, not only for the cultivation and harvesting of cane but also for its processing into sugar in the *engenhos* (mills). Brazilian planters at first tried enslaving the indigenous population along the coast, supplemented with others rounded up from the interior. By 1545, the six sugar mills in the captaincy of São Vicente had a total of more than 3000 native slaves. Indian captives proved undependable, however. The intense labor involved in producing an unfamiliar crop made little sense to them, and native men resisted agricultural tasks because they considered it "women's work." Those who did not succumb to disease fled at the first opportunity. After a particularly severe series of epidemics devastated the native population in the 1560s, Brazilian sugar planters gradually turned to African slaves. The plantation Sergipe do Conde in Bahia was typical. Africans

Inside a Brazilian sugar mill, from a drawing made in 1640.

El Paso

Chihuahua

Parral

Durango
Sombrerete
Gran Chichimeca
Zacatecas
San Luis Potosí

Guanajuato
The Bajío
Querétaro
★Mexico City
Puebla
Jalapa
Veracruz
Cuernavaca

Acapulco

Gulf of Mexico

New Spain

constituted 7 percent of its labor force in 1574 and 37 percent in 1591. By 1638, there were almost no Indians to be found among its workers.

In 1680, the total slave population of Brazil was about 150,000. Judging from the numbers imported, however, we might expect a much higher number. Some 4000 slaves entered Brazil each year between 1570 and 1630, and the annual figures for the period from 1630 to 1680 average nearly double that. Several factors accounted for the relatively slow rate of natural increase in the slave population. Birth rates among slaves were low, in part because males arriving on the slave ships outnumbered females by two to one. Indeed, sugar planters would have preferred an even higher ratio of men to women, but had to accept the mix of males and females offered by their African suppliers. Lack of prenatal care, malnutrition, and other factors contributed to exceptionally high rates of mortality among children born to slave mothers.

The planters' callous reckoning suggested that it was "cheaper" in economic terms to import adults rather than to bear the costs and risks of raising slave

---

Slice of Life   THE SAFRA IN COLONIAL BRAZIL

ON JULY 30, 1651, the sugar plantation called Sergipe do Conde in northeastern Brazil buzzed with activity as slaves, salaried employees and their families, and lavradores de cana from the surrounding countryside gathered to witness the formal inauguration of the harvest season, the *safra*. The priest presiding over the ceremonies prayed for the safety of the workers and a profitable harvest, blessed the mill, and fed the first stalks of sugarcane through it. The same ritual could be seen at engenhos throughout the region year after year in late July or early August. It was a festive occasion for all concerned. Slaves decorated oxcarts with brightly colored ribbons and drove them to the mill for blessing, all the while looking forward to a goodly ration of *garapa* (cane brandy) at the end of the day, while the plantation's owners and their invited guests enjoyed a lavish banquet at the big house.

Festivity soon gave way to nine continuous months of back-breaking, round-the-clock labor. Field hands rose at dawn to begin cutting their daily quota of 2500 to 4000 canes. They worked in teams, typically a male slave who cut the stalks with a heavy scythe and a female slave who then tied them into bundles to be loaded onto boats or carts and transported to the mill. Once cut, the cane had to be processed within 24 hours lest the stalks dry out or the juice become sour. The mill apparatus was a complicated one, driven either by water power or by animals. Seven or eight slaves, usually women, worked inside the mill, some feeding the cane back and forth through a series of heavy rollers until all the juice had been extracted, others hauling away the crushed stalks or cleaning the equipment. The work was dangerous. At one mill, an observer reported that a young woman became completely trapped in the machinery and "milled with the very cane." Many workers lost limbs to the heavy rollers, but even serious injuries did not spare one from the labors of the safra. A one-armed slave named Marcelina worked at the engenho Santana in the 1730s. Her job was to check the oil lamps that permitted her able-bodied companions to continue milling day and night.

From the mill, the juice was transferred to the *casa das caldeiras* (kettle house) to be heated and reheated until all impurities had been removed. Furnaces beneath the floor burned day and night throughout the safra season, consuming enormous amounts of firewood in the process. An Italian Jesuit who visited Engenho Sergipe do Conde in the late seventeenth century described work inside the casa das caldeiras:

> And truly who sees in the blackness of night those tremendous furnaces perpetually burning ... the cauldrons, or boiling lakes, continually stirred and restirred, now vomiting froth, exhaling clouds of steam ... the noise of the wheels and chains, the peoples the color of the very night working intensively and moaning together

(continued on next page)

without a moment of peace or rest; who sees all the confused and tumultuous machinery and apparatus of that Babylon can not doubt ... that this is the same as Hell.

Finally, the purified liquid was poured into cone-shaped forms made of red clay, and slaves carried them to the *casa de purgar* (purging house) where a gradual process of percolation produced crystallized sugar, some of it highly refined and white, some of it lower grade, darker *moscovado,* as well as molasses that was then made into *aguardiente,* or rum. The sugar was then packed in large wooden crates for shipment overseas.

Colonial Brazilians called their engenhos *fábricas,* or factories, and with good reason, for the routines of sugar-making resembled those of modern industry. Men, women, and children all had their assigned tasks. Managers aimed to keep the process moving smoothly and continuously, with workers rotating in shifts. House servants and field hands were often pressed into nighttime duty in the mill. Many mills suspended operations on Sundays and other religious holidays, but some masters, skeptical that the slaves would use their time off for church-sponsored devotions, were reluctant to permit any distractions from the routine. But even the most efficient planning could not prevent a certain amount of down time due to unseasonable rains, shortages of firewood, or equipment breakdowns.

On most days of the safra season, however, slaves had little time to rest. A combination of negative and positive incentives kept them working steadily. Malingerers risked corporal punishment, but overseers hesitated to interrupt milling operations to administer a whipping on the spot. Many slaves had a quota to fulfill, and then they could spend the rest of the day tending to their gardens, where they grew fruits and vegetables for their own consumption or for sale in local markets. They also received periodic rewards in the form of rum or other intoxicants. Slaves who worked in highly skilled or managerial phases of the harvest operations might be given money or some sugar to sell on their own account. Such positions also carried the possibility of upward social mobility within the slave community, and even freedom for a favored few.

The safra ended when the rainy season commenced in early May, but much work remained to be done in the three months until the new harvest began. New canefields were planted and existing ones weeded. Slaves worked at repairing the kettles, forms, and other implements used in the mill. But masters and slaves alike took time in June to celebrate feasts honoring Saints Peter, John, and Anthony. By the end of July, however, it was time for a new safra to begin.

Questions for Discussion

What tactics could the slaves of a sugar mill like Sergipe use to resist the demands of their masters? Would these means have been effective? Why or why not?

children from birth to the age at which they might become productive workers. They calculated further that it took less than 18 months for an adult slave to produce enough sugar to cover his or her purchase price. As long as sugar prices remained high and Portuguese traders enjoyed access to slave markets on the African coast, recent arrivals figured prominently among the labor forces on the sugar plantations of Brazil. Indeed, everywhere that sugar went—Mexico, Peru, and the Caribbean—African slavery usually followed.

Haciendas and Ranches

Meanwhile, other Iberians capitalized on the growing demand for the familiar foodstuffs they had brought to the new continent with them. Spanish colonists in Mexico and Peru began almost immediately to produce the wheat they needed to make bread for the Catholic mass and for their own tables. Early efforts to compel Indians to supply wheat in tribute failed. Encomenderos and others then began producing wheat and crops such as barley, alfalfa, and vegetables on small plots of land, often receiving forced allocations of Indian labor to get them through the demanding harvest season.

As time passed, larger farms, usually known as *haciendas* in the Spanish colonies, appeared wherever people found appropriate ecological niches reasonably close to growing cities and mining centers. The area around Puebla in central Mexico, for example, was well suited to wheat production, and it lay astride the trade route linking Mexico City and the Gulf Coast. Other wheat farms could be found in the immediate environs of New Spain's great capital and in the region known as the Bajío to the northwest. In South America, Cochabamba in present-day Bolivia soon became a major supplier of wheat and other grains to Potosí, while grain from haciendas in Chile was shipped northward to Peru. Increasing demand for wine, another imported dietary and religious staple, also prompted colonists to seek out places suitable for growing grapes. Vineyards were planted in coastal Peru and Chile, and in the Rio Grande Valley near present-day El Paso, Texas, and Ciudad Juárez, Mexico.

Many landowners reaped additional profits from the sale of cattle, horses, oxen, mules, pigs, goats, and sheep. Livestock production stimulated Spanish and Portuguese colonists to settle in areas lacking in mineral resources and unsuitable for large-scale commercial agriculture, places that might otherwise have remained outside the colonial economic orbit. Cattle ranches could be found throughout the arid north-central plateau of New Spain and the plains of Venezuela, as well as the Brazilian interior, where the vast captaincy of Piauí by the late eighteenth century had many more cattle than human inhabitants. The gold rush of the eighteenth century brought cattle ranching to Minas Gerais, Mato Grosso, and Goiás in Brazil, while the region around Tucumán in northwestern Argentina supplied mules and cattle for the mines of Potosí.

Sheep ranching and the production of coarse woolen textiles in factories known as *obrajes* spread to many parts of Spanish America by the late sixteenth century. The highland valleys of Ecuador supplied textiles to markets throughout the Andes. More than 600,000 sheep could be found grazing in the valley of Ambato, for example. The area between Puebla and Mexico City became another important center of textile manufacture. Hispanic colonists also introduced sheep to New Mexico, and they along with their Pueblo Indian neighbors exported large quantities of wool to the south.

Spanish, Portuguese, and Iberoamerican commercial farmers also reaped substantial profits from products indigenous to the Americas. By 1630, most of the maize consumed in Mexico City came from nearby haciendas, and by the late colonial period these estates also supplied much of the city's pulque, the fermented beverage made from the agave cactus that was especially popular among the lower classes. Cacao grown by non-Indian hacienda owners in Guatemala, Venezuela, and coastal Ecuador was shipped to Mexico, where a taste for chocolate spread from the Indian population to Spaniards, mestizos, and blacks. American cacao eventually found rich markets in Europe as well. Haciendas in the Andes produced large amounts of coca for consumption by mine workers at Potosí, as well as chuño, the freeze-dried potatoes consumed since pre-hispanic times. Meanwhile, tobacco from Cuba and Brazil reached growing numbers of consumers throughout the Americas and in Europe, Africa, and Asia. Indigo, native to both hemispheres, provided profits for hacienda owners in Central America, especially in El Salvador.

Most haciendas had resident work forces that varied in size according to the specific products of the estates. Cattle ranches, for example, required a much smaller resident work force than haciendas that produced wheat or grapes. Permanent employees were often mestizos and mulattos, although in central Mexico and the Andes there were many Indians as well. Although they were supposed to continue paying tribute and meeting mita and repartimiento obligations, Indian hacienda residents had an easier time evading these burdens than those who remained in their villages.

Landowners offered various incentives to attract resident workers. Customarily, these permanent employees received food rations and perhaps a small plot of land for their own use, along with wages that were normally paid in commodities rather than cash due to the scarcity of coin throughout the countryside. Employers often extended credits to their workers as well. In theory, workers were bound to their jobs until their debts were paid, and sometimes landowners tried to force the children of deceased employees to work off their parents' debts. In practice, however, many indebted workers fled without ever paying. At harvest time and whenever there was extra work to be done, *hacendados* (hacienda owners) recruited temporary laborers from Indian villages in the surrounding countryside. Sometimes they obtained such workers through forced labor systems such as the repartimiento, while in other cases they offered wages.

Principal sugarcane–
producing areas

Amazon R.

PIAUÍ

PERNAMBUCO

Sertão

BAHIA

Salvador

MATO
GROSSO   GOIÁS

MINAS
GERAIS   •Ouro
Prêto

São Paulo •
São Vicente   Rio de Janeiro

Colonial Brazil

Landownership

Large estates did not appear in Mesoamerica and the Andes immediately following the conquest. Densely concentrated indigenous populations occupied the
best agricultural land, and the most powerful conquistadors simply skimmed off
surplus wealth from the native communities in the form of tribute. Many first-
generation encomenderos acquired modest plots of land near the communities
of their encomienda Indians, and these holdings sometimes became the core of
a hacienda later on. By the latter part of the sixteenth century, however, the
decline in the Indian population and the forced resettlement of many survivors
left vast expanses of land vacant, just as burgeoning cities and mining centers
created new markets for agricultural produce. As tribute receipts dwindled and
many encomiendas reverted to the crown, the heirs of the early conquistadors
had to find other ways to support the privileged lifestyle they had come to
expect. Meanwhile, others who had made fortunes in mining or trade diversified their assets by acquiring rural estates.

The process of estate formation was thus a gradual, piecemeal one. A typical hacienda in the early seventeenth century consisted of a patchwork of properties, not always contiguous and acquired in a variety of different ways. Spanish town councils conferred some of the earliest land grants, often to encomenderos and other prominent Spaniards, while later grants came in the form of titles bestowed by the viceroys of Mexico and Peru. Meanwhile, individual Indians and Indian communities were willing to sell or rent surplus lands to meet past due tribute obligations and other needs. Such transfers sometimes violated protective legislation forbidding non-Indians to acquire land within the indigenous communities. Other aspiring landowners simply squatted on unoccupied land without any formalities whatsoever. Most ambitious landowners accumulated a hefty bundle of papers documenting their holdings. Beginning in 1589 and on various occasions thereafter, the crown allowed them to patch up any irregularities in these titles in exchange for a fee paid to the royal treasury.

The process of land accumulation in Brazil was more straightforward. Many plantations had their origins in land grants (*sesmarias*) that sixteenth-century donatários or royal governors conferred, often with the stipulation that the recipients establish a sugar mill within a specified time. But like their counterparts in the Spanish colonies, aspiring *senhores de engenho* (owners of sugar mills) augmented their holdings through purchase or unauthorized occupation of unclaimed lands.

Religious orders accumulated substantial landholdings throughout Spanish America and Brazil. In Peru, monasteries joined conquistadors in laying claim to lands that had once supported the Inca or the native cults. Franciscans, Dominicans, Jesuits, and others also bought up small parcels of Indian land as readily as laymen. In the early seventeenth century, a Dominican priest in central Mexico purchased for his monastery 31 separate plots, each probably no more than 2 or 3 acres. Individual Indians, villages, and non-Indian hacendados also bequeathed rural property to monasteries and convents throughout Spanish America. The nuns of Cuzco's Convent of Santa Clara received regular shipments of meat, cheese, and tallow from their rural estates.

The Jesuits developed an exceptionally extensive network of rural properties to support their frontier missions and their churches and schools in major cities. Jesuit estates worked by African slaves dominated wine and sugar production in coastal Peru, and it is estimated that the order's haciendas occupied about 10 percent of Ecuador's agricultural land. In Brazil, Jesuits owned several of the largest sugar plantations.

Landed Elites

By the seventeenth century, only those encomenderos who had invested in commercial agriculture, mining, or trade continued to be counted among the elite of

Spanish America. Alongside them stood many others who had derived their fortunes directly from entrepreneurial activity. The most successful landowners came to dominate the cabildos of nearby cities and towns where they maintained their primary residences and where they could be spotted in their linen and velvet finery when they went to mass or other public functions. They frequently consolidated their holdings by arranging marriages of their children to the offspring of other landholding families.

Few families were able to sustain prosperous haciendas or plantations for more than a few generations, however. Marriage alliances helped them build estates, but inheritance laws worked in the opposite direction. A select few landowners won royal permission to create an entailed estate whereby the bulk of their property could pass intact to a single heir, often the eldest son, one generation after another. In most cases, however, a landowner's surviving spouse received half the estate and all children, both male and female, divided the remainder equally. When the other parent died, the children split the remaining half, again in equal shares. Thus, rural properties might be subdivided each time an owner died, unless one heir were in a position to buy out his or her siblings' holdings.

Shifting market conditions and the hazards of weather could also undermine the profitability of a hacienda or plantation. Mounting debts posed yet another problem. Proprietors frequently borrowed from convents and other religious institutions to meet operating costs or to finance capital improvements, using their property as collateral. Pious landowners often imposed additional liens on their estates in order to support spiritual and charitable endowments. In Spanish America, haciendas were commonly mortgaged for well over half their market value. Successive owners rarely repaid the principal and often failed to meet the required 5 percent annual interest charges. Time and again, bankrupt estates went up for sale, offering opportunities for more newcomers to enter the landowning class.

Why would anyone purchase a heavily indebted property with uncertain prospects for profit? Schooled in European seignorial traditions that associated landownership with nobility, buyers certainly wanted land for the prestige it conferred, especially when a bankrupt estate could be had for little more than a commitment to assume interest payments to lienholders. Landownership also enhanced a family's marriage prospects and signified that an individual was deserving of many other coveted status symbols, such as cabildo membership or an officer's commission in the local militia. Many aspiring landowners probably also looked forward to the kind of deference that resident peons were presumed to owe their employers.

Pragmatic considerations also entered the picture. Buyers could restore a property to profitability either by investing in capital improvements or by shifting production to meet changing market conditions. Landowners around Caracas, for example, focused first on producing wheat for the Cartagena market

How Historians Understand   DOCUMENTING COLONIAL ENTERPRISE

Studying the ways in which Iberians transformed their New World in the pursuit of profit is one of the easier tasks confronting historians of Latin America, for the documentation is enormous. The Spanish and Portuguese colonial bureaucracies monitored all manner of economic activity in their overseas empires, with an eye to enforcing mercantile restrictions and maximizing revenues for the crown. Such administrative records have obvious limitations, however. They show taxes collected but not those evaded; they itemize goods shipped legally but not those that were smuggled. Historians can use them as rough indicators for tracking fluctuations in production and exchange, but we can never calculate exact totals.

Other kinds of documents help us to reconstruct the histories of many types of colonial enterprises. As we have seen, landowners maintained detailed records of their land titles, copies of which ended up in government archives whenever ownership of a property became the object of litigation. Owners and overseers kept careful accounts in their daily operation of mines, haciendas, and businesses. Probate records provide a wealth of detail on the successes and failures of individual entrepreneurs. Wills typically included information on a person's place of birth, marriages, children, and other heirs, as well as a declaration of the property brought to a marriage by virtue of inheritance, dowry, or personal earnings. Outstanding debts and accounts payable were also listed. Following the testator's death, a meticulous inventory of the estate was taken, complete with the appraised value of all possessions, often down to individual items of clothing and household effects. When heirs fell to squabbling among themselves, as they often did, the surviving paper trail lengthened.

A document certifying that on February 12, 1693, Blas Albarrán Carrillo took possession of a piece of land that formed a small part of the Hacienda Milpillas near Guadalajara, Mexico. It bears the official stamp required on all legal documents.

These records are, of course, skewed toward those who had property and investments of sufficient scale to record, assets worth a court battle among heirs and creditors. Documents are also weighted toward enterprises that remained in the same hands generation after generation. Studies of haciendas and other properties have often focused on properties belonging to the Jesuits, not only because members of the order were excellent administrators, but also because the governments of Spain and Portugal expelled them from the colonies in the late eighteenth century, confiscating their property and usually depositing their well-kept files in archives that have been accessible to historians. Many of the records detailing the harvesting and processing of sugarcane on Brazilian plantations come from Jesuit estates, and historians have had to take special care in verifying that assumptions made about these properties are valid for others in the region.

The further down the social scale we go, the harder it is to document the activities of specific individuals, but we can track the everyday business of artisans, petty entrepreneurs, and other "ordinary" men and women through the records kept by notaries who certified a wide variety of transactions including apprenticeship contracts, bills of sale for all kinds of property, letters granting freedom to slaves, and wills. Those of humble social status appear in court registers too. Alongside hefty bundles of papers dealing with disputes among the great landowners, miners, and merchants, a researcher will often find a slimmer but highly revealing file detailing a complaint brought by a small farmer whose cow had been stolen, or a worker whose boss had mistreated him. Thanks to the fine penmanship and the meticulous record keeping of the thousands of accountants, notaries, clerks, and scribes who plied their trades in colonial Spanish America and Brazil, we are able to trace the varied enterprises of the Iberians' New World.

Questions for Discussion

Most of the documents described in this feature deal with people's property, and not what they were like as people. But suppose we stumbled upon a chest containing documents that belonged to a hypothetical married couple named Juan and María, who between them owned various haciendas in seventeenth-century Mexico. The chest contains Juan's will and documents pertaining to the probate of his estate following his death; an inventory of goods that María brought to the marriage; land titles and records of a lawsuit with a neighboring landowner; an account book listing the names of workers on their haciendas and debts incurred by those workers; and letters granting freedom to several Afro-Mexican slaves, giving information on the liberated individuals' ages and the types of work they performed. What clues can we get from these documents that might tell us something about the personalities and moral values of Juan and María?

Spanish South America

before moving into tobacco and finally into cacao. Indeed, rural elites displayed considerable willingness to diversify their enterprises in the pursuit of profit. A typical landowner in highland Peru might easily produce wine, wheat, and coca on several different plots, while also investing in mercury mining at Huancavelica and an obraje or two as well.

Owners of haciendas and plantations in colonial Latin America were shrewd entrepreneurs. While they definitely coveted land for reasons of prestige, the lifestyle they aspired to did not come cheaply. Sumptuous townhouses, retinues of slaves and servants, the overseers they hired to manage their properties, and the lavish contributions to religious and charitable causes that were expected of them all required a steady cash flow and unwavering attention to the bottom line. Although they may have been reluctant to toil with their own hands, landed elites could not afford to be idle aristocrats if they hoped to maintain their exalted position in local society.

Rural Society

Large estates were not the only type of landholding in colonial Latin America. Españoles, mestizos, mulattos, and acculturated Indians who worked smaller farms known as *labores* or *ranchos* in Mexico and *chácaras* in the Andes constituted something of a rural middle class. Some held secure title to their lands, while others were squatters, sharecroppers, or tenant farmers. In Brazil, small landholders known as *lavradores de cana* cultivated sugar alongside the great plantations and took their cane to the large mills to be processed. On the outskirts of Salvador and other Brazilian cities, small farms known as *roças* supplied fruits, vegetables, and other staple foods to the urban population and to the sugar plantations.

Lands held by indigenous communities also occupied significant portions of the countryside in many parts of Spanish America. Caciques and kurakas allocated plots of community-owned land to individual Indians, but enterprising non-Indians, including many mestizos and mulattos in Mexico, might receive these allotments by virtue of their residence in the village or their marriage to Indian women. Small farmers known as *labradores* also rented community land. In the Cuernavaca region of central Mexico and in many other places, non-Indian farmers, shopkeepers, and artisans came to outnumber Indians in many villages.

The relative percentages of land held by large estates, small farms, and Indian communities varied considerably from one region to another. In the plains surrounding Bogotá, large estates held about two-thirds of the land by the seventeenth century. In peripheral areas such as Costa Rica and the São Paulo district of Brazil, smallholdings dominated the landscape, while in Oaxaca in southern Mexico substantial lands remained in the hands of Indian villages and their caciques.

Brazilian lavradores de cana sometimes held positions on the governing councils of Salvador and other cities, but most smallholders were not so lucky. They could afford few of the privileges and luxuries enjoyed by the owners of large haciendas and plantations. They remained rural people, without second homes or personal ties to powerful figures in the city. Though they might employ others or even own a slave or two, they could not escape the hard physical labor that agriculture demanded. Nevertheless, they too showed their entrepreneurial side, selling their surplus produce in local and regional markets.

TRADE AND TRANSPORTATION

The Spaniards and Portuguese who crossed the Atlantic and their American-born descendants were no strangers to the profit motive, and we have seen how they eagerly searched for ways to exploit their New World to their economic advantage. They found markets for their produce overseas and in the colonies, and spent their profits on merchandise imported from Europe and from other parts of the Indies. The movement and exchange of all these commodities provided many avenues to fortunes great and small for merchants, accountants, shippers, and haulers of freight—as well as embezzlers and thieves. British, French, and Dutch pirates preyed upon international shipping, forcing Spain and Portugal to spend considerable sums defending cargoes and crews.

International Commerce

Gold and silver were by far the most valuable of all commodities transported in colonial Latin America. A substantial portion of these precious metals wound up in Europe. Iberian law considered all subsoil resources the property of the monarch, who granted mining permits on the condition that recipients surrender a portion of their take, usually one-tenth to one-fifth, to royal agents. Some of this treasure stayed in the colonies to finance the administration of the empire, but every year hundreds of silver ingots reached the king's coffers in Madrid. Merchants engaged in the Indies trade also sent large amounts of silver to Europe to be exchanged for merchandise.

Vessels loaded with silver and other treasure were attractive targets for plunder by English, French, and Dutch pirates. Part of Cortés's first loot from Tenochtitlan wound up in the hands of French pirates, and in 1628, the Dutch captain Piet Heyn made off with the entire Mexican silver fleet off the coast of Cuba. Spain therefore imposed strict controls on shipping to and from the colonies. All ships bound for the Americas had to embark from the port of Seville and travel in convoys with naval escorts, and they were permitted to call on only a handful of ports in the colonies. Each year, two fleets set out from Seville, one bound for Veracruz on the Gulf Coast of Mexico, the other for Cartagena in northern South America and the Isthmus of Panamá. Their cargoes included Spanish wine, olive oil, salt cod, and other foodstuffs; clothing and tools; and a wide array of luxury textiles, such as satins, brocades, lace, and linen, often of northern European manufacture.

Once they reached their destination, merchants traveling with the Veracruz fleet headed inland for the famous trade fair at the town of Jalapa, where the climate was healthier and more comfortable than on the coast. Merchants on the South American fleet stopped first at Cartagena and then proceeded to the hot, humid, fever-ridden town of Portobelo in Panama to exchange European wine, textiles, books, and tools for silver, hides, and sugar brought up from Peru. Vis-

Llamas carrying silver from mines.

itors to the Portobelo fair described how silver lay in heaps in the marketplace as representatives of the most powerful merchants of Lima and Seville haggled over the prices of their merchandise. For the return voyage, all ships from both fleets gathered at Havana before setting off together across the Atlantic.

Mexican and Peruvian silver crossed the Pacific in the famous galleons that sailed from Acapulco to the Spanish colony at Manila in the Philippines, where resident Chinese merchants eagerly exchanged Asian merchandise for American bullion. The Manila trade brought an exotic array of goods to the growing marketplaces of Mexico and Peru, among them fine silks, Chinese porcelains, and spices.

Portugal's empire also spanned the globe. Portuguese merchants carried on extensive trade at Goa in India, Macao on the South China coast, and other markets in Asia, bringing exotic commodities back to Europe and thence to Brazil. Meanwhile, the Portuguese developed a growing trade with Africa that was to endure for more than 300 years. The rise of sugar production in the sixteenth and seventeenth centuries, followed by the gold rush thereafter, created an insatiable demand for African slaves, exchanged for Brazilian gold and tobacco and European tools along the African coast.

Overland Transport

The economy of colonial Latin America also depended heavily on the movement of goods and people over land. Where topography permitted, Iberians introduced ox-drawn wagons and carts. Wagonloads of supplies headed north on the *camino real* (royal road) that stretched along the central plateau of New Spain from Mexico City to Zacatecas and on to Santa Fe, New Mexico. But most freight traveled on the backs of mules, especially where rugged terrain or thick vegetation made wheeled transport impossible—up and down the steep slopes of the Andes, and across the isthmus of Panama, for example. The trail from the port of Guayaquil to Quito was especially treacherous. One observer called it "the worst road in the world, because it always rains on these mountain slopes so that the mules fall into the mire." In dry areas, on the other hand, freight haulers worried about finding enough water and fodder for their animals along the way.

Despite these difficulties, overland transport was a lucrative business and essential to the smooth functioning of the colonial economy. Several thousand mules entered Mexico City each day by the eighteenth century, and in the Andes llamas carried heavy loads to remote mining centers. Many enterprising mestizos, mulattos, and Indians earned their livings as carters and mule-drivers, and a lucky few achieved a modicum of upward economic and social mobility. Take, for example, the case of Miguel Hernández, a free mulatto born in Mexico City about 1550. As an adult he settled in the provincial town of Querétaro, a few days' journey north of the capital, where he began assembling a pack train. The town offered attractive opportunities for profit. Not only was it situated in a fertile agricultural zone and on the camino real that headed north to Zacatecas, but it also boasted numerous obrajes that shipped textiles to many parts of the colony. By the time of his death in 1604, Hernández had acquired an excellent credit rating, several pieces of real estate in and around Querétaro, and even a black slave. He left numerous documents graced with his elegant signature, and his membership in the prestigious religious confraternity of the Holy Sacrament brought him into close contact with leading local landowners, merchants, and government officials.

Merchants

Merchants formed an important component of colonial Latin American society. Most powerful were the great wholesalers of Mexico City, Lima, and other major cities, many of whom had fortunes worth well over 100,000 pesos—the equivalent of millionaires for their time. Rumor even had it that Lima's most successful merchants slept on mattresses atop hundreds of bars of silver. Often of European birth, the great commercial entrepreneurs of colonial Latin America built lavish homes at the center of town, bought cabildo positions for themselves or their sons, and diversified their holdings by investing in land, textile production, and urban real estate. In Mexico City and Lima, they organized themselves into merchant guilds, or *consulados,* that settled disputes among them and lobbied for their interests. They also supplied credit to landowners, miners, and other entrepreneurs.

Merchants in Salvador provided much of the credit to the sugar planters of Bahia and many eventually joined the ranks of the planters themselves. Typical was Francisco Fernandes de Sim, a native of the island of Madeira who established himself in the Brazilian capital as a broker in wine and sugar in the 1620s. By the following decade, he owned two ships that plied the Atlantic. His marriage to the daughter of a *senhor de engenho* brought him into the local elite. When he died in 1664, he left three sugar plantations as well as numerous properties in the city of Salvador. Many New Christians, converts from Judaism or their descendants, could be found among the merchant classes of Brazil and the Spanish colonies. About half of Salvador's merchants in the seventeenth century were New Christians, for example.

Major wholesalers sent goods on consignment to agents, often their own relatives, who retailed them in smaller towns or turned them over to itinerant peddlers who carried merchandise on pack trains to remote villages, mining camps, and haciendas. During the height of its silver boom in the early seventeenth century, Zacatecas boasted between 50 and 100 shops, most of them specializing either in groceries or cloth, and served as the hub of a trading network that extended several hundred miles farther north.

Through a practice known as the *repartimiento de mercancías,* the alcaldes mayores, corregidores, and their lieutenants were particularly active in local trade in heavily Indian districts of Spanish America. These men purchased their offices and expected a return on their "investment" beyond their meager salaries. They did so by receiving goods on credit from city merchants and selling them at inflated prices to Indians, and by obliging Indians in their jurisdiction to sell them items of value at deflated prices—all in violation of laws supposedly prohibiting them from engaging in business activities within their jurisdictions.

Mercantile Restrictions

The prohibition on business ventures by political officials was one of many regulations that the Spanish crown imposed on all levels of trade in the Indies. Only Spanish subjects were legally permitted to engage in the Indies trade, and, as we have seen, merchant vessels had to sail from Seville in convoy with the annual fleets. Merchants paid a variety of taxes, including an export-import duty of 15 percent on all westbound cargoes and 17.5 percent on merchandise shipped from the colonies to Seville and a sales tax of between 2 and 6 percent imposed each time an item was resold within the colonies.

None of these restrictions daunted ambitious merchants or eager consumers. Tax evasion was commonplace, and contraband flourished, especially after rival European nations began setting up colonies in the Caribbean in the seventeenth century. Spain's growing concerns in Europe undermined its ability to enforce trade regulations or defend its colonies against foreign interlopers, while weaknesses in its domestic economy limited the supply of goods available through legal channels. Foreign merchants residing in Seville simply used Spaniards as fronts for their involvement in the Indies trade, and foreign vessels loaded with contraband merchandise regularly called at Spanish American ports, especially in areas poorly served by the fleet system. Along the coast of Venezuela, for example, smuggling flourished. The Dutch, based in nearby Curaçao, exchanged coveted manufactured goods for high-grade Venezuelan cacao.

Portuguese colonists in Brazil had to contend with fewer restrictions on their mercantile ventures than their counterparts in Spanish America. Portugal lacked sufficient shipping capacity to restrict the Brazil trade to its own subjects. Foreign ships were free to travel to and from Brazil as long as they secured a license from the Portuguese crown and paid appropriate taxes. In particular, English vessels often made their way to Brazil. By the seventeenth century, however, mounting defense concerns prompted the introduction of convoys in the Brazil trade as well. The discovery of gold and diamonds in the eighteenth century prompted additional restrictions on economic activity in Brazil.

By exploiting the mineral wealth, varied environment, and cheap labor of the colonies, Spanish and Portuguese Americans generated investment capital and stimulated demand for fine clothing and other luxuries as well as everyday staples—food, shoes, tools, and household utensils. Personal ingenuity turned up new opportunities for profit and creative means of evading constraints on merchants' activities. For example, by the early seventeenth century, the *peruleros* (transatlantic merchants based in Lima) had begun bypassing the Portobelo fairs and the middlemen and tax collectors who did business there. Instead, they went to Spain themselves, purchasing items directly from suppliers in Seville and shipping them back to Peru for resale. Buying and selling were central activities in the Iberians' New World, and the colonial environment furnished ample scope for private initiative.

CITIES AND TOWNS IN THE IBERIANS' NEW WORLD

Colonial Latin Americans, then, derived their fortunes from a variety of sources— from silver mines deep below the surface of the Earth; from fields planted in sugar cane, maize, and wheat; from cattle ranches, goldfields, and textile works;

and from the business of moving people and goods over great distances. Regardless of where the wealth came from, however, much of it ended up in the cities and towns that Iberians established throughout their New World. To their way of thinking, the only civilized and proper existence was an urban one. The most successful miners, merchants, and agriculturists of Spanish America and Brazil established their residences and displayed their wealth in the great cities. Cities were also the seats of civil and ecclesiastical power, headquarters of viceroyalties, audiencias, tribunals of the Inquisition, and diocesan sees, as well as the centers of intellectual and artistic life in the colonies. They also became home to the thousands of working men and women, the artisans and domestic servants who supported the lifestyles of the elites.

Capital Cities

Most important among the cities of colonial Latin America were the three great political capitals established in the sixteenth century: Mexico City, Lima, and Salvador da Bahia. Built on the foundations of Aztec Tenochtitlan, Mexico City was in many respects the premier city of the Western Hemisphere. Its population topped 100,000 in the early seventeenth century. The city depended on the vast hinterland of New Spain to supply its necessities, brought in by oxcarts and mules and by canoes that traversed what remained of the valley's lakes.

At the center of Mexico City stood the massive plaza, the *zócalo* that is still the hub of the modern metropolis, surrounded by visual symbols of the colony's power structure: the viceroy's palace, the cabildo headquarters, the cathedral, and the city's principal market. Like many other cities established in Spanish America, it was laid out on a grid pattern. Within a few blocks of the plaza, one could find the lavish homes of the city's elite and dozens of sumptuous convents, monasteries, and churches, as well as the shops of the most prominent retailers and artisans. Elegant coaches trimmed in silk and gold, driven by black and mulatto slaves in full livery, carried the city's rich and powerful citizens as they went about their business. Two large aqueducts, built by Indian repartimiento workers, brought water from springs at Chapultepec, a few miles west of the zócalo, to the city's many public and private fountains.

Spaniards who settled in Peru intended at first to follow the example of New Spain and use the indigenous capital city as headquarters for their new colony. They soon decided that Cuzco was too inaccessible to serve that purpose, however, and the coastal town of Lima, the "city of Kings," became the capital instead. Lima's population grew to about 25,000 by 1614, and close to 80,000 by the 1680s. Its *plaza de armas,* or central square, was an impressive sight to residents and visitors alike. There, too, hundreds of coaches, some worth more than 3000 pesos, could be seen on city streets. By the eighteenth century, Lima boasted 6 parish churches in addition to its cathedral, along with 11 hospitals, 15 nunneries, and 19 monasteries.

Proudly situated atop a bluff overlooking the entrance to the magnificent harbor known as the Bahia de Todos os Santos, Salvador da Bahia served as capital of Brazil until 1763. There resided the colony's chief political author-ity, known as the governor-general or viceroy, as well as the high court and the Archbishop of Brazil. Wharves and warehouses lined the waterfront, while government buildings, churches, and the homes of the rich occupied higher ground. Salvador had a population of about 25,000 in the early eighteenth cen-tury, and double that number by the end of the colonial period. Leading sugar planters from the surrounding area maintained their principal residences at Salvador, and its local government was dominated by senhores de engenho and lavradores de cana.

Provincial Capitals and Other Towns

Other important cities grew along key transportation routes. Puebla de los Ange-les, situated along the road from Mexico City to Veracruz, ranked second only to the viceregal capital among the cities of New Spain and matched Lima in pop-ulation by the eighteenth century. Puebla's cathedral boasted bell towers higher than those of Mexico City, and its tightly woven local elite tried to outdo their counterparts in the capital in staging elaborate ceremonies to welcome a new viceroy to the kingdom of New Spain.

In South America, Huamanga (known today as Ayacucho) also traced its growth to its strategic position along the route linking Lima with Upper Peru. La Paz, the principal city of modern Bolivia, lay astride the road linking Potosí, Cuzco, and Chuquisaca. Oruro in Bolivia owed its existence to the success of its silver mines and its location along major trade routes, for the cheapest mode of transporting mercury from Huancavelica to Potosí involved shipping it by sea from Lima to Arica and then overland through Oruro.

Though many a ghost town could be found in the mining regions, major cities developed wherever precious metals proved sufficient in quantity to sus-tain mining and associated economic activities for more than a few decades. In the seventeenth century, Potosí was easily the largest city in South America, and Zacatecas ranked as New Spain's third largest city, with a population that reached eighty thousand. In the gold fields of Brazil, Ouro Prêto's population numbered upwards of 50,000 in the heyday of the mining bonanza (see Plate 7). Communities throughout Minas Gerais boasted elegant, richly ornamented churches.

Still other towns served as regional markets and administrative centers. Quito, today the capital of Ecuador, was the seat of an audiencia and a center of distrib-ution and supply for the many obrajes that could be found in the surrounding val-leys. Its Franciscan monastery and Jesuit church remain to this day among the most impressive examples of colonial church architecture in all of Latin America.

Cuzco, no longer the center of political power that it had been in Inca times, nonetheless remained an important Spanish city. Spanish churches and convents with pre-colonial foundations can still be seen in the center of town.

While most of Brazil's important cities were seaports on the Atlantic coast, the heavily fortified port cities of Spanish America–Veracruz, Acapulco, Havana, Portobelo, Cartagena, Guayaquil, Callao–ranked among the least impressive of the colonies' urban centers. Most people of any means preferred to live inland, away from the heat, tropical storms, recurrent diseases, and threat of pirate attacks that plagued coastal settlements. The French explorer Samuel Champlain proclaimed Portobelo "the most evil and pitiful residence in the world." An Italian visitor was equally unimpressed with Acapulco, describing it as "a humble village of fishermen," and noting that merchants coming up from Lima had to prevail upon the town's poor mulattos to provide them temporary lodging.

Urban Amenities

Urban life afforded comforts and amenities not readily available in rural areas. Major cities had paved streets, at least at the center of town, as well as public parks like Mexico City's Alameda. By the end of the sixteenth century, most cities had a number of social welfare institutions, including hospitals, orphanages, and shelters for women, all supported by the church, the state, or pious benefactors drawn from local elites. Mexico City even had an asylum that catered to the special needs of the mentally ill.

The viceregal capitals and major provincial towns of colonial Latin America were also active centers of intellectual and artistic life. Printing presses turned out theological and devotional materials in Mexico City, Lima, La Paz, Puebla, and other cities. Santo Domingo, Mexico City, and Lima all had universities dating from the sixteenth century, and by the end of the seventeenth century, universities had also appeared in Quito, Córdoba in Argentina, Guatemala City, and Cuzco. Major cities such as Lima, Salvador da Bahia, and Mexico City, as well as smaller towns such as Cuenca and Latacunga in present-day Ecuador, had Jesuit colleges that trained sons of the elite for the priesthood and other careers. No universities were established in Brazil, but the colony's wealthiest planters and merchants sent their sons to Portugal to study at the distinguished University of Coimbra. Convents located in major urban centers served the intellectual needs of a select group of women. Not only did many convents offer primary instruction for young girls, but they also provided an opportunity for some nuns to pursue literary or scholarly interests.

Architects and artists found ample outlets for their talents in building and adorning the churches and convents in cities and towns throughout the colonies. In Spanish America, the silver bonanza of the late sixteenth and seventeenth centuries spurred an ecclesiastical building boom. Foremost were the great cathedrals

Interior of a church in Salvador, Brazil.

that took a century or more to complete. In Mexico City, for example, work on the cathedral began in 1563 and was not concluded until 1700. Richly detailed exterior facades and elaborate gilded altarpieces characterized the baroque style that predominated in the church buildings of the seventeenth century.

Urban Working Classes

The cities of colonial Latin America were home not only to highly visible political, ecclesiastical, and economic elites, but also to thousands of skilled and unskilled workers of all racial groups. In the larger cities, one could observe large numbers of silversmiths, painters, tailors, shoemakers, barbers, candle makers, silk weavers, jewelers, carpenters, masons, bakers, blacksmiths, and other artisans who organized themselves into guilds in order to maintain the standards of their trades. By the end of the sixteenth century, there were more than 200 guilds in New Spain, most of them located in Mexico City. Hundreds of young men of all racial backgrounds apprenticed themselves to master craftsmen certified by the guilds. Skilled tradespeople played a somewhat less prominent role in Brazilian cities, but in Salvador a popular tribune (*juiz do povo*) represented their interests to the town council.

Blacks and mulattos, both slave and free, could be found in cities everywhere, most notably in Brazil but also in Spanish America. Urban slaveowners often found it profitable for a slave to learn a trade and work for wages, which the master then pocketed. In many cases, however, skilled artisans could accumulate sufficient funds of their own to purchase their freedom or that of their loved ones. Slaves also performed domestic service in the households of urban elites. Blacks were particularly prominent in port cities such as Salvador, Acapulco, Veracruz, Callao, and Cartagena, where they performed a great deal of the labor as porters and stevedores. In the government shipyards of Callao and Guayaquil, black slaves worked as carpenters, joiners, shipwrights, and caulkers, often side by side with their owners.

The urban poor vastly outnumbered the rich and enjoyed few of the comforts that elites took for granted. In Mexico City and elsewhere, many lived in crowded quarters rented from convents and other religious establishments or from wealthier residents of the town. They enjoyed little privacy, and they spent much of their leisure time in the streets, plazas, and marketplaces, and in the many taverns that catered to a lower class clientele. Many city dwellers were reduced to begging or petty crime to survive.

At the same time, however, city life offered everyone, even the poor, elaborate spectacles and other diversions. Religious holidays and ceremonies held to honor incoming viceroys and other dignitaries gave elites a chance to show off their wealth and curry favor with powerful leaders of the church and state, but these occasions also featured popular entertainment such as parades, bullfights, and fireworks. As some of the most privileged members of the working classes, members of artisan guilds marched in processions and sponsored comedies for the amusement of the crowds. Festivals also gave the urban poor an opportunity to let off steam and ridicule the pretensions of their prominent and prosperous neighbors. Urban life, then, offered something for everyone, and for this reason, cities were among the most important features of the new world that Iberian Americans created for themselves.

CONCLUSION

From California to Tierra del Fuego, Spanish and Portuguese immigrants found a stunning variety of resources they could exploit: fertile lands suitable for producing crops they had known back home, mineral wealth beyond their wildest expectations, and dozens of exotic new commodities that could be marketed in the "Old" World and the "New." Shrewd and innovative entrepreneurs, they turned rainforests into sugarcane fields, blasted tunnels deep beneath the surface of the Earth, and turned their livestock loose everywhere they went.

Over the three centuries that followed Columbus's landfall in 1492, Iberian colonists, their African slaves and American-born descendants, and the British, French, and Dutch settlers who followed, transformed the physical environment of the hemisphere, making it a "New World" for indigenous peoples and newcomers alike. However much or little they knew of the world beyond the sea, the natives of the Americas became part of a global economy. In Mexico and Peru, they risked suffocation underground and mercury poisoning above, all to provide silver coins that paid Spanish armies in Europe and filled the pockets of merchants as far away as China and India. Europeans became avid consumers of the Aztecs' chocolate, flavored with sugar grown by Africans transported across the Atlantic in chains, while addiction to American tobacco spread throughout Europe and to Africa and the Far East.

To be sure, Mesoamericans and Andeans had engaged in long-distance trade well before 1492, but Spanish colonists refashioned pre-existing routes to suit their own purposes, over the Isthmus of Panamá and across the forbidding Gran Chichimeca to the mines of northern New Spain, for example. The Nahuas of central Mexico had once obtained their cacao from Colima on the northwest coast and Soconusco in present-day Guatemala, but by the seventeenth and eighteenth centuries their colonial descendants were consuming chocolate produced on haciendas as far away as Caracas and Guayaquil. Spanish and Portuguese Americans carved new trade routes that carried American produce to distant markets in both hemispheres. Transformed into a new world of the Iberians' making, the people and resources of the Americas now answered to the imperatives of an emerging global economy.

LEARNING MORE ABOUT LATIN AMERICANS

Couturier, Edith Boorstein. *The Silver King: The Remarkable Life of the Count of Regla in Colonial Mexico* (Albuquerque, NM: University of New Mexico Press, 2003). Biography of a Spaniard who made a fortune in silver mining in eighteenth-century Mexico.

Higgins, Kathleen J. *"Licentious Liberty" in a Brazilian Gold-Mining Region: Slavery, Gender, and Social Control in Eighteenth-Century Sabará, Minas Gerais* (University Park, PA: Pennsylvania State University Press, 1999). Shows how the lives of slaves, especially, were shaped by the specific context of Brazil's gold-mining region.

Hoberman, Louisa Schell, and Susan Migden Socolow, eds. *Cities and Society in Colonial Latin America* (Albuquerque, NM: University of New Mexico Press, 1986). Collected essays by leading historians on various groups of people who lived in colonial Latin American cities, including merchants, nuns, artisans, servants, slaves, and criminals.

Hoberman, Louisa Schell, and Susan Migden Socolow, eds. *The Countryside in Colonial Latin America* (Albuquerque, NM: University of New Mexico Press, 1996). A companion volume to *Cities and Society in Colonial Latin America;* essays explore such topics as material culture, conflict, and changing agricultural technology.

Lane, Kris. *Quito 1599: City and Colony in Transition* (Albuquerque, NM: University of New Mexico Press, 2002). A glimpse into the lives of merchants, workers, slaves, and shipwreck victims in colonial Ecuador at the end of the sixteenth century.

Martin, Cheryl E. *Rural Society in Colonial Morelos* (Albuquerque, NM: University of New Mexico Press, 1985). Traces the interaction of native villages and sugar haciendas in the region around Cuernavaca, Mexico.

Schwartz, Stuart B. *Sugar Plantations in the Formation of Brazilian Society: Bahia, 1550–1835* (Cambridge, U.K.: Cambridge University Press, 1985). A prize-winning book that examines life and work on Brazilian plantations.

5

THE AMERINDIANS' CHANGING WORLD

IN 1577, KING PHILIP II of Spain decided that he wanted more detailed information on his American possessions. To accomplish this goal, he sent a lengthy questionnaire to local Spanish officials throughout Mesoamerica and the Andes. The recipients in turn consulted with Catholic priests and indigenous leaders in hundreds of communities. A total of 208 reports, 167 of them from New Spain, reached the king within a few years. Known collectively as the *Relaciones Geográficas,* these documents graphically demonstrate the profound changes that the native peoples witnessed in the first several decades that followed the arrival of the Europeans in Mexico and Peru.

Typical was the testimony of the Indian caciques of Oaxtepec in what is now the state of Morelos in Mexico. By 1580, the people of Oaxtepec grew an abundance of Spanish fruits such as melons, figs, oranges, limes, and quinces. They had become enthusiastic participants in the emerging market economy, with much of their produce destined for sale in Mexico City. Like many other communities, Oaxtepec provided a brilliantly colored map, with both a Catholic church and the indigenous symbol for the community at its center (see Plate 8). But the caciques could not hide their nostalgia for the "good old days" before the coming of the Spaniards, when people worked hard, bathed three times a day, and "did not know what sickness was."

Few of Oaxtepec's caciques were old enough in 1580 to have direct personal memories of pre-conquest days, and they may well have idealized the years of Mexica domination. But they were certainly correct in their notion of the profound changes the indigenous peoples of the Americas had experienced since 1492. Their material environment had altered forever as Europeans introduced exotic plants and animals and reshaped the landscape to accommodate haciendas, plantations, and mines. The structure of their community life had changed too, as they now answered to new rulers and prayed to new gods.

At the same time, Native Americans retained many features of life as they had known it before the arrival of the Spaniards and Portuguese. Long-familiar crops still provided the bulk of their subsistence, and most people continued to speak only the languages their forebears had known for centuries. Behind a facade of adaptation to European forms of community life, the indigenous peoples continued many traditional practices and beliefs when they governed themselves and communicated with the supernatural.

This chapter examines both continuity and change among native peoples under Spanish and Portuguese colonization. We will look first at the people who lived in the cores of the great pre-hispanic empires of the Aztecs and Incas. The presence of mineral and agricultural resources and a native population accustomed to paying taxes and performing forced labor made Mesoamerica and the Andes especially attractive to Spanish colonists. We will turn next to natives of the frontiers of northern Mexico and southern South America, areas that were less densely settled in pre-colonial times and less inviting to European colonists. Indians in these regions were often gathered into mission complexes operated by Franciscan and Jesuit clergy, an experience that triggered even more drastic alterations in their way of life than those experienced by natives in Mesoamerica and the Andes. Finally, we will examine how the indigenous peoples of the Americas resisted and adapted to the many changes they experienced during three centuries of Spanish and Portuguese rule, and how they reformulated their individual and group identities over time.

NATIVE COMMUNITIES IN MESOAMERICA AND THE ANDES

Spanish colonizers of the sixteenth century gravitated to the highland interiors of Mexico and South America. The real and imagined wealth of the Aztecs and Incas drew the first conquistadors to Tenochtitlan and Cuzco. They marveled not only at the material splendor of these grand capitals, but also at the sophisticated social and political organization of the great indigenous empires. The simultaneous discovery of huge silver deposits in northern Mexico and Upper Peru in the 1540s gave the Spaniards ample incentive to stay in Mesoamerica and the Andes, and they looked upon the native peoples of these regions as a convenient source of labor for mining and other enterprises. The colonizers

TIMELINE	
1549 First Jesuits arrive in Brazil	**1615** Felipe Guaman Poma de Ayala completes his history of Peru
1568–1572 Jesuits arrive in Peru and Mexico	**1680** Pueblo rebellion in New Mexico
1570s Viceroy Toledo orders massive relocation of Peru's Indian population	**1690s** Jesuit missionaries active in Sonora and southern Arizona
1573 Franciscan missionaries begin work in Florida	**1692** Rebellion of Indians and other lower classes in Mexico City; Spaniards begin reconquest of New Mexico
1598 Franciscans begin work among the Pueblos of New Mexico	**1712** Indian rebellion in Chiapas
1610 Jesuit missionaries begin work among the Guaraní in Paraguay	**1769** Franciscans begin building missions in California

quickly set about reorganizing indigenous community life and adapting traditional systems of forced labor and taxation to their own imperatives.

As a result, the highland peoples of Mexico and Peru experienced more immediate Spanish intrusions into their daily lives than did natives of areas that were more marginal to the European agenda. But Andeans and Mesoamericans also possessed a rich and complex indigenous culture that they could draw upon in fashioning their responses to their changing world.

Shifting Populations in the República de Indios

Official Spanish policy divided colonial society into two separate "repúblicas," one of Indians, the other of Spaniards. In Mesoamerica and the Andes, the "república de indios" was made up of hundreds of peasant communities with no real connection to one another. In theory, these villages were shielded from harmful outside influence, with mestizos, blacks, and españoles other than priests, corregidores, and alcaldes mayores forbidden to reside within them, while protective legislation supposedly safeguarded community lands. In practice, however, non-Indians infiltrated everywhere, eventually outnumbering the native population in some villages. Meanwhile, labor drafts forced natives from their communities of origin, and the need to supply tribute and other perquisites to the Spaniards drew them into the emerging cash economy of the "república de españoles."

The demographic makeup of the so-called Indian communities was anything but static. European diseases continued to reduce the indigenous population for a century or more until the native peoples began developing greater resistance to smallpox and other Old World illnesses. In order to facilitate missionary efforts and collect tribute, Spanish officials consolidated the survivors numerous times in the sixteenth and early seventeenth centuries, forcing those living in outlying areas to move to more centrally located villages and sometimes lumping together people who spoke different indigenous languages. This combination of epidemics and forced resettlements left vast tracts of land vacant, facilitating the consolidation of Spanish-owned haciendas.

The most sweeping relocations occurred in the Andes, mandated by Viceroy Francisco de Toledo in the 1570s. In the province of Huarochirí, 100 or so settlements were concentrated into just 17, and in Upper Peru (present-day Bolivia), Toledo "reduced" some 900 hamlets and 129,000 people into just 44 villages. Toledo's resettlement program undermined traditional Andean survival strategies. Prior to the arrival of the Europeans, each community held lands at different elevations up and down the mountainsides, giving them access to several different microclimates and allowing them to grow a variety of crops. Communities created by Toledo's decrees often lost control of outlying ecological niches. The viceroy's program also disrupted cooperative labor arrangements that native peoples had developed over the course of many centuries.

Native peoples did not always comply with forced resettlements. In Peru, some communities lodged official protests with the viceroy and audiencia even before they received their formal orders to relocate, while other groups complied but returned to their former homes less than a decade after Toledo's program went into effect. Indians in New Spain appealed to colonial courts and sometimes secured reversals of relocation orders. In 1603, the village of Anenecuilco in the present-day Mexican state of Morelos successfully resisted removal to the village of Cuautla. Three hundred years later, as Mexico's Revolution of 1910 began, the famous agrarian rebel Emiliano Zapata rallied his fellow townsmen in Anenecuilco to fight persistent encroachments of nearby sugar haciendas on village lands.

Other groups moved voluntarily in the years following the conquest. Andean peoples forcibly relocated by the Incas took advantage of the new colonial regime to return to their places of origin. Particularly notable were the Cañaris, whom the Incas had uprooted from southern Ecuador and resettled in the Yucay Valley near Cuzco and elsewhere. By the 1580s, however, the Cañari population of the province of Cuenca in Ecuador had grown to 12,000, a fourfold increase since the conquest.

Many people also moved individually or in small groups. In the Andes, a man who left his community of origin and settled in another native village could escape being drafted for the Potosí mita. Known as *forasteros,* these men were denied both membership in the ayllu (the traditional native community organization) and allocations of community land. However, they were also exempt from the payment of tribute. As a result, forasteros often accumulated greater wealth than the *originarios,* as those native to the community were called. Many forasteros also gained access to land by marrying local women or making informal arrangements with kurakas (traditional chiefs) in their adopted communities. Kurakas thus found ways to profit from the influx of forasteros, exacting labor and other personal favors in exchange for these concessions.

Many native people left the república de indios altogether, settling in Spanish cities, haciendas, and mining camps. Meanwhile, favorably situated Indian communities attracted large numbers of mestizos, blacks, mulattos, and españoles. By the late eighteenth century, for example, nearly two-thirds of Oaxtepec's people were non-Indians. Though officially barred from political positions in the república de indios, many of these newcomers acquired community lands through purchase, rental, squatting, or marriage to Indian women, and they wielded considerable influence in the Indian villages.

Local Government in the República de Indios

Local government in the villages of Mesoamerica and Peru rested in the hands of an indigenous ruling class deputized by the Spanish to supervise tribute collection, marshal workers for labor drafts, and maintain order within their villages. At first, the encomenderos, clergy, and crown officials dealt with whatever hereditary rulers they found in place, as long as these individuals were willing to cooperate with the new regime. Soon, however, they began attempting to recast the structure of local government to more closely resemble models of municipal organization they had known in Europe.

In each community, the Spanish designated a single individual, always a male, to be the *gobernador* or head of local government. Sometimes the person chosen was a cacique (or kuraka in Peru), with a legitimate tie to pre-hispanic rulers, but in many other cases someone else assumed the position. Other leading figures in the village became *regidores* and *alcaldes* that together formed a governing body that the Spanish called a cabildo, similar to the town councils created in major Spanish municipalities. Native cabildos also included a bailiff and a scribe trained to record community business in indigenous languages but using the European alphabet. Cabildo members not only received a salary from the village treasury; they also claimed food, personal service, and other perquisites from community members and were usually exempt from tribute payment and labor drafts. With such incentives, the number of officers tended to multiply.

The Indian gobernador and his cabildo exercised a wide variety of duties within their jurisdictions, often following pre-hispanic custom. They handled the allocation of village lands, supervised the sale and rental of lands by private individuals, and oversaw the operation of local markets. They also punished community members for misdemeanors that included public drunkenness, theft, and domestic violence. Local government in the indigenous communities rested primarily in native hands, although Spanish district magistrates (the corregidores or alcaldes mayores whom we met in Chapter 3 and their lieutenants) could and did meddle in village business.

Spanish assumptions that political offices should be reserved for males did not mean that women were completely marginalized from politics in the república de indios. Women raised money to finance lawsuits in defense of community lands and were often at the forefront in village rebellions against colonial authorities. Numerous hereditary *cacicas* (the feminine form of caciques) could be found in the Mixteca region of southern Mexico, and there are scattered references to female kurakas in the Andes. Though excluded from holding office or participating in elections, these women wielded considerable influence within their communities.

Spanish authorities maintained the fiction that indigenous cabildo officers were elected, usually for one-year terms. Pre-hispanic custom usually dictated that new rulers were chosen only on the death of an incumbent, so in many places the same individuals were elected year after year. Voting was restricted to a select circle of elite men. In the Cuernavaca region of central Mexico, for example, electors usually numbered about 10 percent of the adult males living in the village. Factional disputes abounded in colonial Indian communities, and local elections were sometimes punctuated by violence.

In some places, especially in Mexico, mestizos and others served as village gobernadores and other officers. The Hinojosa family, caciques of Cuernavaca, dominated local politics in the república de indios for several generations in the seventeenth and eighteenth centuries. Biologically mestizos, they perhaps descended from a Spaniard named Francisco de Hinojosa who settled in Cuernavaca in the sixteenth century. They spoke Spanish and maintained close ties with the priests at the Franciscan monastery and with local españoles, including owners of sugar haciendas in the area.

The first Hinojosa to be elected gobernador of Cuernavaca was Don Juan de Hinojosa, who attained the office in 1629. Twenty years later, his younger brother Agustín also held the post. Juan boasted descent from the conquistadors of Cuernavaca. Both men openly acknowledged their status as mestizos, although Agustín also called himself an español on numerous occasions. Agustín married Doña Juana Jiménez, granddaughter of a sixteenth-century gobernador and the sole heir of one of the region's most powerful native families. Their son Antonio served as gobernador for many years. People said he looked like an español, and his wife was the daughter of a prominent Spaniard and a cacica from Texcoco. Their children's baptisms were recorded not in the book reserved for Indians, but in the volume used for españoles and other non-Indians.

The complicity of native officials with the Spanish power structure and their dogged pursuit of personal interests frequently eroded whatever legitimacy they might have in the eyes of their constituents. Kurakas in Peru who collected tribute and rounded up men to work in the silver mines at Potosí were either unwilling or unable to provide the reciprocal benefits that their forebears had supplied to the commoners, for example.

Subsistence and Survival in the República de Indios

The plants and animals brought by Europeans to their New World and the varied enterprises of Spanish and Portuguese colonists brought profound changes to the physical landscape of the Americas, but Indian peasants continued their traditional modes of subsistence while borrowing selectively from the foreigners. Native crops such as maize and beans in Mesoamerica and potatoes in the Andes remained staples in their diets, and Indians were slow to adopt plows and other tools as long as their familiar techniques continued to meet their needs. Customary patterns of land tenure officially prevailed, with ownership of most lands vested in the community and native officials in charge of allocating plots to heads of households. In practice, though, the passing years saw the increasing privatization of lands, as caciques and kurakas, along with enterprising commoners and non-Indian residents, accumulated more and more lands for themselves.

The greatest challenge the repúblicas de indios in Mesoamerica and the Andes faced was the encroachment on their lands by Spanish estates. In the late sixteenth and early seventeenth centuries, when the Indian population was at its lowest, coexistence was possible, but once native numbers began to increase in the eighteenth century, competition for land and water intensified, especially in areas where Spanish penetration was heaviest. Villages also contended with one another for access to these vital resources, often perpetuating disputes that dated back hundreds of years.

Indian peasants employed a variety of tactics, including forcibly occupying lands, damaging irrigation works, and physically attacking hacienda overseers and employees, in an effort to reclaim lands they believed were rightfully theirs. Community leaders also mastered the intricacies of the Spanish legal system and often traveled to Lima or Mexico City to present their complaints in person to the viceroy or the audiencia. They carefully safeguarded sixteenth-century maps and other credentials that supported their case. These papers are replete with references to lands possessed "from time immemorial," long before the arrival of the Spaniards.

Natives also made frequent use of the courts to get relief from excessive tribute, forced labor obligations, and other abuses that undermined their ability to support themselves. On many occasions they won, in part because the authorities may have still harbored sympathy for the Indians based on the ideals of Bartolomé de las Casas and other sixteenth-century advocates. More importantly, Spanish officials understood the strategic importance of sustaining the native population, for Indians could pay their tributes and serve their labor obligations only if they retained enough land to provide for themselves. Although wealthy

Slice of Life   THE INDIANS OF OAXTEPEC DEFEND
THEIR LAND AND WATER

AT THE BEGINNING of this chapter, we met the native leaders of the Mexican village of Oaxtepec, who in 1580 looked back on the manifold changes they had witnessed since the Spanish conquest—changes that in many ways shattered life as the caciques' forebears had known it. Little did these caciques know that their community would face continued challenges to its survival for generations to come. These challenges would force their descendants to capitalize on the resources available to them, to enter the cash economy by selling produce native to their land as well as crops brought by the Europeans, and to seek help from sympathetic outsiders.

As the caciques gave their testimony in 1580, the area around Oaxtepec—today, the Mexican state of Morelos—stood on the brink of a major shift in patterns of landholding. In the final two decades of the sixteenth century, non-Indians acquired substantial lands near Oaxtepec, lands left vacant by the precipitous decline in the indigenous population, and expanded the cultivation of sugarcane to supply the markets of Mexico City and other urban centers.

From the beginning of the seventeenth century until Mexico's Revolution of 1910, the villagers of Oaxtepec had to compete with sugar haciendas for access to the land and water they needed for their own subsistence and for the fruit, vegetables, and sugarcane they produced for sale. Meanwhile, the village's fertile soil and agreeable climate attracted growing numbers of non-Indians who bought or rented lands from Indian leaders and became permanent residents in violation of royal prohibitions. Officially, however, Oaxtepec remained part of the "república de indios."

Over time, the community's leaders developed a variety of approaches to deal with the haciendas. Litigation was one tool they often employed, although the courts did not always render the decision they desired. Other tactics included acts of violence against specific targets and strategic alliances with non-Indians who might help them in their struggle to maintain their community.

A particularly troublesome adversary was a hacienda named Pantitlán, and the object of contention was not land, but water coming from a spring located near the church in Oaxtepec. For many years, Pantitlán lay in ruins, and the villagers enjoyed exclusive use of the water. In 1750, a new owner of Pantitlán decided to refurbish the property's sugar mill and expand production. At first, the two parties struck a compromise that allowed each to have access to the water, but by 1776 the hacienda's owner took the villagers to court, charging that they had taken most of the water, halting his sugar mill at the height of the harvest. Protracted litigation and several out-of-court settlements over the next two decades failed to produce a lasting accord. Hacendados in the region

(continued on next page)

THE INDIANS OF OAXTEPEC DEFEND THEIR LAND AND WATER *(continued from previous page)*

circulated rumors that the villagers were planning a general uprising with support from other indigenous communities. Perhaps fear of an insurrection prompted the owner of Pantitlán to agree to build an aqueduct that would enable him to draw water from a nearby river instead of relying exclusively on the contested spring. In this case, then, the villagers won something of a victory; their only concession was to allow a part of the aqueduct to cross their land. The villagers and the hacienda owner continued to bicker over the use of water from the spring, however.

Meanwhile, the villagers carried on a long-standing water dispute with the owner of another hacienda, who accused them of damaging his aqueducts in order to divert water to their crops and to the thousands of banana plants cultivated by the town surgeon, the parish priest, and many other non-Indians who rented village lands. This feud reached particularly acrimonious levels in 1786, central Mexico's famous "year of hunger," when the warm, fertile valleys of present-day Morelos were able to produce extra crops of maize after a devastating crop failure in less favored locales. For centuries, the Indians and other residents of Oaxtepec had produced irrigated crops of maize in the winter and sold it in the months when supplies were lowest and prices highest, and they stood to make an especially good profit as famine spread and maize prices escalated. A court decision awarded the Indians access to extra water in 1786, but two years later the hacendado won a reversal of that verdict. Oaxtepec's response was to renew its battle with Pantitlán over the spring water, continuing their litigation into the first decade of the nineteenth century.

Questions for Discussion

Suppose that the indigenous people of Oaxtepec had decided to close their community to non-Indians and to withdraw completely from the cash economy. Would this strategy have even been possible? Why or why not? Would it have enabled them to better survive the effects of Spanish domination? Why or why not?

landowners might easily bribe a judge to rule in their favor, Indians often proved adept in playing various power figures against one another. They could frequently count on help from their parish priest, whose livelihood depended on the continued viability of the village economy. These victories came at a price, for in resorting to Spanish courts and Spanish laws to defend their livelihoods, native communities tacitly and probably unwittingly acknowledged the legitimacy of colonial rule. On the other hand, one could also say that the authorities' willingness to hear and sometimes act on their complaints earned them a certain measure of legitimacy in the eyes of native plaintiffs.

When litigation and other means of rectifying abuses failed, a community might resort to violence. Men and women picked up rocks or machetes and attacked a specific target, usually a person or object directly associated with a particular grievance—a priest, government official, or hacienda overseer, a village jail or a hacienda's irrigation works. Colonial officials met these challenges with a judicious blend of repression and appeasement. Usually, they singled out a few alleged ringleaders for exemplary punishment that might include forced obraje service, fines, public whippings, or exile from the area. They sometimes ordered the construction of a stone gallows in the center of a village to remind residents of the power of the state. Most often, however, the incidents ended with some sort of conciliatory gesture on the part of the authorities. The natives might win at least one round of an ongoing land dispute or gain reprieve from a new increase in taxes, labor obligations, or church fees.

Rarely did these revolts extend beyond a single village, much less challenge the colonial order as such. Most native peoples simply did not see themselves as "Indians" in a way that would have prompted them to unite with neighboring villages with which they had outstanding land disputes and other quarrels. Historian William B. Taylor, who has studied this kind of violence in central Mexico and Oaxaca, concluded that the native villagers in these areas were "good rebels but poor revolutionaries."

Native Communities and the Cash Economy

Even as they waged spirited legal battles with outsiders, Indians also made numerous and profitable compromises with the evolving cash economy. Income from the sale of agricultural produce and craft items in local markets and in Spanish towns and wages earned laboring in mines and on haciendas provided natives with cash to meet tribute obligations, pay legal fees, buy personal items, make improvements on their churches, and finance community fiestas. In the seventeenth and eighteenth centuries, vendors from Huarochirí in Peru supplied the Lima market with apples, peaches, guavas, chirimoyas (a fruit native to the Andes), maize, and chile peppers, as well as cattle, sheep, goats, and llamas. When they went to Potosí to serve their labor obligations, mita workers carried coca, freeze-dried potatoes, and other commodities to sell at the inflated prices that prevailed in the mining center. Caciques and kurakas used their connections to foster their personal commercial ventures.

A kind of mutual accommodation between haciendas and nearby Indian villages characterized rural society in central Mexico. Large landowners needed extra workers during planting and harvesting seasons, but they wished to avoid the expense of maintaining a large resident labor force. The villages provided a handy reservoir of temporary labor, and it behooved the landowner to see to it that the Indians retained enough land to support themselves during much of the year, but not to the point where they could supply all of their needs without recourse to the cash economy.

Forces other than the need for cash also drew Indians into the larger economy. The *repartimiento de mercancías,* whereby corregidores and alcaldes mayores pressured natives into buying commodities from them, was common throughout Mesoamerica and the Andes. Sometimes they furnished mules and other items vital to the Indians, but this trade might also involve items for which the natives had no use. Local officials also forced Indians to sell produce to them at prices well below market rates.

In some places, however, Indians willingly participated in the reparto de mercancías because it served their economic interests. In Oaxaca in southern Mexico, for example, Mixtec and Zapotec peasants supplemented their household income by producing cochineal, a red dye extracted from insects that lived on cacti native to the region. Cochineal was highly coveted in markets throughout Europe, and by the eighteenth century it ranked second only to silver among exports from Mexico. The actual production of this valuable commodity remained almost entirely in native hands throughout the colonial period, but most Indians needed credit to participate in the trade. At the beginning of each annual production cycle, local officials advanced them funds to buy the "nests" of pregnant insects that they placed on the cacti. In return, when they harvested their product, they gave their creditors one pound of cochineal for each 1.5 pesos they had received. The Mixtecs and Zapotecs could have gotten higher rates of return by selling their cochineal in the open market. Without credit, however, they would not have been able to produce it in the first place, and few people other than the corregidores were willing to lend money to poor peasants. The 1.5 pesos they received at the start of the season usually exceeded the cost of producing a pound of cochineal, so the arrangement helped them meet other expenses as well. From the natives' point of view, doing business with the corregidores made economic sense.

Families and Households in the República de Indios

The basic unit of production and subsistence in the república de indios was the household. European colonization had brought important changes to indigenous family life. Missionaries undermined parental authority by encouraging young natives to reject the religious practices of their elders. In place of the extended families and other kinship networks common in indigenous society, missionaries attempted to impose the patriarchal nuclear family. They exhorted their converts to accept premarital chastity, monogamy, and the lifelong bonds of Christian matrimony. In the privacy of the confessional priests evidently probed the most intimate details of the Indians' lives. A confessional manual written in 1631 suggested more than 200 questions that confessors might ask penitents about sexual thoughts and behavior.

The demands of colonialism also upset traditional kinship networks. Widespread mortality left many old and young people without close relatives. Men were gone for weeks or months at a time while they performed their forced labor service, and many never returned. Women therefore shouldered heavier burdens maintaining the household. When tribute obligations came to include quantities of woven cloth, women's work further increased. The imposition of highly patriarchal Spanish legal and religious concepts throughout the colonies and the breakdown of the ayllu in Peru disrupted the cooperative and complementary arrangements between men's work and women's work that had characterized gender roles in pre-hispanic society. Women also found it more difficult to hang on to inherited property in the Spanish legal system.

There is evidence that high levels of domestic violence accompanied the nuclear family arrangement. Priests and civil authorities saw the nuclear family as a microcosm of the larger society. Men "governed" their households as the king governed society as a whole. Social and legal norms recognized a man's right, in fact his obligation, to administer physical "correction" to his wife, children, and other members of the household. Only when such punishments exceeded the bounds considered appropriate did the authorities intervene, and many cases went unreported. Native women were frequent victims of homicide, usually at the hands of their husbands.

Native society thus experienced multiple pressures at the level of the family and the household. Indigenous people nonetheless found new ways to build and maintain kinship networks. Particularly important was the Spanish practice of *compadrazgo,* literally co-parenthood, whereby a special bond existed between the parents and godparents of a child. Godparents might also assume guardianship of a child if the parents died. Compadrazgo thus provided an alternative family when migration, disease, and other calamities tore apart natural kinship networks.

There is evidence too that the persistence of native notions of community life mitigated against some of the more harmful effects of Spanish patriarchalism. The Mixtec and Zapotec peoples of southern Mexico, for example, continued as before the conquest to identify women as members of the community as a whole rather than simply as the wives of specific men. When a husband inflicted physical injury on his wife, he had to answer to the entire community.

Native peoples also ignored the church's teachings on sexuality. In Peru, for example, they persisted in the practice of *sirvinacuy,* or trial marriage, in which young couples lived together to test their mutual compatibility before formally marrying in the church. Those who decided not to marry went their separate ways without any loss of personal honor. Children born of these unions, illegitimate in the eyes of the church, bore no such social stigma in Andean society.

RELIGION AND COMMUNITY LIFE IN THE REPÚBLICA DE INDIOS

The evangelization of native peoples in Mesoamerica and the Andes began almost as soon as the Spanish arrived. For many Indians, the first European they met was a priest, whether Franciscan, Dominican, Jesuit, or a member of the secular clergy.

Missionaries initially claimed great success in converting the natives, but their early optimism soon waned. They often accused natives of backsliding into pagan rituals and gave up on the idea of creating a native priesthood. Although Catholic teaching proclaimed the equality of all souls in the eyes of God, Church authorities came to view Indians as "niños con barbas" (literally, "children with beards") capable of grasping and practicing only the most basic elements of the faith.

Even though colonial Indians were relegated to a decidedly inferior standing within the church, Catholicism as they understood it came to occupy an important place in their lives. The local church was often a focus of community pride, and Christian festivals gave them regular opportunities to come together and reinforce the ties that bound families and villages together. In an effort to make sense of their continually changing material and cultural world, native peoples freely combined Catholic symbols and dogma with elements derived from pre-hispanic religious custom.

Natives as Catholics

Most Indians received rudimentary instruction in the intricacies of the faith. Parents usually brought their infants to church to be baptized within a few days of birth. Children attended catechism classes, where they memorized prayers such as the Our Father and the Ave María and precepts such as the Articles of Faith and the Ten Commandments. Bilingual catechisms used to instruct native children in the Andes suggest that these youngsters were presented with a simplified version of Christian doctrine, reflecting the priests' skepticism about natives' intellectual and spiritual capacities. Priests in Indian parishes enforced regular attendance at Sunday mass.

Catholics were supposed to receive the sacraments of confession and the Eucharist once they reached the age of reason, about seven or eight, although many Indians, especially in the Andes, never did participate in these rites. Perhaps because their indigenous religions had nothing comparable to Christian notions of individual sin and guilt, many Nahuas in central Mexico reportedly avoided the sacrament of confession whenever they could. The incompetence of priests in native languages could also limit the quality of confessions. If a touring bishop reached their community, they might also be confirmed, and whenever possible, priests administered the last rites to the dying. Many adults participated in the sacrament of matrimony as well, although priests continually complained of the number of couples living together without the official blessing of the church.

Relations between Indian peasants and their priests often became strained. Priests demanded perquisites from their parishioners over and above the customary fees they charged for their services. Native women were required to perform domestic chores in the priest's household, for example. Priests sometimes used physical punishment in disciplining errant members of their flocks. When secular priests replaced the regular clergy in Indian parishes, they frequently spent so much time on their personal business ventures that they neglected their spiritual duties. Parishioners also complained that their priests meddled in village politics and failed to live up to the ideals they preached, especially in the area of sexual behavior. Many priests fathered children by native women.

Belief and Practice in the República de Indios

Native persistence in what priests viewed as vestiges of their old religion, including clandestine rituals that involved the use of hallucinogens and the sacrifice of small animals, proved to be a major source of tension between priests and their Indian parishioners, especially in Peru. Andeans venerated their *huacas*–traditional sacred places and the divinities that inhabited them. Although Indian men often fell under Spanish scrutiny as their performed their obligatory labor service, women found chances to retreat to remote mountain locales where they conducted elaborate rituals in honor of these local deities, just as they had done

Priest interrogating an alleged Indian idolater, from the manuscript of the native Andean historian Felipe Guaman Poma de Ayala, who served as an interpreter and assistant to a Spanish priest charged with investigating native idolatry in Peru.

Sixteenth-century drawing made by Indians of Huejotzingo, Mexico, showing the Virgin Mary and the child Jesus, with men and supplies they provided to Cortés in the conquest of Mexico.

in pre-hispanic times. Native peoples in the Andes also revered the mummified remains of ancestors. They exhumed the corpses of relatives from church cemeteries, dressed them in traditional garb, offered sacrifices of llamas, guinea pigs, maize, and coca, and reinterred them in their old burial grounds.

Numerous campaigns aimed at what churchmen called the "uprooting of idolatry" occurred through-out Peru in the seventeenth century, and a special jail in Lima confined the most recalcitrant offenders. The clergy justified such measures by pointing out that the natives had been converted to the true faith but had relapsed–the same ratio-nale used when non-Indians faced prosecution by the Inquisition. But priests dif-fered among themselves as to what actions constituted dangerous heresy worthy of prosecution and what customs were harmless elements of indigenous culture, inferior to European folkways but not socially disruptive in and of themselves.

What actually occurred in the hearts and minds of native peoples was a complex and ongoing process whereby they accepted certain elements of Chris-tianity, retained many old practices and beliefs, and in the end created something new that served basic personal and community needs through con-tact with the supernatural. They were more receptive to Christian teachings that fit well with traditional beliefs. Historians have noted, for example, that native peoples showed particular enthusiasm for the Catholic devotion to the souls in purgatory, perhaps because it meshed with their customary reverence for their dead ancestors.

As time passed, the distinction blurred between that which was pre-hispanic and that which was Catholic. Native Americans showed great devotion to Catholic saints without discarding traditional notions that assumed the presence of the sacred in many animals, plants, and inanimate objects. People in central Mexico, for example, revered bees that produced wax used in the candles that burned on the church altar. Like so many aspects of their life as colonial subjects, the religious experience of Native Americans was a vibrant and highly creative mix of indigenous elements, European Catholicism, and daily adaptation.

Religion and Community Identity

Whatever the natives' level of doctrinal sophistication or religious orthodoxy, villages took pride in the size and beauty of their principal church, often spending lavish sums on church bells, altarpieces, and other adornments. At the urging of the famous Franciscan missionary Gerónimo de Mendieta, the Indians of Huejotzingo in central Mexico commissioned a Flemish painter from Mexico City to fashion an altarpiece for their church. Completed in 1586 at a cost of more than 6000 pesos, the altarpiece featured statues of 15 different saints and numerous paintings showing scenes from the life of Christ. Rituals that were at least superficially Catholic, from regular Sunday mass to special feast days, brought the community together on many occasions throughout the year.

A cadre of Indian laymen, usually known as *fiscales,* assisted the priest in maintaining the church and led devotional services in the absence of a priest. Others served as *cantores* (singers) or sacristans. In central Mexico, these officers were known collectively in Nahuatl as *teopantlaca,* literally, "church people." These positions often carried exemption from tribute, considerable social prestige, and numerous opportunities for personal profit. Fiscales in one community near Mexico City required children to bring them gifts of maize when they came to church for catechism class. Following Catholic custom, these positions were restricted to males. Women's roles in official worship services were not as well defined, but in many places they took responsibility for sweeping the church and cleaning the altar linens.

Central to religious life in the república de indios were the *cofradías,* organizations that were formed to foster devotion to a particular saint and to provide spiritual and material benefits to members. Cofradías and the celebrations they sponsored became vehicles for community solidarity. They also provided a kind of life insurance, paying for the funeral rites of deceased members. Women were very active in the Indian cofradías, sometimes outnumbering male members. Leadership positions, however, were usually restricted to men, and they conferred considerable personal prestige. Indeed, a community's political officials often served in key cofradía offices as well. Specially designated village lands supported cofradía activities. Villagers either rented out these lands or cultivated them collectively, selling the produce and turning the proceeds over to cofradía officers. The Mayan cofradías of Yucatán were noted for their extensive cattle ranches, for example.

Religious holidays that were nominally Catholic became an outlet for indigenous cultural expression. Once the obligatory mass and other solemnities that required the presence of a priest had been dispensed with, natives often preferred to carry on the celebration by themselves. Priests decried what they viewed as excesses—bingeing on food and alcohol, elaborate processions and fireworks displays, bullfights, dancing, and lewd behavior—as well as the blatant or subtle traces

| How Historians Understand | MEASURING ACCULTURATION USING INDIGENOUS LANGUAGE SOURCES |

As indigenous peoples learned to write their own languages in the European alphabet, they became adept at using their literacy to defend and advance their interests. Community leaders kept written records of the proceedings of their cabildos and cofradías, and composed documents that purportedly substantiated village land claims. Men and women of many different social ranks enlisted native scribes to write their wills. Historians have used all of these sources to gain perspectives on changes within the native communities during three centuries of colonial rule.

Nahuatl speakers of central Mexico produced many native language sources. These documents reveal nuances of colonial life that cannot be detected from documents written in Spanish. We learn, for example, what rituals accompanied land transfers within the native community, what kinds of polite formalities people exchanged in various social encounters, how men and women organized their households, and how on their deathbeds they divided their personal possessions among their kin. Historians using Nahuatl sources have also shown greater continuity in the practice of local government from pre-conquest to colonial times than what researchers working exclusively from Spanish documents had supposed.

Introduction to Nahuatl will and testament of the Indian Juan Fabián, from the town of San Bartolomé Atenco, August 1, 1617.

Scholars have also tracked the process of native acculturation by examining the gradual incorporation of Spanish loan-words into Nahuatl. The Spanish brought many objects and concepts for which no Nahuatl equivalent existed. At first, the natives simply used their own words. For horse they said *macatl,* the word for deer, and a firearm was a "fire trumpet." Baptism was *quaatequia,* literally, "to pour water on the head." They did, however, begin adopting a Nahuatlized form of the Spanish word Castilla (Castile), which they added to indigenous words to describe other Spanish imports. Wheat thus became "Castile maize."

Within a couple of decades, Spanish nouns began to make their way into Nahuatl. Natives learned to call a horse a *caballo,* and used the words *vaca* (cow) and *mula* (mule) as well. The Spanish *trigo* (wheat) replaced the earlier "Castile maize." By the end of the sixteenth century, nouns such as *cuchillo,* the Spanish word for knife, and *camisa* (shirt) had been so thoroughly absorbed into Nahuatl that most Indians probably did not even recognize these items as innovations introduced by the Spaniards.

Natives also adopted words associated with Catholicism such as *compadre, misa* (mass), *cruz* (cross), and *Santa Trinidad* (Holy Trinity), along with the days of the week and the months of the year. When Juan Fabián of the town of San Bartolomé Atenco wrote his Nahuatl will in 1617, he began by noting that the day was Monday (*lunes*), the first of August. He then proceeded to invoke the three persons of the Holy Trinity and referred to *Dios* (God) throughout his text.

Terms such as *gobernador, virrey* (viceroy), and *obispo* (bishop) also began appearing regularly in Nahuatl documents by the late sixteenth century. Frequent appearances of the word *pleito* (lawsuit) reflected their growing recourse to the Spanish legal system. In the seventeenth century, Spanish verbs, conjugated as if they were Nahuatl words, began appearing. Especially common were such verbs as *pasear* (to stroll), *confirmar* (to confirm, a reference to the sacrament of confirmation), and *prendar* (to pawn). Even Nahuatl grammar showed some Spanish influences.

This incipient bilingualism reflected native peoples' growing contacts with the cash economy, as wage laborers in mines and on haciendas or as sellers of merchandise in markets frequented by Spanish-speakers. Scholars have also noted, however, that certain Spanish words failed to appear in Nahuatl. Particularly notable for its absence is the word "indio." The Nahuas persisted in identifying themselves in terms of their local community, despite the strong Spanish tendency to lump all natives together in this category.

Comparisons between Nahuatl sources and colonial documents written in other indigenous languages have suggested that the natives of central Mexico probably experienced far greater exposure to European influence than

(continued on next page)

MEASURING ACCULTURATION USING INDIGENOUS LANGUAGE SOURCES *(continued from previous page)*

their counterparts elsewhere in Latin America. Sources from Yucatán, for instance, show far fewer Spanish loan-words incorporated into the Mayan language, and none of the grammatical adaptations common in Nahuatl by the late colonial period.

Questions for Discussion

What similarities and differences are there between the ways Nahuatl speakers began incorporating Spanish words into their speech and the ways people today adopt words from other languages with which they come in contact?

---

of traditional custom that accompanied the festivities. The exuberance of their religious fiestas shows how Indians in Mesoamerica and the Andes truly made Catholicism their own, picking and choosing those aspects of the faith that served the spiritual and temporal needs of individuals and communities.

MISSION INDIANS

European colonization took somewhat different forms outside the core areas of Mesoamerica and the Andes. The northern frontier of New Spain beyond Zacatecas, southern South America, and the interior forests of Brazil attracted fewer permanent Spanish and Portuguese settlers. People native to these regions did not escape the negative effects of conquest, however. They too fell victim to imported diseases, and many survivors were rounded up and taken away as slaves to work in distant mines and sugar plantations. Those who remained in their original homelands became the focus of an intense missionary effort. No longer free to roam as they chose, they now derived their subsistence from intensive agriculture rather than hunting and gathering.

Jesuit and Franciscan Missions

The regular clergy spearheaded missionary efforts in Mexico and Peru during the sixteenth century. The presence of orders such as the Franciscans, Dominicans, and Jesuits in Indian parishes was supposed to be temporary. Once they had completed the initial conversion of an area, royal policy dictated that secular clerics replace them and that the orders move on to new frontiers awaiting Christianization. In practice, the regular clergy remained in control of many Indian parishes in Mesoamerica and the Andes until well into the eighteenth century. Meanwhile, though, the orders maintained an active missionary program on the fringes of Spanish and Portuguese settlement. By far the most prominent among these frontier missionaries were the Jesuits and the Franciscans.

Drawings published in 1614 of Tupi Indians before and after conversion at a mission in Brazil.

Founded in 1534 by the Spaniard Ignatius of Loyola, the Society of Jesus–the Jesuits–attracted highly educated men from throughout Europe. Ignatius and his followers embraced a militant Catholicism and stressed the need to gain new converts for the faith in order to compensate for the inroads of Protestantism in Europe. The new colonies of Spain and Portugal offered them an ideal field for their missionary enterprise. The first Jesuits in the Americas were the six who accompanied Governor Tomé de Sousa to Brazil in 1549. They quickly set to work gathering Tupi and other native peoples into the mission villages they called *aldeias.* In 1554, they established one of their most important missions, São Paulo de Piritininga, at a site that would later become the city of São Paulo. The numbers of Jesuits working in Brazil grew steadily, reaching 110 by 1574 and 165 in 1610.

Although their detractors accused them of exploiting the native peoples of Brazil, Jesuits could also be found among the most outspoken defenders of the Indians. The most famous of these was the Antonio Vieira, who had once served as King João IV's personal confessor and diplomatic emissary. In the mid-seventeenth century, Vieira worked with the Indians of Maranhão and Pará, deep within the Amazon territory. Echoing the words of Bartolomé de las Casas and other Spanish Dominicans of the previous century, he declared that those who captured or owned native slaves lived in a state of mortal sin and faced eternal damnation unless they mended their ways. Meanwhile he and his fellow Jesuits rounded up 200,000 natives from the Amazon basin and settled them into 54 mission aldeias close to the coast, near Belém.

Jesuits arrived in Peru in 1568 and Mexico in 1572. They became especially active in ministering to Indians in the Andes. They also worked briefly in what is now the southeastern United States, setting up missions from Virginia to the present site of Miami, Florida, until native hostility forced them to abandon their efforts. Beginning in 1610, the Jesuits established a large mission complex among the Guaraní of Paraguay, who saw the missions as a safe refuge from other hostile tribes and Spanish colonists in the region, as well as a place to acquire useful European goods such as iron tools and livestock. By the early eighteenth century, more than 100,000 Guaraní lived in 30 separate mission units, called *reducciones.* These missions extended well beyond the present-day borders of Paraguay, into Brazil and Argentina.

Northwestern Mexico was another important focus of the Jesuits' program. They moved up the coasts of Sinaloa and Sonora and into Baja California in the seventeenth century. By the 1690s, Jesuits had reached the present-day Sonora–Arizona border, where the Austrian-born Eusebio Francisco Kino founded a number of missions among the Pima people. To the east of the Sierra Madre, Jesuit missions included such native groups as Tarahumaras, Tepehuanes, and Conchos.

Franciscan missionaries were also active on the frontiers of Spanish America, especially in areas that would one day became part of the United States.

Plate 1 A mural at the Maya site of Bonampak showing a battle scene.

Plate 2 Mummified remains of a Moche woman who died about 450 C.E., discovered by archaeologists in 2005. She was a woman of high status, but what is most remarkable about her tomb is that it contains not only needles and other artifacts usually associated with female gender roles, but also war clubs and spear throwers, suggesting that perhaps she was a warrior or a ruler. Note the tattoos on her arms.

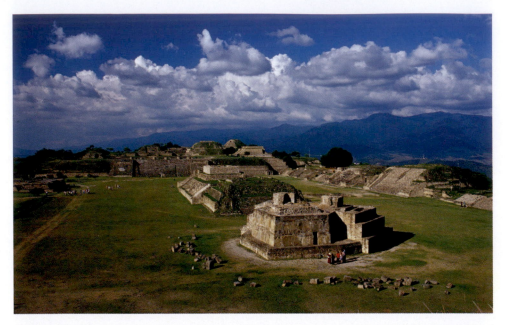

Plate 3 The temple complex at Monte Albán, Oaxaca, Mexico. Archaeologists believe that the building in the foreground served as an observatory.

Plate 4 A textile from the fifteenth century C.E. depicting jaguars, a recurrent motif in Andean artwork. This piece is from Chancay, north of present-day Lima. Chancay was conquered by the Incas at about the time the textile was made.

Plate 5 The mosque of Córdoba, reconsecrated as a Catholic church in the mid-thirteenth century. In the 1500s, Spanish Catholics tore down a portion of the mosque and built a cathedral in its center. The arches seen in the photo's foreground are from the original mosque; in the background is a painting of the Child Jesus and two Catholic saints.

Plate 6 During the late twentieth century archaeologists unearthed the remains of the chief Aztec temple in downtown Mexico City, just a block from the central plaza and the cathedral. Adjoining the archaeological site is the Templo Mayor museum, where visitors can see many artifacts found during the excavation.

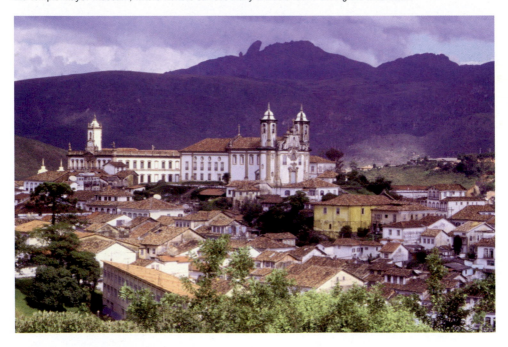

Plate 7 Ouro Prêto, Brazil, showing colonial buildings dating from the mining boom of the eighteenth century.

Plate 8 Relación Geográfica map of Oaxtepec, Morelos, an Indian community in central Mexico, 1580. Drawn by an indigenous artist, it formed part of a report commissioned by King Philip II of Spain. The symbol beneath the church tower at the center of the map stands for the name of the place: "Hill of the huaxin tree."

Plate 9 *Mulatto Gentlemen of Esmeraldas, Ecuador.* The central figure in this painting, dated 1599, is 56-year-old Don Francisco de Arobe, a mulatto who served as governor of a community of 35 mulattoes and 450 Indians on the coast of Ecuador. The artist was an Indian named Andrés Sánchez Gallque.

Plate 10 Drawing from a book written by Zacharias Wagener, a German who lived in Brazil from 1634 to 1641. He wrote, "The wives and children of notable and wealthy Portuguese are transported in this manner, by the two strong slaves, to the houses of their friends or to church; they hang the beautiful cloths of velvet or damask over poles so that sun does not burn them. They also take behind them a variety of beautiful and tasty fruits as a present for those that they wish to visit."

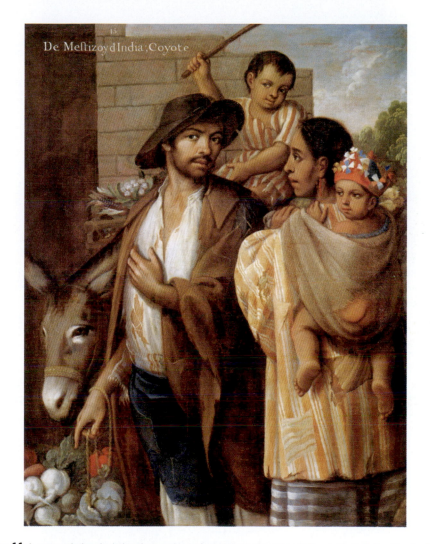

Plate 11 A casta painting depicting the marriage of a mestizo man and an Indian woman. As in virtually all the other paintings showing racial mixture in eighteenth-century Mexico, the man is of a higher racial status than the woman, even though this couple is obviously very poor.

Plate 12 Portrait of King Charles III by Spanish artist Francisco de Goya. Like many other monarchs and noblemen of his time, King Charles enjoyed hunting when not attending to affairs of state.

Ruins of a mission church established by Franciscans in 1626 at Quarai, southeast of present-day Albuquerque, New Mexico. The Quarai church and two others together comprise the Salinas Pueblo Missions National Monument. The church was abandoned in the 1670s and never reoccupied.

They arrived in Florida in 1573, and by the mid-seventeenth century, their missions extended along the Atlantic coast from St. Augustine north to just below the present site of Savannah, Georgia, and westward across what is now the Florida panhandle. The growth of British colonies in South Carolina and Georgia forced them to scale back their efforts in the eighteenth century, however.

The Franciscans also began work in New Mexico at the end of the sixteenth century. There the natives already lived in sedentary villages, and Spaniards accordingly called them the Pueblo Indians—the word "pueblo" in Spanish means village or town. Therefore, the people of New Mexico continued to live in the same settlements, even the same clustered apartment-like complexes of their ancestors. Indeed, the people of Acoma, New Mexico, today proudly assert that theirs is the longest continuously occupied community in the United States. Still, the transition to Franciscan tutelage spelled enormous change for the Pueblo peoples. As the only ecclesiastical personnel in New Mexico, the friars wielded substantial power, so much so that some historians have called their regimen a virtual theocracy. The Franciscans quarreled frequently with Spanish authorities in New Mexico, even excommunicating the governor on more than one occasion.

The Franciscans established colleges in Querétaro, Zacatecas, and Mexico City to train future missionaries for the northern frontier. In the early eighteenth century, they extended their work to Texas, founding a cluster of missions near present-day San Antonio, some of which are still in use as parish churches today. After 1769, Franciscans established a chain of missions extending up the California coast from San Diego to San Francisco. In South America, Franciscans established missions in Paraguay, the Chocó region of New Granada (modern-day Colombia), and in parts of Brazil.

Native Peoples in the Jesuit and Franciscan Missions

Resettlement in a mission exposed native peoples to the ravages of European diseases while often requiring the survivors to make drastic changes in their lifestyles. For many Indians, mission life meant a difficult transition from hunting and gathering or semi-sedentary, slash-and-burn agriculture to residence in a fixed location where their livelihood came from more intensive agriculture and from craft specialties learned from the missionaries. This change might in turn alter the natives' customary divisions of labor between males and females. Among the Tarahumara in northern Mexico, men abandoned hunting and warfare and assumed a greater share of agricultural labor under the Jesuit regimen, while women spent more time tending livestock introduced by the Spanish. Resistance was common, and natives were often "reduced" to mission life by force.

Life within the missions was much more structured than what the native peoples had known, even for the Guaraní of Paraguay, who already lived in well-ordered sedentary villages before the coming of the Jesuits. Here as elsewhere, the missionaries set up native governing bodies that at least superficially resembled the cabildos of the república de indios in Mesoamerica and the Andes. Social distinctions became more marked than they had been in pre-colonial times, as men appointed to these positions claimed exemption from routine labor and other privileges. Denied formal roles in this new hierarchy, native women found their access to community resources reduced as well.

Mission Indians and Colonial Society

In theory, the missions were cut off from contact with the outside world, but in fact the native peoples congregated within them were hardly isolated from the larger colonial society. The Jesuit reducciones of Paraguay offered particularly tempting targets for Brazilian slavers, known as bandeirantes, who operated out of São Paulo. To defend against such attacks, the Jesuits organized mission Indians into militia units. Elsewhere, however, missionaries tolerated or even facilitated the drafting of Indians for various labor obligations and relied on military forces to assist them in rounding up and disciplining their charges.

From Paraguay to Arizona, the missions formed one component of a complex network of Jesuit enterprises. Throughout Latin America, Jesuits accumulated substantial property in the form of haciendas, plantations, and obrajes, using the proceeds to support the missions and the *colegios* where young men trained for the priesthood and other professions. In Brazil and elsewhere, Jesuit estates owned numerous African slaves. As landed proprietors, the Jesuits became shrewd businessmen, and they applied their managerial acumen to their missions as well. Crops and craft items produced by mission Indians sold in regional markets from Sonora to southern South America. The Paraguayan missions became famous for the production of *yerba mate,* a native plant used to make tea. Franciscans showed a similar entrepreneurial bent, shipping mission-grown foodstuffs from Florida to Cuba, for example.

Mission Indians were also pawns of Spanish and Portuguese imperial ambitions. The possibility that the French and the English might somehow penetrate their northern frontier and make off with the treasure of Zacatecas was a constant preoccupation of the Spanish. To secure that frontier, the crown made repeated efforts to lure colonists from the mother country and from central Mexico. Few potential settlers responded, for the bustling cities, fertile agricultural fields, and mining centers to the south offered more attractive possibilities. Many undoubtedly agreed with the Franciscan missionary who called Texas "the land so bad that nobody would want it," and it was just as hard to lure settlers to California later on.

Spanish officials therefore saw no alternative but to make loyal Christian "colonists" out of the peoples already native to the northern frontier. The missionary enterprise thus served the king's political purposes, and for this reason the crown provided financial support for the Franciscans in New Mexico, Texas, and California. Local officials in these provinces enlisted pacified natives such as Pueblos and Opatas to join them in fighting Apaches and other recalcitrant tribes.

NATIVE PEOPLES AND THE COLONIAL ORDER

The native peoples of the Americas responded to Spanish and Portuguese colonization in many different ways. Some became so fluent in Spanish that they became known as *ladinos,* a word used in medieval Spain to describe nonnative speakers of Castilian. Quite a few Indians became so thoroughly acculturated that they "passed" as mestizos and no longer functioned as members of the república de indios. Others, like the caciques and kurakas of Mexico and Peru, found powerful incentives to retain their "Indian" identity while actively collaborating with colonial authorities and wealthy Spaniards. Still others actively participated in the expansion of European hegemony. The Tlaxcalans of central Mexico participated in Cortés's initial victory over the Aztecs, and their descendants helped colonize the northern frontier of New Spain in the sixteenth, seventeenth, and eighteenth centuries. At the opposite end of the spectrum were those who remained outside the effective control of the Spanish and Portuguese states.

In the sixteenth century, there were still men and women alive who could remember the days before the coming of the Europeans, and they certainly passed on these recollections to children and grandchildren too young to know anything but the new order of things. Some communities preserved these memories in oral and written traditions that have survived to the present. But in many places, the passing centuries blurred the divide between "pre-Columbian" and "post-conquest" in the historical memory of individuals and communities.

Indians in the República de Españoles

Spanish towns and cities quickly became magnets for Indians. Men wishing to abandon life in their home communities could easily find work in construction, transport, or craft specialties, while native women were in great demand as domestic servants and wet-nurses. Native elites sometimes established second residences in Spanish cities and sent their sons to be educated at the Jesuit schools in Mexico City, Cuzco, and Lima.

Mexico City and Cuzco were built on the sites of important pre-hispanic population centers, and they continued to be home to thousands of natives in the post-conquest period, but newly created cities such as Lima in Peru and Puebla in Mexico also had sizable native populations from the very beginning. In its early years, Lima's Indian population included many natives of New Spain and Central America, especially Nicaragua, brought as slaves by the conquistadors, but soon migrants from the Peruvian highlands joined them in the City of the Kings. The population of Bogotá included 10,000 Indians and only 3000 Hispanics at the end of the seventeenth century.

Colonial authorities tried to adhere to the principle of separating the república de españoles from the república de indios even in the cities. They officially reserved some quarters, most often at the center of town, for Spaniards, and required Indians to live in designated neighborhoods on the outskirts. Separate parish churches were set up to minister to Indians and non-Indians. In Mexico City, the cabildo marked off a 13-square-block area at the center of town and declared this the *traza,* the area for españoles. Four native barrios surrounded the traza and together comprised the community known as San Juan Tenochtitlan, and to the north lay another Indian settlement, Santiago Tlatelolco. Both of these communities had a native gobernador and other officers, just like those of villages in rural areas. Residents of these urban Indian *barrios* (neighborhoods) were subject to tribute and forced labor obligations.

In practice, segregated living patterns were impossible to enforce. As early as 1555, the Mexico City cabildo permitted Spaniards to acquire land within the Indian sector, and Indians had already begun residing in the traza. Most of those who were employed as domestic servants lived in the homes of their employers. By the end of the sixteenth century, Indians and non-Indians often lived side by side, both inside and outside the traza, and worshipped together at "Spanish" and "Indian" churches alike. In many other cities, local authorities failed to establish even the fiction of separate quarters for the two groups.

Mining towns also drew thousands of Indians, some as forced workers under the mita and repartimiento and others who became permanent wage laborers. Mitayos often brought their families with them when they went to work at Potosí, and many of them stayed on after completing their obligatory service. Native settlements known as *rancherías* surrounded the town. For example, 14 parish churches served the native rancherías at Potosí in the seventeenth century. Similar clusters of Indian residences could also be found on the outskirts of Zacatecas at the height of its mining boom. In the eighteenth century, residents of the northern Mexican mining town of Chihuahua used the generic term "indios mexicanos" to refer to Indians who had migrated there from central New Spain.

Urban Indians mingled not only with Spaniards but with mestizos, mulattos, and blacks as well. Many learned Spanish, not only to speak with non-Indians, but also to converse with Indians who spoke different languages. In the process, ethnic distinctions among various groups dissolved. These indios ladinos often found work as court interpreters and town criers. City dwellers adopted many other trappings of a Europeanized lifestyle and became adept at a wide variety of crafts. As early as 1569, one observer noted that the Indians of Mexico City had mastered virtually every trade imaginable. They made swords, saddles, and European-style clothing and hats for the city's growing Spanish population. Spanish artisans came to view them as competitors and did whatever they could to exclude Indians from membership in their guilds. Indians countered by setting up their own guild-like organizations.

Despite their considerable acculturation, most natives living in cities maintained a certain identity as Indians, especially through the cofradías that were as important to them as to their counterparts in rural areas. Here as in the peasant villages of the república de indios, native cofradías excluded Spaniards and other non-Indians. In 1585, Lima had seven Indian cofradías, along with six for Spaniards and ten for blacks and mulattos.

Local custom often assigned native individuals and their cofradías prominent roles in the public ceremonial life of Spanish cities and towns. Representatives of 82 Indian cofradías from Mexico City and nearby pueblos marched in a procession marking the funeral of King Philip IV in 1665. In 1723, the city of Lima staged an elaborate celebration of the marriage of a member of Spain's royal family. Twelve Indian men, most of whom could claim cacique lineage, marched in the city-wide parade dressed as Inca kings. In Cuzco, representatives of the Inca nobility marched in the processions held on the feast of Corpus Christi and other Catholic religious holidays.

The authorities maintained an ambivalent attitude toward urban Indians. On the one hand, the presence of large numbers of native workers was essential to the quality of urban life. On the other hand, Indians were seen as a threat to social stability in the cities. In 1692, Indians and other lower classes of Mexico City openly rebelled, protesting food shortages and setting fire to the viceregal palace. In the wake of the uprising, city authorities banned the sale of pulque and took other strongly repressive measures against Indian residents, whom they characterized as "lazy, vagabond, useless, insolent, and villainous people."

"Indios Bárbaros"

Despite the sustained efforts of church and crown to bring all the colonies' natives under Spanish and Portuguese tutelage, many groups remained more or less permanently outside their control, living *sin rey, sin fe, sin ley*–without king, without faith, without law. Even the determined Franciscan and Jesuit missionaries failed to subdue these people. Because they rejected Christianization and subjugation to Spanish rule, Apaches, Araucanians, and others remained *indios bárbaros* (literally, barbarian Indians) in the eyes of settlers and authorities alike.

The Apaches of the northern frontier of Mexico were one group who successfully resisted Spanish encroachments. From the seventeenth century forward, they preyed upon Hispanic settlements in New Mexico and Pueblo villages, carrying off foodstuffs, horses, guns, and tools. In the eighteenth century, as British and French colonies in North America pushed other groups westward into Apache territory, raids extended farther south and west, to Chihuahua and beyond. The many *presidios* (military posts) that appeared along the frontier did little to stop Apache depredations.

In southern Chile, the Araucanians posed a similar threat to European settlement throughout the colonial period. Alonso de Ercilla y Zúñiga, a sixteenth-century Spanish military officer who fought against the Araucanians, immortalized their bravery and tenacity in a poetic epic of more than 2000 verses, *La araucana.*

The ability of these peoples to resist was surely abetted by the fact that they lived in regions that were relatively marginal in the eyes of colonists, lacking precious metals and not well suited to the production of valuable export crops. At the same time, however, they also showed considerable ingenuity in using the tools of the Europeans to preserve their autonomy. Frontier groups acquired Spanish horses early on, and they soon became expert horsemen. By 1600, the Araucanians reportedly had more horses than the Spanish settlers in Chile did. The Araucanians also changed their military tactics, not only learning to fight on horseback, but also attaching the tips of Spanish swords to their lances. They even made their own gunpowder to use in weapons they captured from the enemy.

These so-called barbarians skillfully adapted their culture to meet the needs of their changing situation. Only with the development of new technology–barbed wire, repeating rifles, railroads, and telegraphs–in the late nineteenth century did the national governments of Chile, Argentina, Mexico, and the United States succeed in finally subduing the natives of their respective frontiers.

Their ability to fend off Spanish rule did not mean that the Apaches and Araucanians were exempted from the hardships and abuses of colonialism. Like other indigenous peoples, they fell victim to the diseases brought to the Americas by Europeans and Africans. Laws forbidding the establishment of new encomiendas or the outright enslavement of native peoples carried no weight on the frontier. Leading citizens of New Mexico, often including the governor himself, reaped substantial profits from the sale of captured Apaches, especially women and children. A similar trade characterized frontier life in Chile. Persistent resistance thus brought no reprieve from the devastating impact of the European invasion of America.

Regional Revolts

In addition to the challenges posed by unsubdued "barbarians," Spanish and Portuguese authorities also had to reckon with acts of open defiance on the part of natives who had supposedly accepted colonial rule. We noted previously that Indians in Mesoamerica and the Andes sometimes employed violence to gain relief from specific taxes, land alienation, or abusive priests and government officials, but seldom did these rebellions spread to surrounding villages. From time to time, however, native revolts assumed a regional character and questioned the fundamental basis of civil and ecclesiastical authority, and these actions provoked more drastic responses from colonial officials. Some were millenarian movements with the stated goal of overturning the existing social order, reminiscent of such early colonial revolts as Taqui Onkoy in Peru, which we discussed in Chapter 3. These late colonial rebels made much more extensive use of Christian religious symbols than their sixteenth-century counterparts.

One such upheaval briefly swept Chiapas in southern Mexico in 1712. People from the Tzeltal and Tzotzil Mayan villages rallied around María López, a 13-year-old native girl who claimed to have seen a vision of the Virgin Mary. Her father Agustín, who served as sacristan in the local parish church in his home village of Cancuc, joined other men in building a chapel on the spot where the Virgin had reportedly appeared.

There María took up residence and preached to growing numbers of Mayan pilgrims from other villages. Worsening economic conditions, recent attempts by the Spanish authorities to curb what they viewed as excessive drinking and feasting associated with cofradía celebrations, and the continued abuses of colonialism, many of which fell disproportionately on Mayan women, all enhanced the appeal of a cult led by natives without the intervention of Catholic priests.

Alarmed, officials of church and state pronounced the movement to be the work of the devil, jailed some of Cancuc's native officials, and mustered militia forces to put an end to this challenge to Spanish authority. Agustín López and other Mayan men vowed to defend their shrine with armed resistance of their own, while María reportedly ordered her followers to seize all silver and other

ornaments from their churches and bring them to her, "because now there is neither God nor King." In the end, however, Spanish military force prevailed,
crushing the rebellion some four months after it began.

Sometimes these regional rebellions succeeded in casting off colonial rule altogether, at least temporarily. In 1680, the Pueblo peoples set aside the language barriers and long-standing feuds that had traditionally divided them and mounted a
concerted revolt against the Hispanic presence in New Mexico. A long period of
drought and the colonial authorities' growing intolerance of the natives' continuing
use of pre-hispanic religious symbols were among the immediate causes.

The Pueblo uprising began on August 10, 1680. The rebels burned churches,
destroyed Catholic religious images, and slaughtered some 400 Hispanic residents of Santa Fe and other communities, including several Franciscan priests.
Hundreds of refugees fled southward to El Paso del Norte—today's Cuidad
Juárez, Mexico, on the border with the United States. The nominal leader of the
rebellion, a man called Popé, called for the destruction of all things Spanish, even
to the point of uprooting European fruit trees that had flourished in New Mexico. He enjoined his followers to wash off their Christian baptism, destroy their
rosaries and religious images, and remarry in traditional Pueblo rites. As word
of the Pueblos' rebellion spread throughout the northern frontier, other native
groups followed their example.

The Pueblos won their freedom from Spanish rule for more than 12 years.
In 1692, however, colonial authorities began a counteroffensive that restored
their control of New Mexico. Numerous factors contributed to the rebels' defeat.
For one thing, once they had driven out the Franciscans and secular Hispanic
officials, the unity they had achieved in 1680 began to crumble. Not everyone
was willing to give up all material objects and rituals associated with Spanish
domination. Meanwhile, Apaches stepped up their attacks on the sedentary
Pueblos, prompting them to renew their alliance with the Spanish for their own
protection.

Their rebellion won the Pueblos some important concessions, however.
They secured an end to the encomienda, and eighteenth-century authorities
often looked the other way as descendants of the 1680 rebels kept a number of
indigenous religious rituals alive. Although Pueblo warriors now accompanied
Hispanic soldiers in campaigns against the Apaches and other hostile tribes, they
wore their traditional battle gear and war paint as they went.

Native Historical Memory and the Colonial Order

The natives of Latin America have sometimes been called "people without history," in the sense that traumas of the conquest and the deliberate actions of
European missionaries and political authorities destroyed indigenous manuscripts and blurred the historical memories contained in oral traditions passed

from one generation to another. Although these difficulties should not be underestimated, the indigenous peoples in the Spanish and Portuguese colonies in fact preserved at least some memory of their own history.

A cadre of Indian and mestizo intellectuals in Mesoamerica and the Andes produced lengthy treatises documenting their people's history in pre-hispanic and colonial times. One such individual, Domingo de San Antón Muñón Chimalpahin, was born in 1579 in Chalco on the outskirts of Mexico City. Educated in the capital, in 1620 he completed a lengthy Nahuatl history of his ancestral community. The mestizo Fernando de Alva Ixtlilxochitl, a descendant of Texcoco's ruling family and its gobernador in the early seventeenth century, also wrote a chronicle of his hometown. In Peru, the native historian Felipe Guaman Poma de Ayala composed a monumental history that chronicled the transition from Inca to Spanish rule. His mestizo contemporary Garcilaso de la Vega, son of a Spanish conquistador and an Inca noblewoman, penned another commentary on the history of Peru.

Not many native commoners read these histories, of course, and in some cases the manuscripts were deposited in libraries and archives only to be discovered centuries later by historians. But this did not mean that "ordinary" Indians possessed no notion of their own past. Although only a handful of their pre-hispanic books survived, the Maya of colonial Yucatán recorded their history in what became known as the Books of Chilam Balam. In each community, elders familiar with ancient oral traditions recited what they could remember, and young men trained in European script wrote down what they heard. From generation to generation, village elders guarded them from Spanish authorities. When native peoples went to court to defend their land and water, they presented elaborate files documenting their historical claim to these resources. Rituals in honor of their ancestors also kept ancient memories alive, and Andean peoples reenacted vestiges of Inca hegemony on many ceremonial occasions.

The histories preserved, retold, and reenacted by native peoples did not always coincide with what we might regard as objective historical fact. The land titles they presented in court were often blatant forgeries or fanciful parodies of Spanish legal documents. Native elites sometime recast community histories to suggest that they had always been Christians. In the seventeenth century, the Otomí caciques of Querétaro in Mexico composed an account that emphasized the contributions of their forebears in the city's founding a century before. Their account never mentioned the coming of the Spanish, and the Otomí are identified as the Catholic conquerors who wrested control of the Querétaro region from the savage, pagan Chichimecas. The caciques did what most other societies have done, blending fact and wishful thinking to create a "usable past" that enabled them to explain their world and cope with the challenges they faced.

LATIN AMERICAN LIVES

FELIPE GUAMAN POMA DE AYALA

BORN IN THE PROVINCE OF Ayacucho just a few years after Pizarro's arrival in Peru, Felipe Guaman Poma de Ayala often stated that his father was an Andean nobleman and his mother the daughter of the Inca emperor Tupac Yupanqui. No historical documentation supports his claims to such a lofty pedigree, but whatever his antecedents, Guaman Poma became a prime example of the indio ladino, or acculturated Indian in Spanish Peru. At the same time, he fashioned a worldview that accommodated both Christian and indigenous Andean teachings.

A native speaker of Quechua, Guaman Poma received a good education, probably under the tutelage of missionaries. He became reasonably fluent in Spanish, learned to write the European alphabet, and read widely in fields such as Spanish theology, history, and law. This training made him an ideal candidate to serve as an interpreter for Spanish officials. On one of his most important assignments, he accompanied the priest Cristóbal de Albornoz, commissioned to investigate idolatry in the Andes in the wake of the Taki Onkoy rebellion. There is also substantial evidence that he interpreted at important meetings of the Peruvian Church held in Lima.

Guaman Poma was not simply a servant of the Spaniards, however. He used his language skills to present lawsuits on behalf of native peoples attempting to defend their lands. On various occasions, he presented native complaints directly to the viceroy in Lima. Some of his grievances against colonial authorities were driven by his own self-interest, however, and pitted him against other indigenous people. He waged a long and ultimately unsuccessful battle against the Chachapoyas, natives from northern Peru whom the viceroy had resettled on lands claimed by Guaman Poma's extended family. His stubborn refusal to accept the viceroy's orders not only discredited his case but earned him a penalty of a public whipping and a 2-year banishment from his home town of Huamanga.

Toward the end of his life, Guaman Poma penned a lengthy history of Peru under Inca and Spanish domination entitled *Primera nueva crónica y buen gobierno*, addressed to King Philip III and completed about 1615. Here he voiced a clear nostalgia for an idealized pre-hispanic past and denounced the many abuses of the new regime. Though he admired Viceroy Francisco de Toledo, he deplored the forced resettlements that had removed entire communities from "sites selected by the most important native wise men, doctors, and philosophers and approved by the first Incas for their climate, lands, and water." He had little good to say about corregidores and encomenderos and their black slaves who interacted with Indians on a daily basis. With the coming of colonialism, he wrote, the Andean world had turned upside down.

The book also reveals much about Guaman Poma's religious attitudes. Though he embraced Catholicism, he criticized the clergy for their pursuit of worldly gain and their notorious sexual misconduct, especially their forced liaisons with native women. While praising his employer Cristóbal de Albornoz, he condemned other officials of church and state who used excessive force in their efforts to extirpate idolatry. He singled out for special criticism a native fiscal who destroyed traditional religious objects under Albornoz's command. Particularly appalling to Guaman Poma was the fact that this fiscal was later made a cacique.

Moreover, Guaman Poma did not reject Andean notions of spirituality. He dismissed the leaders of Taqui Onkoy as false shamans who had subverted traditional healing rituals, which he viewed as valid and beneficial. He recommended that dances customarily performed for the old gods be continued, but now in honor of "the true God and all that the holy Roman church demands." Indeed, he believed his people had been part of the Christian story of redemption all along. One of the three magi who visited the Christ child at Bethlehem, he claimed, was an Andean.

Nearly 1200 pages in length and featuring 398 pen-and-ink drawings, Guaman Poma's manuscript was lost for three centuries until scholars discovered it in the Royal Danish Library in Copenhagen. Historians and anthropologists have used his chronicle as a rich primary source about the indigenous people of sixteenth-century Peru.

Questions for Discussion

Felipe Guaman Poma de Ayala's book, including all 398 of his illustrations, can be viewed on the Internet, with commentary in English and in Spanish, at www.kb.dk/elib/mss/poma. What do these images tell us about the times in which he lived?

CONCLUSION

Over the course of three centuries, indigenous peoples responded to their colonization by Spain and Portugal in a variety of ways that ranged from open defiance to self-serving accommodations detrimental to their long-range personal and collective interests. Whatever tactics they chose, they succeeded at least in capturing the attention of colonial authorities, both civil and ecclesiastical. The Spanish and Portuguese governments had to spend substantial revenues on subsidies for missionaries whose job it was to teach the natives to obey proper authorities, on courts to handle native complaints, and on military forces to repress overt challenges to colonial rule. Likewise, the Church expended time and money on periodic prosecutions of natives accused of idolatry. Nor could the owners of the mines, haciendas, plantations, and obrajes ignore the native peoples in their vicinity. Heavily dependent on Indian labor, owners of these enterprises spent considerable time and effort finding the right mix of compulsion and compensation that would turn reluctant natives into dependable workers.

Without question, the natives of the Americas suffered mightily under Spanish and Portuguese colonial rule, but they also played a crucial role in shaping the history of Latin America. As one leading historian has put it, they also "conditioned the evolution of colonial society and limited the options of the European ruling class." Meanwhile, they borrowed selectively from the cultural baggage that the Iberians brought with them. Over the course of three centuries, they formed a new cultural synthesis, one that made sense of their changing world and that enabled them to survive and to preserve their families and their communities. For most Indians, life as colonial subjects was a complex mix of accommodation and resistance to European norms and institutions. They came to accept certain demands made upon them by the Church, the state, and individual entrepreneurs, but they might revolt when those demands exceeded customary expectations. The natives of the Americas were not passive victims of European colonization.

LEARNING MORE ABOUT LATIN AMERICANS

Andrien, Kenneth J. *Andean Worlds: Indigenous History, Culture, and Consciousness Under Spanish Rule, 1532–1825* (Albuquerque, NM: University of New Mexico Press, 2001). A well-written overview showing how the natives of Peru adapted to life under Spanish colonial rule.

Ganson, Barbara. *The Guaraní Under Spanish Rule in the Río de la Plata* (Stanford, CA: Stanford University Press, 2003). An excellent history showing how the Guaraní adapted to life in the Jesuit missions of Paraguay, Argentina, and Brazil.

Haskett, Robert. *Indigenous Rulers: An Ethnohistory of Town Government in Colonial Cuernavaca* (Albuquerque, NM: University of New Mexico Press, 1991). Drawn largely from Nahuatl sources, this book shows how native peoples managed their local communities in colonial Mexico.

Knaut, Andrew. *The Pueblo Revolt of 1680: Conquest and Resistance in Seventeenth-Century New Mexico* (Norman, OK: University of Oklahoma Press, 1995). Examines the causes and consequences of the Pueblo rebellion.

Schroeder, Susan, ed. *Native Resistance and the Pax Colonial in New Spain* (Lincoln, NE: University of Nebraska Press, 1998). Six leading historians discuss resistance to colonial rule in Yucatán, Chiapas, Oaxaca, and northern Mexico.

Stern, Steve. *Peru's Indian Peoples and the Challenge of Spanish Conquest: Huamanga to 1640*, 2nd ed. (Madison, WI: University of Wisconsin Press, 1992). Describes the internal changes that occurred in indigenous society during the first century following the Spanish conquest.

6

A NEW PEOPLE
AND THEIR WORLD

LATIN AMERICAN SOCIETY began with a handful of European sailors landing on
the shores of tropical America from the Bahamas to Brazil. To them, the natives
they encountered were simply *indios*. Within a short time—usually not much more
than nine months—the ethnic mix became more complicated as the first mestizos
and mamelucos were born to native mothers and European fathers. Most early
European voyages also included a few African-born slaves, and Spanish and Portuguese colonists soon began importing large numbers of slaves to work their fields
and perform household chores. New Christians (recent converts from Judaism) and
a scattering of non-Iberian Europeans also made their way to the colonies despite
official pronouncements aimed at excluding them. Along the west coasts of Mexico and South America, one could also find Asians who had crossed the Pacific on
the Manila galleons. Meanwhile, more and more people of mixed African, Indian,
and European ancestry appeared. Many terms were coined to describe them. In
Spanish America they were often simply called *pardos,* meaning dark-skinned people, or *castas,* or people of *color quebrado* ("broken color"). Other labels included *lobos*
(literally, wolves) and *coyotes* in the Spanish colonies and *cabras* (goats) in Brazil.

Colonial Latin America was, then, a racially diverse society, but not everyone enjoyed equal access to power and privilege. Spanish and Portuguese immigrants and their American-born descendants claimed the premier positions for
themselves and attempted to keep "inferior" people in their places. Ethnicity was
not the only determinant of a person's standing in colonial society, however.
Wealth was important too, and while the richest people were usually white, ambitious mestizos and mulattos could sometimes advance their positions if they were

177

successful in mining or trade. Another criterion was honor, measured by the degree to which individuals conformed, or at least appeared to conform, with written and unwritten standards governing personal behavior. These rules were highly gender-specific and relegated women, regardless of their wealth or ethnicity, to subordinate positions in colonial society.

Colonial Latin Americans lived in a hierarchical society where they were expected to defer to their social betters, command respect from those who ranked beneath them, and above all to adhere to the norms of conduct appropriate to their class, gender, and ethnicity. Yet many people found ingenious ways to flout the rules or bend them to their own advantage. In the process, they created a vibrant and ever-changing society and culture.

THE MAKING OF MULTIETHNIC SOCIETIES

The first Europeans arrived in the Americas with a very clear sense of "us" and "them." They believed that the natives of this new world were so different from themselves that some of them doubted whether these strange people even had souls. From the very beginning, authorities of church and state began dictating how Europeans and "Indians" should relate to one another. Some of these rules were intended to protect the natives from exploitation, and others stipulated taxes and labor obligations that they owed to their new masters, but all of them upheld the sharp distinction between indigenous Americans and European newcomers. Law and custom also set African slaves apart from people who were free.

Officially, then, the Iberian colonies in the Western Hemisphere began with the assumption that there were three sharply distinguished categories of people: Europeans, Indians, and African slaves. Social reality was far more complex. European immigrants did not always identify with those who came from a different region of Spain or Portugal, and they usually viewed themselves as socially superior to people of European stock born in the Americas. Not everyone of African descent was a slave. The appearance of so many people of mixed ancestry further complicated the picture.

Spanish and Portuguese Immigrants

The influx of Spaniards and Portuguese continued throughout the colonial period and was especially strong whenever and wherever new mining bonanzas or other get-rich-quick opportunities appeared. These immigrants are often called *peninsulares* because they came from the Iberian Peninsula, but to their contemporaries they were *españoles europeos* (European Spaniards) or *españoles de los Reinos de Castilla* (Spaniards from the kingdom of Castile) in Spanish America, *europeus* (Europeans) or *reinóis* (from the kingdoms) in Brazil. A majority of these immigrants were male, especially during the early years. Between 1509 and 1519, for example, only about 10 percent of the European immigrants to the

Spanish colonies were female. By 1600 that proportion had grown to more than 30 percent, but in the eighteenth century, a time of heavy immigration, women constituted only about 15 percent of those arriving in the Spanish colonies.

The ratio of women to men among Portuguese immigrants to Brazil was always significantly lower—so low, in fact, that in 1549 a leading Jesuit even suggested that the numbers of white women in the colony could be increased if prostitutes were allowed to emigrate from Portugal. Not until the late seventeenth century did Portuguese authorities permit the founding of a convent in Brazil, preferring that white women choose marriage and procreation rather than a life of celibacy.

Many of the Spanish and Portuguese immigrants were young bachelors eager to make their fortunes in the Indies, while others were married men whose wives remained in Europe, at least until their husbands established themselves in their new homes. While immigrant men often had casual sex and longer-term relationships with Indian, African, and mixed-race women, when it came to marriage they usually preferred women of European descent, often the daughters or nieces of previous newcomers. Spanish and Portuguese immigrants formed tightly knit communities, often settling near relatives or people from their own hometowns and choosing fellow Europeans to be the baptismal sponsors of their children.

Europeans never constituted more than a tiny minority in any given place—typically less than 2 percent of the population in major cities and even less in smaller towns and rural areas. Their economic, social, and political influence far outweighed their numbers, however. High-ranking positions in the church, the government, and the military typically belonged to peninsulares, and town councils were often top-heavy with Europeans. The most powerful merchant companies were headed by peninsulares, many of them New Christians in the sixteenth and seventeenth centuries. Europeans also figured heavily in the landowning class. More than 60 percent of Bahia's sugar planters in the period from 1680 to 1725 were either Portuguese immigrants or the sons of immigrants.

Those born in Spain and Portugal based their claims to power and prestige on their presumed purity of blood, which in the colonies came to mean European ancestry untainted by African or Indian mixture. European immigrants could be found in many social ranks, however. Many were master artisans, government clerks, and itinerant merchants, but some were vagabonds and criminals. Whatever their place in society, they often displayed arrogance toward those born in

America. For their part, Americans of all racial groups mocked the immigrants for their speech and their unfamiliarity with the culture and terrain of the colonies. Mexicans called them *gachupines,* while Peruvians used the word *chapetones.*

Creoles

Far more numerous than the peninsular immigrants were those born in the colonies who claimed pure Spanish or Portuguese ancestry on both the paternal and maternal sides. Historians usually label these people "creoles," though in practice Spanish Americans usually just called themselves *españoles* (Spaniards). In Brazil, Americans of Portuguese descent were known as *americanos* or *brasileiros.* Some Americans of European stock became quite wealthy, as prosperous merchants and owners of mines, haciendas, and plantations. A select few attained high offices, serving as judges of the superior courts and occasionally even as viceroys. In Brazil, despite official regulations that supposedly denied such positions to those born in the colonies, between 1652 and 1752 ten Brazilians sat on the high court (*relação*) of Bahia. Other prominent creole families formed business partnerships or marriage alliances with high-ranking peninsular officials, even though both the Spanish and Portuguese crowns explicitly forbade such practices. Twenty-five judges of the high court in Bahia married the daughters of sugar planters and other well-placed members of local society.

Large numbers of creoles occupied less prestigious positions in the civil and ecclesiastical bureaucracies, while many others could be found in the ranks of artisans, petty merchants, and small landowners. Peninsular immigrants often scoffed at their pretensions to "pure" European descent. In fact, many people successfully hid their Indian and African ancestors and "passed" as whites. Those creoles who had little else going for them in the way of wealth or connections often proved the most touchy in defending their "whiteness," their sole claim to preferential status in society.

Mestizos and Mamelucos

The first Spanish American mestizos and Brazilian mamelucos were the offspring of European men and native women. Virtually all of them bore the stigma of illegitimacy, and colonial authorities viewed their growing numbers with alarm. Young males in particular were seen as troublemakers. As time passed, however, more and more mestizos and mamelucos were simply the children of racially mixed people. If their parents were married in the church, they could claim legitimacy, an important marker of social standing.

By the seventeenth and eighteenth centuries, large numbers of mestizos lived in the cities and towns of Spanish America, and even in many "Indian" villages. They worked at many different kinds of jobs. In cities, many were skilled craftsmen, even though artisan guilds often tried to exclude them. Urban mestizos also worked as domestic servants, shopkeepers, and street vendors, while in rural areas they were small farmers, overseers of haciendas and plantations, cowboys, muleteers, and itinerant peddlers (see Plate 11). Spanish law, with its neat division of colonial society into separate "republics" of Spaniards and Indians, had no official place for mestizos, so by default they became part of the Spanish community. As such they were considered *gente de razón,* or "people of reason," and they were exempt from tribute and other obligations required of Indians. Mestizo men of legitimate birth could become priests, especially if they were fluent in an indigenous language. Higher positions in the church were closed to them, however, and they were most often assigned to poor parishes in the most remote rural locations.

The situation of mamelucos in Brazil differed somewhat from that of their counterparts in Spanish America. Most of colonial Brazil's principal cities were located along the coast, where the drastic decline of the native population left comparatively few Indian women available to mate with Portuguese men and give birth to the first generation of mamelucos. In frontier areas farther inland, however, people of mixed European and indigenous ancestry were more numerous. They served as cultural intermediaries between the Portuguese and the natives and played a crucial role in the founding of the city of São Paulo.

African Slaves

Wherever sufficient numbers of dependable native workers could not be found, proprietors of plantations, mines, and haciendas relied on the slave labor of Africans or of their American-born, often racially mixed descendants. Slavery was especially common in Brazil, the Caribbean, and the coastal areas of Central and South America. With the important exceptions of Cuba, Santo Domingo, Puerto Rico, and Venezuela, the importation of Africans into the Spanish colonies began to slow after 1650, as the developing British colonies in the Caribbean and eastern North America outbid Latin American buyers. In Mexico, the native population began to rebound ever so slightly in the mid-seventeenth century. They and the growing numbers of racially mixed people supplied more and more of the colony's labor needs, so that by the eighteenth century slavery had virtually disappeared in many parts of Mexico. In Brazil and Cuba, on the other hand, the importation of slaves and the institution of slavery remained viable until well into the nineteenth century (see Plate 10).

Slaves occupied key positions in the colonial economies. Recent arrivals from Africa performed heavy unskilled labor, while American-born slaves often acquired valuable specialized skills. On plantations, for example, slave men often held the coveted post of sugar master, entrusted with overseeing the entire process of sugar manufacture. Slaves also worked in many of Mexico's textile factories. Master artisans such as shoemakers, blacksmiths, and tailors acquired slaves and employed them in their own shops. In urban areas, masters often found it profitable to hire out skilled slaves and pocket their earnings. These slaves might enjoy considerable control over their own time and living conditions. In sixteenth-century Havana, one observer noted that slaves "go about as if they were free, working at whatever they choose, and at the end of the week or the month they give the masters the *jornal* [wages] … some have houses in which they shelter and feed travelers, and have in those houses, slaves of their own."

Slaves in Brazil and Spanish America were usually baptized as Catholics, sometimes at their point of departure in Africa and sometimes on arrival in the colonies, but received very little formal religious instruction. In Brazil and other areas with high concentrations of slaves and a continued influx of new Africans, slaves managed to retain many elements of African culture, including religious practices and beliefs, diet, music, dance, and traditional medicine. African women played especially important roles in the transmission of their native culture to future generations of slaves and free blacks in the New World.

Slaves were permitted to marry in the church, although Brazilian sugar planters often discouraged their slaves from receiving the sacrament of matrimony, especially if it involved a partner who belonged to another master. Marriage between slaves and free persons was also permitted, with children of these unions taking the status of their mother, slave or free. Family ties could be ruptured, of course, when slaves were sold.

As Catholics, slaves were subject to prosecution by the Inquisition, and indeed the inquisitors often looked askance on their continued practice of African folkways and their incomplete grasp of orthodox Catholic teachings. Because there was no Inquisition tribunal in Brazil, slaves were sometimes taken to Portugal for trial and punishment by the Inquisition and then returned to the colony. Such was the fate of José, a mulatto slave who worked in a sugar mill in northeastern Brazil. In 1595 he was convicted of denouncing God and cursing the church when his master refused to give him enough to eat. His sentence included a public whipping in the streets of Lisbon. After he returned to Brazil, his blasphemous protests continued, so vehemently that local officials ordered him to serve 4 years on the king's galleys.

Slave Resistance

Slaves found various ways to resist or protest their condition. Many employed what scholars have called the "weapons of the weak," subtle acts of defiance that included feigning illness and sabotaging work routines. Slaves could appeal to government authorities if they were mistreated, and they might persuade a judge to order them sold to a more lenient master. In extreme cases, women resorted to abortion and infanticide to save their children from a life of slavery. Slaves also used African spiritual practices, actions the Europeans called "witchcraft," to assert some degree of power over their masters and other whites. Some Brazilian slaves became so well known for their powers of divination and casting spells that they were able to sell their services to other slaves and even to whites.

Collective slave rebellions also occurred from time to time. In the region around Córdoba in eastern Mexico, some 2000 slaves from several different sugar and tobacco plantations rose in revolt in June of 1735. The rebels killed plantation overseers, destroyed crops, and carried off equipment used in processing sugar. Property losses totaled an estimated 400,000 pesos. Only after 5 months of fighting did militia units succeed in quelling the rebellion, but 6 years later another slave upheaval again brought the local economy to a standstill.

Still other slaves found freedom through escape, often to frontier areas where they might easily gain paid employment with no questions asked. In some cases, especially during the early years of European colonization, runaways joined Indian communities and helped the natives resist conquest. As early as 1503, Governor Nicolás de Ovando reported that some of Hispaniola's slaves had escaped and were living with native rebels.

Maroon Communities

Sometimes runaways (known as *cimarrones* in Spanish, maroons in English) formed their own settlements in remote jungle or mountain locations. Known as *palenques* in Spanish America, runaway communities could be found in eastern and western Mexico, the Isthmus of Panamá, and especially in Venezuela, where the runaway population reportedly reached 20,000 in the early eighteenth century. The region around Cartagena in present-day Colombia was another favored location for the formation of maroon settlements. In eastern Cuba, palenques proliferated in the mountain range known as the Sierra Maestra, where Fidel Castro's rebels would launch their resistance movement in the 1950s. Spanish authorities in Cuba attacked one such settlement, known as El Portillo, in 1747, taking 13 prisoners. Records of their arrest provide a rare glimpse into the type of people to be found living in runaway settlements. The group included six men, five women, and two small children who had been born at El Portillo. All but one of the adults was African-born, and all had been smuggled illegally into Cuba.

Maroon communities supported themselves through subsistence agriculture, by bartering their produce for other needed items at local markets, and by raiding nearby haciendas and towns. In coastal areas, they traded with pirates of many nationalities who ventured into Iberian American waters and sometimes joined them in sacking towns and plundering treasure ships. They augmented their population by inviting Indians and other marginalized people to join in their communities. In some parts of Mexico, male residents of palenques seized Indian women from neighboring villages.

Hundreds of runaway settlements known as *quilombos* formed in the vast interior of colonial Brazil. The Dutch occupation of northeastern Brazil in the mid-seventeenth century prompted many masters to desert their plantations, creating especially favorable opportunities for slaves to flee the sugar zone and form their own communities. Perhaps the most famous of all Brazilian quilombos was Palmares, whose population may have numbered 30,000 or more at its height around 1670. Despite repeated attacks from both Dutch and Portuguese forces, Palmares endured for most of the seventeenth century until it was finally routed in 1694. Zumbi, one of its last leaders, is today honored as a hero by Afro-Brazilians, who observe the anniversary of his execution each November 20 as a National Day of Black Consciousness.

Even though Palmares was destroyed, the remnants of numerous maroon communities survive to this day in many parts of Latin America. Brazil has as many as 1,000 former quilombos, whose residents have struggled in recent years to gain title to their lands. The town of Cuajiniquilapa in the Mexican state of Guerrero had its origin in a colonial palenque. Today, the descendants of the original settlers maintain a small museum dedicated to the town's history.

Free Blacks and Mulattos

Some slaves found their way to freedom through a legal process known as manumission. Owners might free an especially favored slave, perhaps a female domestic servant, in their wills. Slave children fathered by masters frequently won manumission as well, especially if their fathers lacked legitimate heirs. Some slaves were able to accumulate funds to purchase their own freedom. In the mining regions of Brazil, slaves were often required to deliver a stipulated quantity of gold to their masters each day but could keep anything over and above that amount. Female slaves who worked as street vendors could also pocket a portion of their receipts. and free blacks might buy the liberty of their kin. In contrast to the southern United States in the nineteenth century, Latin American society assumed a relatively permissive attitude toward manumission.

Manumission, flight, and intermarriage between slaves and free persons all contributed to the growing numbers of free blacks in the colonies. Many of these people were racially mixed, with Native American and/or white ancestry. They were usually called mulattos, though a host of other terms existed. Colonial authorities everywhere viewed mulattos as a socially disruptive group, even more so than mestizos. A governor in Minas Gerais summed up this attitude: "Mulattos being unstable and rebellious are pernicious in all Brazil; in Minas they are far worse because they are rich, and experience shows us that wealth in these people leads them to commit grave errors, chief among them being disobedience to the laws."

Free blacks and mulattos experienced multiple forms of discrimination. Often, they were mistaken for slaves, and they had to go to great lengths to assert

Image of Santo Antônio de Catagerona, venerated by members of a black brotherhood in northeastern Brazil. This saint was born in Africa and taken to Sicily as a slave. He won his freedom and later became a Franciscan.

their status as free men and women. In the Spanish colonies, they were required to pay tribute, just as Indians were. Although artisan guilds tried to exclude them, free black craftsmen played prominent roles in the colonial economy, and some managed to accumulate considerable wealth (see Plate 9).

Free persons of African descent were vital to the defense of the Iberian colonies. Skilled black stonemasons helped construct the heavy fortifications that guarded Cartagena, Havana, St. Augustine, and other port cities. Some free blacks served in racially integrated militia units, but many more filled the ranks of black and mulatto militia companies. They fought alongside Spanish and Portuguese units in defending coastal regions against enemy attack and helped maintain order in major cities. In Mexico, black militia forces helped repel pirates from Veracruz in 1683. Military service gave free blacks important advantages, including pensions, certain legal rights, exemption from tribute in Spanish America, and a stake in colonial society.

Free people of color built a sense of group solidarity in their militia companies and in the many religious brotherhoods they established in cities and towns throughout Brazil and Spanish America. The brotherhoods often included slaves as well as free blacks and mulattos. In the city of Salvador, Brazil, for example, there were six such organizations for blacks and five for mulattos at the beginning of the eighteenth century. Like the Indian *cofradías* of Spanish America, these groups sponsored religious celebrations and provided members with many social services, including funeral expenses, dowries for young women, and help in times of illness. In the Brazilian district of Minas Gerais, functions sponsored by these organizations provided the only opportunities for large numbers of blacks to assemble legally. Events sponsored by the brotherhoods often provided venues for the continued practice of African traditions.

RACE AND CLASS IN COLONIAL LATIN AMERICA

Colonial Latin America was a racially stratified society, with what might seem to be a straightforward pecking order. Whites usually occupied the most prestigious ranks, followed in descending order by mestizos, free mulattos, Indians, and slaves. Social reality, however, was not that simple. Wealth, skills, and connections to powerful people could help an individual advance beyond the status held by others of his or her race. Enterprising mestizos could and did enjoy a social standing superior to that of their creole neighbors, and in fact they often came to be regarded as white, even when their physical features suggested otherwise.

Still, colonial Latin American society placed a high premium on whiteness, and people of mixed ancestry often took care to distance themselves as much as possible from their African and Indian origins. Consider, for example, Beatriz de Padilla, a woman accused of murdering her lover in Guadalajara, Mexico, in the mid-seventeenth century. She insisted that court records list her as a *morisca,* meaning that she was more white than black. Although her mother was a mulatta, Padilla proclaimed that her father belonged to one of the city's leading white families. In similar fashion, lighter-skinned mestizos began calling themselves *castizos,* supposedly indicating that they were three parts white and only one part Indian. A sure way to insult someone was to cast doubt on his or her pretensions to whiteness.

Social and Cultural Definitions of Race

Beatriz de Padilla's claim to be a morisca shows that some people created subcategories when defining their racial identity. By the mid-eighteenth century, artists were producing the so-called castas paintings, images that depicted a bewildering range of possibilities that could result when people of different categories produced offspring. In fact, very few of these fanciful terms were ever used in everyday conversation, and the paintings were curiosity pieces coveted

A casta painting, *De Español y Mestisa, Castiza*, by Mexican artist Miguel Cabrera, 1763.

by European art collectors rather than accurate representations of social reality in the colonies.

Few people could trace their lineage as precisely as the subjects in the castas paintings or even as well as Beatriz de Padilla. Members of the high elite proudly touted genealogies that spanned many generations and included conquistadors and peninsular grandees, but most people were lucky if they knew their family's history at all. Like most Indian commoners, many blacks, mulattos, and even mestizos lacked surnames. Migration, the death of parents, and the abandonment of children all worked to erase whatever memories might have existed. Because there was no civil registry of births, people could "prove" their ancestry only by obtaining a copy of their baptismal record or by producing witnesses who could attest to their parentage.

How Historians Understand

Parish Registers and the Study of Colonial Society

The kinds of written sources most readily available to historians are heavily weighted in favor of the literate, the wealthy, and the powerful. The Catholic Church's insistence that everyone be baptized, however, assured virtually every person at least a cameo appearance in the documentary record. Priests were required to keep careful records of all the baptisms, marriages, and funeral rites they performed, regardless of the social standing of the individuals involved. The Genealogical Society of Utah in Salt Lake City has microfilmed many of these parish registers, and copies are available to researchers worldwide.

Parish registers are, of course, extremely valuable for people wishing to trace their own family genealogy, but historians have also used these records to learn a great deal about colonial Latin American society. Baptismal records give the infant's parents' names and ethnicities and note whether or not their parents were married. Some children, however, were listed as *hijos de padres no conocidos* ("children of unknown parents") or *espósitos* ("abandoned"). Still other records give one parent's name while omitting the other.

A document dated June 5, 1807, regarding the marriage of María Teresa Salazar of Los Angeles, California, and Leandro Galindo, a soldier, originally from San Francisco, California.

From these notations, historians have been able to gather information about fluctuations in the rates of illegitimacy and abandonment.

Baptismal registers also name the child's godparents, offering important clues to patron–client relationships and other social networks. Even the names chosen for newborns indicate important trends in colonial society. For example, historians have traced the growing devotion to the Virgin of Guadalupe in Mexico by noting the increasing popularity of the name "Guadalupe" in eighteenth-century baptismal registers. Contrary to the popular belief that this cult arose first among Mexican Indians, they have found the name to initially have been much more popular with españoles.

Burial registers offer grim reminders of recurrent epidemics–page after page of hastily scribbled notations, with many of the deceased described as infants or small children. If time and energy permitted, priests might include the cause of death. Many women died in childbirth and were buried alongside their newborns. Priests in frontier areas might note that a person had been killed by hostile Indians. Often too, priests noted whether a person was buried with a simple ceremony or with more elaborate pomp–an indicator of wealth and social status.

Marriage documents have proven particularly useful to historians of colonial Latin American society. When a couple presented themselves to a priest asking to be married, they had to show what Spanish Americans called *diligencias matrimoniales,* documents proving that they were not close blood relatives of one another or already married to others. If they were not natives of the place where they were marrying, they had to prove where they had previously resided, which has enabled historians to track migration patterns. The frequency of marriage across racial lines offers important clues to social mobility.

There are limits to what we can learn from these documents, however, especially about specific people of lower social standing. Indian commoners, slaves, and many racially mixed people either had very common surnames or none at all, thus making it difficult to trace an individual from one record to another. Many people of limited means also spared themselves the expense of a church wedding. Still, our knowledge of colonial Latin American society is immeasurably richer thanks to these sources.

Questions for Discussion

Consider again the case of Juan and María, the hypothetical Mexican couple we thought about in the "How Historians Understand" section of Chapter 4. Using the church records from their home parish along with the documents we found in that imaginary "trunk," how full a picture of their lives could we reconstruct?

In any case, ethnic identities were fluid and highly subjective, depending on personal appearance, reputation, hearsay, occupation, and who was making the identification. If several different people were all asked to specify the race of an individual, they might all give different answers. Historians have discovered numerous cases in which the same individual might be listed as a mestizo in one document, an español in another, and a mulatto in yet another. Priests could be persuaded to go back and alter a baptismal record, and a person moving to a new place might be tempted to "whiten" his or her ancestry, especially in areas where there were few European immigrants who might contest their claims.

In fact, racial identity was often defined as much by behavior and culture as by biology. Someone called a mestizo might look very much like an Indian, but if he or she spoke Spanish and functioned as a member of the república de españoles, then he or she was not an Indian. "Indians" were people who lived in Indian communities, paid tribute, spoke indigenous languages, and dressed like Indians, regardless of their actual parentage. Mestizos residing in Indian villages sometimes found it advantageous to "pass" as Indians in order to gain access to community land or office. When factional disputes erupted within Indian communities, a sure way of discrediting an adversary was to accuse him or her of being a mestizo or a mulatto.

An example from the province of Latacunga in the Ecuadorian Andes shows how cultural artifacts served as markers of ethnic identity. Indians were supposed to belong under the ecclesiastical jurisdiction of the Franciscans, while secular clerics ministered to españoles, but church officials quarreled over where mestizos should worship. In 1632 the bishop ordered that all mestizos who wore Indian-style clothing to go to the Franciscan church. Even this seemingly simple solution did not settle the issue, however, for many Indian and mestiza women favored a skirt known as a *faldellín,* a style that combined native and European elements. An arbiter finally decided that all women who wore a *lliclla,* a shawl widely used by indias and mestizas alike, should belong to the Franciscan parish.

Ethnicity, then, was imprecise and subject to modification throughout a person's lifetime. How much or how little an individual cared about his or her ethnic classification apparently varied considerably as well. People with tenuous claims to whiteness were often especially sensitive to any aspersions cast on their ancestry. Race also mattered to someone like Beatriz de Padilla, perhaps because she could better defend herself against criminal charges if the court regarded her as almost white. Many others, however, realistically perceived that they had little likelihood of moving up the social ladder, and thus no reason to quibble about their racial identity.

Class and Ethnicity

Great wealth could buy many status symbols in colonial Latin America—a spacious and well-furnished townhouse, a rural estate, fine clothing, jewelry, an elegant coach, and slaves. Such luxuries went a long way toward convincing one's neighbors that anyone who could afford them deserved an elevated standing in the community. Money could also buy other less tangible but perhaps more important markers of social distinction. Men could purchase a seat on the town council or even the governorship of an entire province. Wealthy parents could provide their daughters with sizable dowries and increase their chances of marrying into a prominent family. Those with fortunes to spare could greatly enhance their prestige by becoming patrons of a convent or hospital. In Spanish America even titles of nobility were for sale, although as we saw in the case of Antonio López de Quiroga in Chapter 4, not everyone who entered a bid actually got a title.

Further down the social ladder the benefits of financial success were more modest but still significant. The mulatto muleteer Miguel Hernández of Querétaro, Mexico, used his hard-won earnings to acquire rural property, a slave, and a membership in one of the city's most prestigious cofradías. Blacksmiths, tailors, jewelers, and other craftsmen who accumulated enough funds to acquire their own shop took a big step in advancing their standing in the community. A mestiza or a mulatta who possessed a modest dowry might hope to marry a respectable artisan or shopkeeper. By the eighteenth century, class—a person's access to wealth—was becoming an increasingly important criterion of social status. Yet there were clear limits to the upward mobility of Indians, mestizos, blacks, and mulattos, and limits also to the downward mobility of people who could plausibly claim pure European ancestry. Lighter-skinned people had more chances to marry "up" and found it easier to get loans to finance a daughter's dowry or the purchase of a shop.

Wealth and ethnicity also played a role in the so-called patron–client relationships that operated at virtually all levels of society. A person's patron was someone of higher social standing who provided help of many kinds. A peninsular immigrant seeking a job in the colonial bureaucracy, a journeyman carpenter hoping to set up shop for himself, a free black seamstress or cook trying to round up enough money to buy a loved one's freedom—all of these people would look to someone a rung or two higher on the social ladder to assist them in achieving their goals. The higher up one stood to begin with, the more powerful patron he or she could summon and the more generous favors he or she could expect. Both class and ethnicity were crucial in setting the upper and lower boundaries of a person's social mobility.

HONOR, GENDER, AND PATRIARCHY

If class and ethnicity set the parameters of social mobility, a person's reputation could raise or lower his or her standing within those parameters. Reputation depended in large part on how much one adhered to a comprehensive code of honor that prescribed rules of proper behavior for males and females at all stages of their lives. The rules covered nearly every aspect of a person's life, from marriage and sexuality to honesty in business dealings. People had endless opportunities to become familiar with these rules: Priests expounded on them from the pulpit and in the privacy of the confessional, and civil officials echoed the same message as they carried out their duties.

The frequency and consistency with which authorities of both church and state invoked these rules did not guarantee that everyone observed them. For many people, a strict adherence to all of the norms was impractical given the circumstances of their lives. Others simply went their own way. Those who enjoyed relatively high social standing might try to conceal their transgressions, but men and women who had little to lose had less reason to cover them up. Still, people at even the humblest ranks of society often cared very much about their personal reputations. For many, it was the only way they could gain a measure of respect in the eyes of their neighbors and perhaps the support of a patron.

Honor and the Patriarchal Family

Central to the notion of honor was the principle of patriarchy, the idea that all authority is society rested in the hands of fathers or father-like figures. The patriarchal nuclear family, headed by a male with all women, children, and servants subject to his governance, was considered both the building block and the prototype of a stable society. The king and his appointees were supposed to rule their jurisdictions in paternal fashion—firmly but benevolently. In theory, each male head of household acted as the king's deputy, charged with controlling the behavior of everyone living under his roof. His prerogatives included administering corporal punishment, within certain limits, to errant family members and servants.

Priests and civil officials stressed how important it was that men monitor and discipline their wives, daughters, and female servants, paying special attention to their sexual behavior. As daughters of Eve, women were seen as morally inferior to men—dangerous temptresses who, if left unsupervised, could easily lead men to "the precipice of perdition," as one observer in eighteenth-century Mexico put it. Ideally, wives and unmarried daughters were expected to observe what Spanish Americans called *recogimiento,* or seclusion within the walls of their homes, leaving only to attend mass or family gatherings, and then only when chaperoned by a male guardian. Widows and women who never married were urged to join the household of some male relative—father, uncle, brother, even an adult son.

Unseemly conduct by a man's wife, daughters, servants, or other female relatives reflected negatively on his honor and therefore on his standing in the community. Spanish Americans used the phrase *hombre de bien,* literally, man of good, to describe the honorable head of household. Such a man was fair and honest in his business dealings, loyal to the king, and conscientious in fulfilling his civic obligations. He was also expected to support his family as best he could. Most of all, he effectively "governed" his household. The surest way to insult a man was to suggest that he was a cuckold, unable even to control the sexual behavior of his own wife. A man who caught his wife in an adulterous affair could kill her or her lover with little fear of prosecution. In short, a man's honor depended on his family's conduct and reputation, while a woman's honor was contingent on her submission to her father or other adult male relative.

Marriage and the Family

Because the nuclear family was considered so important to the stability of society, both church and state paid careful attention to marriage as the means through which families came into being. For a marriage to be considered valid, it had to be witnessed by the church, which involved a number of formalities. Both parties presented documents showing that they were not currently married to anyone else and that they were not close relatives of one another. Then the couple's intention to marry was publicly announced in church so that anyone with information to the contrary could come forward. In theory, men and women were free to marry whomever they chose, but in practice, parents—especially those with great wealth and or even slight pretensions to elevated social status—often exerted powerful pressure on their children to make matches advantageous to the family's honor. In their efforts to ensure that their sons and daughters chose "proper" spouses, they often petitioned the church for exemptions to customary bans on marriages between first cousins or other relatives.

Families of means provided their daughters with a dowry in money or other property. This endowment might consist of a few animals, furniture, dishes, and other household items, but the wealthiest brides brought to their marriages huge fortunes, including haciendas or plantations, slaves, and abundant silverware and jewelry. The daughter of the Bolivian silver magnate Antonio López de Quiroga received a dowry valued at 100,000 pesos when she married in 1676. In general, the more lavish the dowry, the better the woman's chances of marrying someone of high social standing.

Almost without exception, once the marriage ceremony was performed, the union was for life. It was possible to secure an annulment if one could prove that the marriage had been invalid in the first place, in the case, for example, that one party proved physically incapable of performing the conjugal act or was found to have another spouse living somewhere else. A husband or wife could also secure an ecclesiastical divorce, which permitted one to live apart from an abusive spouse but did not include freedom to remarry as long as the spouse survived. Such concessions were quite rare, however. Priests and civil officials alike generally concurred that their duty was to see that couples stayed together for the greater good of society. Colonial archives are full of complaints of domestic violence, almost always from women, who sought recourse when their husbands exceeded what society considered appropriate levels of physical "correction." More often than not, authorities of both church and state summoned the husband and exhorted him to use more "gentle" means of persuasion in governing his household. They would then urge the wife to return home and take special care in performing her domestic and conjugal duties. The authorities reasoned that a woman allowed to live apart from her husband would have no means of support for herself and her children and would become a burden to the community.

Honor and Sexuality

The church forbade all sexual activity outside of marriage or not intended for procreation. Women were expected to be virgins at the time of marriage, although it was assumed that men would have had prior sexual experience. An honorable man was permitted, indeed expected, to break an engagement if he learned that his fiancée was not a virgin. In practice, however, many couples saw nothing wrong with having sex once they had become engaged by exchanging a *palabra de casamiento* ("word of marriage").

When a pregnancy resulted before a marriage ceremony actually took place, what happened next depended a great deal on the relative social status of the man and the woman. If both parties held similar standing in the community and their families approved the match, the marriage proceeded as planned, with few consequences for anyone's reputation, and the child was considered legitimate. If the woman's parents considered her fiancé socially inferior, they faced a dilemma: Which would do greater damage to the family's honor—to have their daughter bear a child out of wedlock or to accept a man of questionable status as a son-in-law? When the man's social rank was notably higher than the woman's, his family might well pressure him into breaking the engagement and leaving her to fend for herself. She could, however, sue him for breach of contract, and force him to marry her or at least provide her with a dowry to enhance her chances of marrying someone else.

Women who bore children out of wedlock suffered great dishonor, and those with pretensions to some standing in the community often went to great lengths to conceal their pregnancies. Abortion and even infanticide were not unknown, but it is difficult to determine how frequently these practices were employed by desperate women—certainly often enough to prompt repeated comment from the clergy. Much more commonly, a woman who could manage to do so kept hidden from view throughout the pregnancy, and then either "adopted" the child as if it had been born to another woman, gave the baby to someone else to raise, or left it on the doorstep of a church or convent. Colonial baptismal books typically contain numerous entries for "children of unknown parents." Most major

cities had foundling hospitals for abandoned infants. Mortality rates in these institutions often ranged as high as 90 percent.

Even the more fortunate of children born out of wedlock bore a social stigma
that greatly hampered their own claims to social standing. The priesthood and
other prestigious careers were usually closed to men of illegitimate birth, while
women might find fewer chances of marrying into an elite family. It was possible, however, for a person to gain legitimacy after the fact, if the biological parents subsequently married. Those who could afford the long paper trail involved
could also obtain an official certification from the Spanish crown declaring them
legitimate, regardless of the circumstances of their birth.

Men's sexual activities were far more difficult to monitor than women's, of
course, and even men who openly acknowledged that they had fathered children out of wedlock suffered few consequences, as long as they provided for their
offspring's care. In some cases, fathers took their illegitimate children into their
own homes and never publicly revealed the identity of the mother. Respectable
bachelors could preside over their own patriarchal households, exercising control over servants and others who lived under their roof. This double standard
did not mean that men's sexual indiscretions went completely unpunished. Rape
was prosecuted, but the rigor of the prosecution varied according to the social
standing of the victim and her male relatives. The victim usually bore the burden of proof, and her past sexual history weighed heavily in determining the
guilt or innocence of the accused. Authorities of church and state were especially
concerned with the problem of bigamy, which most often involved married men
who migrated across the ocean or to a new part of the Americas and took new
wives, passing themselves off as widowers or bachelors.

Honor and Homosexuality

Homosexual behavior was punished in the civil and church courts, and punishment sometimes went as far as the execution of those found guilty. Men reputed
to be homosexuals also became targets of gossip and ridicule. The social standing of the accused and the amount of discretion he exercised definitely played
a role in determining his fate, however. Doctor Gaspar González was a priest in
La Plata (today, the city of Sucre, Bolivia) prosecuted for sodomy in 1595 and
again in 1608. The jobs he held during his long and distinguished ecclesiastical
career included the conduct of a general *visita,* or inspection, of the entire diocese of La Plata. His open affair with a young man named Diego Mexía caused
quite a scandal. They lived in the same house, shared sleeping quarters, and publicly displayed their affection for one another. Mexía accompanied González on
his inspection tour, and the priest later purchased him a seat on the city council
of La Plata as well as numerous expensive gifts.

Had González been more circumspect about his personal life, his education
and occupation might have spared him from the consequences of his actions.

Indeed, some witnesses hesitated to reveal evidence against him because of his standing in the community. Ecclesiastical authorities normally preferred to handle such matters quietly in order to protect the church's reputation, but González's outright defiance of accepted standards left them little choice but to prosecute. When the church court in La Plata found him guilty of sodomy and ordered him defrocked and turned over to secular authorities for punishment, González used his connections to appeal the sentence before a superior tribunal in Lima. That court ruled that there was insufficient evidence to convict him of sodomy, but because he had scandalized the community, he should be banished from the diocese of La Plata. He did not, however, lose his claim to the privileges and benefits accorded to priests.

As for Diego Mexía, his lower social rank and prior legal troubles brought him stiffer penalties. He had been a prisoner in the Potosí jail before González befriended him and secured his release. As a layman, Mexía faced prosecution in the stricter civil courts rather than the ecclesiastical tribunals that handled González's case. During the course of the investigation, authorities tortured him, hoping to convince him to admit his transgressions. The procedure left him permanently disabled in both arms. Although he refused to confess, the court found him guilty, and sentenced him to 6 years' unpaid service on the galleys. He also lost his city council position. The man with whom González had been involved at the time of his earlier trial, a 20-year-old apothecary's assistant, fared even less well. He was convicted and publicly executed. Attributes such as wealth, occupation, and education, then, influenced the kind of treatment a person might receive if he or she violated society's sexual norms.

The Limits of Patriarchy

However much the clergy, civil officials, and families might stress the importance of observing the norms of honor and patriarchy, many people found these rules impractical or irrelevant. Often, couples ignored the teachings of the church and never formally married, even though they lived together for many years and had several children. A church wedding cost money, including fees for the priest who performed the ceremony and the expense of getting certified copies of documents required to prove eligibility for the sacrament. Many people decided that they would rather spend their scant resources on other things. In many communities, between one-fourth and one-half of all children baptized were listed as illegitimate. Ironically, it was only at the highest and lowest rungs of the social ladder where formal marriage was close to universal—among the elites and among Indians living in missions or villages under the strict control of the clergy.

The demands of daily life meant that most women simply could not remain secluded in their homes, even if they did live with a husband or other male relative. Women who lacked servants left the home several times a day just to perform their domestic chores. They walked to the market and hauled water from streams or from public fountains in larger cities. They gathered at the rivers to do their laundry as well. Those who lived in crowded urban tenements, where an entire family might share a single room, spent much of their time in the streets and plazas of their neighborhoods. Women in rural areas did most of their work outside as well.

Many women, wives as well as widows and single women, also had to go out and earn a living. Rural women took produce from their gardens and fields to markets in town. Women also operated businesses, such as bakeries, taverns, inns, and retail stores, which brought them into contact with many people. Many other women worked as midwives and healers, seamstresses and cooks. Elite families hired young mothers as wet nurses. Wives of shopkeepers and artisans worked alongside their husbands and often carried on the business themselves if their husbands died. A few women even became members of artisan guilds. In Lima, for example, the potters' guild counted 1 woman among its 14 members in 1596, and another woman was an active member of the hatters' guild. By the late colonial period, a few cities even had guilds comprised entirely of female artisans. In 1788, Mexico City's guild of women silk spinners included 23 masters, 200 journeymen, and 21 apprentices. The port of Cartagena in present-day Colombia had a guild of female brandy producers.

Working women could not easily conceal an out-of-wedlock pregnancy, and in general they had a harder time defending their honor and reputation than women who remained secluded. Even women who stayed home and supported themselves by taking in laundry or mending might be accused of having illicit relationships with their male clients. Some women did resort to prostitution, in brothels in the larger cities and on a more freelance basis elsewhere, perhaps because they could earn much more by selling sexual favors than they could in other occupations. Ana María Villaverde, for example, was a young widow who worked in Mexico City's tobacco factory in the late eighteenth century. When she was laid off from her job, she turned to prostitution, tripling her earnings. Despite the social stigma they suffered, prostitutes seldom ran the risk of prosecution by civil or church authorities.

If they survived the dangerous childbearing years, women usually outlived men, especially because wives were often much younger than their husbands. Iberian inheritance laws provided widows with half the property that the couple had accumulated during the marriage, with the other half divided equally among all children, sons and daughters alike. A woman also retained full rights to any goods she had brought to the marriage as a dowry. Wealthy widows lived comfortably and sometimes wielded enormous economic influence as owners of mines, haciendas, and plantations, although the norms of patriarchy strongly urged them to live with an adult son or other male relative. If they cared to marry again, they usually did not lack for willing prospects.

For poor women, however, generous inheritance laws meant nothing, and their relatives were often unable to take them in. Unmarried women, including

LATIN AMERICAN LIVES

JUANA DE COBOS, BAKER IN CHIHUAHUA

ON THE EVENING of September 3, 1752, Mariana Muñoz de Olvera went for a walk through the streets of the northern Mexican mining town of Chihuahua. Passing by the home of a prosperous widow named Josefa García de Noriega, she caught the eye of Miguel Rico de Cuesta, a peninsular Spanish merchant and García de Noriega's fiancé. He called out to Mariana, taunting her with questions about how she could afford the new clothes she was wearing and insinuating that she had traded sexual favors for the money to buy them. She responded with a couple of choice insults aimed at the arrogant Spaniard. A few hours later her mother, Juana de Cobos, heard about the incident and confronted Josefa García de Noriega about her fiancé's rude remarks and questioned the widow's own sexual conduct.

The next morning, García de Noriega filed criminal charges against the "troublesome and scandalous" Cobos and her daughter. Thus began a legal battle that would last for several months and eventually result in their being ordered to move their home and business to the other side of town, where they would be less likely to have further altercations with Rico de Cuesta and García de Noriega. The local authorities were clearly biased against Juana de Cobos. Indeed, the official who first heard García de Noriega's complaint served as a witness when she and her fiancé married a few months later.

Juana de Cobos and Mariana Muñoz de Olvera were easy targets for the scorn of a man like Miguel Rico de Cuesta and his allies on the town's cabildo, for they lived outside the confines of patriarchal households. Though both were married, both lived apart from their husbands without official church permission. Juana, born in a farming community south of Chihuahua in 1706, had migrated to the town with her husband Juan Muñoz de Olvera during its silver boom of the late 1720s. Sometime thereafter, she and Juan separated, and for the remainder of her long life she supported herself, her children, and several grandchildren by operating a bakery. Like so many other women of her time, she never learned to read or write, but one of her adult sons took care of the necessary paperwork. Mariana married in 1746, when she was 21, but within a few years, she too left her husband and she and her two young children went to live with her mother.

By refusing to live in patriarchal households, Cobos and Muñoz de Olvera forfeited a good measure of their claims to honor and respectability. Their frequent quarrels with other people in town did not help their reputations any, and Juana's rivals in the bread trade did not appreciate her periodic attempts to undercut prices set by the town's cabildo. She found it hard to compete with male bakers, many of whom were well-placed peninsular Spaniards who ran larger operations and profited from economies of scale. Her competitors routinely asked her to contribute to activities of the town's loosely organized bakers' guild, but allowed her and other female bakers no say in the proceedings. Not surprisingly, Cobos often refused to help. In 1748, for example, she declined to help underwrite a comedy that the guild sponsored during festivities belatedly marking King Ferdinand VI's accession to the Spanish throne.

Despite her many difficulties, Juana de Cobos managed to win a certain standing in her community. Most people took her for an española, although a few documents refer to her as a mestiza, and Josefa García de Noriega called her a mulatta during their protracted feud. At least some of the time, people addressed her using the honorific title of "Doña." Perhaps the greatest measure of her social standing came when city officers decided that she was sufficiently respectable that they could use her bakery as a place where young women accused of sexual misconduct might be disciplined while learning a useful trade. When she died in 1797, at the age of 91, she was buried "de cruz alta" ("with a large cross"), an honor reserved for those of sufficient means to afford a deluxe funeral.

Questions for Discussion

Did Juana de Cobos and Mariana Muñoz de Olvera violate all of the gender norms of their society, or only some of them? What mattered most in determining their social position in Chihuahua: class, ethnicity, or gender?

many single mothers and wives who had been abandoned by their husbands, often lived on their own as well. By choice or necessity, then, large numbers of women lived in households headed by females, especially in urban areas where it was easier for women to find work to support themselves. Often, two or more women might pool their meager resources to form a single household. Eighteenth-century censuses taken in the cities of Mexico show that women headed as many as one-third of the households. In the Brazilian town of Ouro Prêto, women were in charge of 45 percent of all households as of 1804, and 83 percent of these women had never been married.

Women who headed their own households could still not escape the fact that they lived in a patriarchal society. While widows certainly enjoyed somewhat greater respectability than unmarried women, any woman not under some kind of male supervision had to overcome public suspicions that she lived dishonorably. Still, many women had no choice but to live with this stigma and concerned themselves more with the practical necessity of supporting themselves and their children than with what their gossipy neighbors had to say about them.

Convents: "Islands of Women"

Life in a convent provided some women with a respectable alternative to living in a male-dominated household. In fact, convents amounted to what one historian has called "islands of women," with populations as high as 1000 in some of the larger establishments in Mexico City and Lima. These women had little or no contact with men other than the priests who administered the sacraments or perhaps members of their immediate families. Nuns took perpetual vows of poverty, chastity, and obedience to their superiors. Cloistered nuns were supposed to spend their time almost exclusively in prayer and contemplation. Contact with outsiders occurred in the convent's *locutorio,* a meeting room where an iron grille separated the cloistered nun from physical contact with visitors. The public might also attend mass at a convent chapel, but here too the nuns remained sequestered behind a grille.

Life in the convents, however, was not always as austere as these rules might suggest. Nuns' failure to observe proper decorum and their refusal to live in strict accord with their vows of poverty was a frequent subject of concern for church officials. Many nuns, especially those who came from wealthy families, eschewed communal dormitories and lived in comfortably furnished private rooms or even small apartments, some complete with private patios and gardens, within the convent. In her quarters, a nun could create what amounted to a matriarchal household that might include several servants or slaves, one or more orphan girls whom she personally raised, and perhaps a female relative or two.

The locutorios of major convents often witnessed lively social events featuring spirited conversation, music, and other entertainment. Visitors at these gatherings were treated to fine delicacies from the convents' kitchens. Popular legend maintains that the famous Mexican mole–a flavorful sauce combining American ingredients such as chiles, chocolate, and tomatoes with cloves, cinnamon, peppercorns, coriander, and other Old World spices–originated in one of Puebla's principal convents.

Not everyone who lived inside a convent was a nun. In seventeenth-century Cuzco, for example, the city's two convents together housed more than 500 women, and fewer than half of them were nuns. In addition to servants, slaves, and orphans, one could find young girls from respectable families who were there to learn reading, writing, arithmetic, needlework, and other basic skills in a society that offered few other formal educational opportunities for females. Victims of domestic violence, widows, and other women on their own might find temporary or permanent shelter within the convents' walls, sometimes of their own accord and sometimes "deposited" by their male relatives. Church authorities might also remand a woman to a convent as punishment for sexual improprieties or other wrongdoing.

Within the convents' walls nuns had certain opportunities not customarily available to them in the outside world. Convents as institutions typically controlled substantial wealth. As "brides of Christ," novices brought dowries when they entered religious life, and these became the property of the convent. Through bequests and other donations, nunneries also acquired assets in the form of real estate, both rural and urban, and they also figured among the most

Portrait of Sor Juana Inés de la Cruz, at work in her library.

FIEL

Copia de otra que de sì hizo, y de su mano pintò la R. M. Juana Ynés de la Cruz Fenix de la America, Glorioso desempeño de su Sexo, Honrra de la Nacion deeste Nuevo Mundo, y argumento de las admiraciones, y elogios de el Antiguo. Nació el dia 12. de Nov. de el año de 1651. à las onse de la noche. Reciuió el Sagrado Habito de el Maximo D.S.S. Geronimo en su Convento de esta Ciudad de Mexico, de edad de 17. años. Y murió Domingo 17. de Abril de el de 1695. de edad de 43. años, y quatro meses, et cinco dias, y cinco horas. Requiescat in pace. Amen.

important sources of credit in the colonial economy, making loans to merchants and landowners and garnering an annual interest rate of 5 percent.

Women who headed the convents exercised considerable leverage in managing these assets, along with power over the internal operation of the nunneries. These positions thus provided leadership opportunities available nowhere else to women in colonial society. Abbesses and other convent officers were chosen in periodic elections by the highest-ranking nuns themselves, and elections were sometimes hotly contested. Powerful creole families took an active interest in convent elections because of the prestige and economic benefits that might accrue to them if a family member were elected abbess of a wealthy convent.

Convents also afforded a select few women a chance to pursue intellectual interests. The most famous colonial nun was Sor Juana Inés de la Cruz

(1648–1695) of Mexico. Although universities and other institutions of higher learning were closed to women, she studied on her own. Her interests ranged from music, physics, and mathematics to theology and philosophy. She corresponded with leading intellectuals of her time and wrote poetry, drama, and essays, often with a decidedly feminist spin. One of her most widely quoted verses, for example, posed the question of the relative morality of prostitutes and their male clients. Who sins more, Sor Juana asked, she who sins for pay or he who pays for sin? Hundreds of other nuns also left numerous writings, including poetry, plays, histories of their convents, and lengthy spiritual autobiographies written at the suggestion of their confessors. Still others became expert musicians, singers, and composers.

Convents and Colonial Society

No matter how much economic power or intellectual distinction these favored nuns received, they could not escape the fact that they lived in both a patriarchal and hierarchical society. They always remained subordinate to male church authorities, from their personal confessors to the bishops of their dioceses. Toward the end of her life, Juana Inés de la Cruz renounced her intellectual pursuits, giving away her books and scientific instruments, in part because a bishop had warned her that these activities put her soul at risk. Cloistered nuns also had to rely on male majordomos, who were often close relatives of the abbesses, to take care of their business affairs.

Convents also reflected the class and ethnic divisions of society. Only women able to provide a dowry could become professed nuns. The entrance fee in Lima in the early seventeenth century was 6000 pesos, and double that if a nun wanted her own private quarters. In addition, her family usually had to provide an annual stipend to cover her living expenses. Smaller towns, especially in frontier areas, usually lacked convents, thus restricting the options of many women. In Brazil, the religious life was out of reach for all but the most affluent women. Until 1677, when Salvador's first convent opened, wealthy families sent their daughters to convents in Portugal.

Inside the convents, there were numerous social distinctions. The most prestigious nuns were those who wore the black veil. They came from respectable and often wealthy families of Spanish or Portuguese descent. Only they were eligible to vote and hold office, and they were exempt from all menial work. Next came the sisters of the white veil. Their dowries were lower and their social backgrounds less distinguished than those of black-veiled nuns. To them fell many of the housekeeping duties inside the convent. The convents also housed many Indian, mestiza, and black women known as *donadas*. They took informal vows of chastity and performed the most onerous chores.

A few convents were specially created for Indians and mestizas, but these institutions did not escape the strictures of a racially stratified society either. As we saw in Chapter 3, even though Cuzco's convent of Santa Clara had been founded originally for mestizas, within a few decades nuns of Spanish origins had captured control of the convent's leadership and relegated mestiza sisters to second-class status. Mexico City's convent of Corpus Christi, founded in 1724 for Indian women, was reserved for the legitimate daughters of caciques and other Indian nobles. It owned no property. The nuns survived exclusively on alms they gathered and were not permitted to have private quarters or servants.

Women unable to enter a convent but still wishing to pursue a religious life might find shelter in a *beatario,* an informal institution that resembled a nunnery but had no recognized standing in the church and none of the prestige associated with convents. The Catholic Church eventually conferred sainthood on two colonial *beatas,* Rosa of Lima and Mariana de Jesús of Quito. In general, however, church authorities distrusted these women for seeking spiritual enlightenment outside of official ecclesiastical channels. Many beatas found themselves accused of heresy and brought before the Inquisition.

CONFORMITY AND DEFIANCE IN COLONIAL SOCIETY

Colonial Latin Americans received constant reminders that they lived in a society that made fine distinctions of ethnicity, honor, class, and gender. Whenever they appeared in court, whether as defendant, plaintiff, or witness, a notary carefully noted their ethnicity, or at least what he perceived it to be. Church records also stipulated the race of persons baptized, married, or buried. Class differences were clearly visible to anyone who walked the streets of any city. The wealthy could be seen parading about in elegant coaches and dressed in fine clothing while the poor were lucky if they had a roof over their head. And while class and ethnic identification could sometimes change, gender distinctions were the most obvious and enduring. Outside of convents, women held no official positions in the church, nor were they eligible for public office or admission to higher education or the professions. Men and women alike were repeatedly exhorted by priests and civil officials to behave in ways appropriate to their gender.

For most people the routines of daily life entailed interaction with people who ranked above them or beneath them socially, and elaborate rules of etiquette supposedly governed these encounters. On special occasions, the pecking order of colonial society went on public display as high dignitaries of church and state marched in procession through city streets, followed by representatives of other groups, all lined up according to rank. Men, women, and children also regularly witnessed what happened to those judged to be social outcasts. Executions and whippings were carried out in public, as were the punishments of nonconformists condemned by the Inquisition, to provide an object lesson for all. Despite all these rules and lessons, however, people found ways to defy the conventions of their society, sometimes in full view of their presumed social betters, more often in safer, more private settings.

The Social Etiquette of Everyday Life

The rules of etiquette began with the forms of address used in everyday conversation but also included grammar and general demeanor. "Remember to whom you are speaking" was a frequent admonition to people of lower social standing whenever they found themselves in contact with people who ranked above them. In Spanish America, men and women who possessed a certain measure of social standing presumed that the title "Don" or "Doña" would precede their names whenever anyone talked to them or about them. Government officials expected to be addressed with even loftier terms, such as "Your Excellency" or "My Most Excellent Lord," and those who held academic titles used them as well. Even in casual conversation, Spanish and Portuguese speakers were expected to use the appropriate version of the pronoun "you," as each language has two words for the term. One connotes respect, or at least social distance between the speaker and listener, and the other is used among equals or when the speaker considers himself or herself superior in rank to the listener. Men were also expected to doff their hats in the presence of their social betters.

As clear as these guidelines might seem, situations might arise, particularly in the world of petty commerce, where the rules were not at all straightforward. Peninsulares or creoles often owned tiny retail shops that sold a wide variety of merchandise to people of many different ethnic backgrounds. By virtue of their own rank in society, shopkeepers expected deferential behavior from Indians and mulattos, but their livelihoods depended on treating their customers with a certain amount of respect. The merchants' clientele often understood that spare cash in their pockets gave them the leverage necessary to defy customary social conventions.

One such encounter took place in the shop of the Spaniard Martín de Echaquibel in the mining town of Chihuahua in northern Mexico in 1753. A mulatto came into the store, asked to see some merchandise, and then turned to leave without buying anything. Insulted, Echaquibel exclaimed, "Look, dog, you are a mulatto and I am very much a Spaniard," using the familiar second-person pronoun. The customer could hardly dispute the difference in their racial identities but defiantly pointed out that he was not the shopkeeper's slave and that he would do as he pleased.

Other people were less openly so but just as disrespectful as Echaquibel's customer. In the privacy of their homes and in other protected spaces, they surely mocked the pretensions of those who claimed to be their social betters. They found safety in numbers, too. The lower classes in late colonial Buenos Aires, for example, often gathered to watch the creole militia drill, and laughed whenever these weekend warriors made a mistake. And, as we shall see, public

An eighteenth-century drawing of an open-air tavern or *pulquería* in Mexico City.

celebrations offered ideal opportunities to mock any and all symbols of rank and authority in colonial society.

The Administration of Justice

Authorities of church and state in colonial Latin America found plenty of occasions to remind everyone who was in charge and how those in subordinate positions should behave. The administration of justice, vested in city councils, in local officials serving in rural districts, and in the viceroys and high courts of Lima, Mexico City, Salvador, and other major cities provided numerous such opportunities. In the sixteenth century, the central square of every newly founded Spanish American town had a *picota,* a stone or wooden pillar that symbolized the king's authority. Whenever local officials set out to arrest someone, they carried with them a special baton that signified their right to mete out justice.

Punishments for crime varied according to the social standing of those convicted. Whites were usually spared corporal punishment and ordered to pay a fine instead. Whippings and executions were usually carried out in the central plaza of town. Petty criminals such as thieves and those found guilty of assault might be given dozens or even hundreds of lashes. Convicted murderers were often executed, but only after they were paraded through the streets of town, accompanied by members of the clergy, representatives of the civil authorities, and a town crier who publicly announced their crimes. Their corpses were then left on display for the presumed edification of those who had not witnessed the actual execution.

Civil and church officials were certainly concerned with impressing people with the long arm of the law, but they also had to convince the public that they were wise and just rulers. For this reason they tempered the administration of justice with a fair amount of leniency and attention to prescribed procedures. Although there was no such thing as trial by jury, the accused were usually provided with a defender who summoned witnesses to testify on the defendant's behalf and argued in favor of leniency when guilt was not in doubt. Civil authorities and inquisitors resorted to the death penalty only occasionally. Serious crimes were often punished by banishment from the community or a term of forced labor in a textile factory, silver refinery, bakery, or sugar mill. Men might also be sent to serve in a remote military post for ten or more years.

The Inquisition and Deviant Behavior

In addition to the civil government, the Holy Office of the Inquisition played a role in enforcing many of society's rules. The formal establishment of tribunals in Lima and Mexico City came in the early 1570s, although monastic orders and bishops had previously conducted inquisitorial proceedings, particularly against Indian converts accused of backsliding into their old ways. After the 1570s, Indians were exempt from the Inquisition's jurisdiction, but the church found other ways to prosecute native "idolaters." Every other baptized Catholic, from the most prestigious ranks of the Spanish nobility to mestizos, slaves, and free people of color, was fair game for Inquisition scrutiny, however. Brazil never had a formal tribunal, but Inquisition authorities from Portugal paid occasional visits to the colony, and sometimes the accused were sent to Portugal for trial.

The Inquisition's official charge was to root out deviant beliefs and behavior, including heresy, blasphemy, bigamy, witchcraft, superstition, and the secret practice of Jewish rites. Powerful New Christian merchant families were rounded up in a series of trials held in Lima and Mexico City in the late sixteenth and early seventeenth centuries. Women, especially those who claimed to have special spiritual or magical powers, were often subject to prosecution. Scores of English pirates captured at Veracruz, Cartagena, and other ports were brought to trial as "Lutheran corsairs."

In fact, however, the Inquisition proved less oppressive in the colonies than in Spain and Portugal. Given the huge territorial expanse of Spanish America and Brazil, it could reach only a small number of people. The tribunals of Mexico City and Lima, as well as a third one set up at Cartagena in 1610, covered huge territories, with agents in principal cities who were supposed to report offenses to their superiors. The inquisitors followed regular procedures, carefully questioning witnesses, punishing those who falsely accused others, and dismissing many charges for want of sufficient evidence. Those found guilty faced penalties that ranged from wearing penitential garb in public for those who reconciled themselves to the faith to confiscation of their property and even execution for those who stubbornly refused to recant their errors. Executions were rare—about 50 were ordered by the Mexico City tribunal in the 250 years of its existence, another 30 in Lima, and probably not more than 100 in all of Spanish America. According to one estimate, not more than 1 percent of all persons prosecuted by the Inquisition received death sentences. Others, however, died in Inquisition jails while awaiting trial. Sentences were carried out in public ceremonies so that all could see the consequences of violating religious and behavioral norms.

Rituals of Rule

Public executions and whippings offered gruesome reminders of the power of the church and state, but on other occasions colonial Latin Americans witnessed more pleasing portrayals of the social and political order in which they lived. Throughout the year there were numerous religious holidays when the pecking order of society went on public view in the colorful processions that passed through the streets and plazas of all major towns. These occasions also provided good opportunities to portray the teachings of the church in brilliant visual fashion to the assembled crowds. Reenactments of the medieval battles between Christians and Muslims underscored the message that the church had triumphed over its enemies.

In many cities, the feast of Corpus Christi was the most spectacular of these religious holidays. Celebrated in late May or early June, this holy day honored the sacrament of the Eucharist. A solemn procession carried the consecrated host, displayed in a golden and bejeweled monstrance, through the streets and plazas, accompanied by representatives of many different segments of society—all male, of course. Participants included the viceroy in capital cities, the bishop and the rest of the secular clergy, the city council, members of male religious orders, Inquisitors, cofradías, trade guilds, Indians, blacks, and mulattos, all carefully arranged according to their rank in society, with places closest to the Eucharist considered the most prestigious. The Mexico City procession was often more than a mile long, and even included students from the school of San Juan de Letrán. City governments went to great expense to mark the occasion. In 1621, for example, Mexico City spent 21 percent of its budget on the Corpus Christi celebration.

Other occasions provided opportunities to reinforce the allegiance of the people to their king. The death of a monarch and the coronation of his successor called for solemn funeral rites, followed by public demonstrations of loyalty to the new king. Lavish and costly spectacles marked the arrival of a new viceroy, or a marriage or birth in the royal family. Others heralded Spanish successes in warfare, such as the celebrations held throughout the empire following the defeat of a British assault at Cartagena in 1741. In Mexico City, an annual observance was held on the anniversary of Cortés's victory at Tenochtitlan in 1521. All of these rituals were designed to teach the king's subjects that they lived in a great empire. To symbolize the benevolent, paternal generosity of their sovereign, those who marched in the processions often tossed coins or other trinkets to the crowds.

Scatological Songs and Dances of Defiance

Solemn processions were only part of the festivities that marked special religious and civic occasions. There was plenty of popular entertainment, including fireworks, theatrical pieces, cockfights, and bullfights. Many festivals gave people the opportunity to dance in the streets, drink heavily, and ridicule the powerful and pretentious. Their songs and dances often had explicit sexual content. In the streets of eighteenth-century Mexico, men and women favored a lascivious dance called the *chuchumbé,* performed while singing suggestive verses, such as this one: "A monk is standing on the corner, lifting his habit and showing the chuchumbé." Holidays also allowed people to don costumes and act out ritual inversions of the social order. Men dressed as women, and laymen disguised as members of the clergy pretended to bless the crowds. The pre-Lenten carnival season was especially noted for such excesses.

Authorities worried that these large gatherings might spill over into popular riot. In June of 1692, such fears materialized when an angry crowd stormed the viceroy's palace and set the building on fire during the Corpus Christi celebration in Mexico City. People were angry because food prices had skyrocketed and the viceroy had failed to provide the relief they expected. Their protests soon gave way to generalized looting of shops throughout the central district of the city. The authorities responded by rounding up alleged ringleaders and ordering several of them to be executed. They also attempted to ban the sale of the popular intoxicating beverage known as *pulque.*

Religious and civil festivals certainly brought large numbers of people together and allowed them a temporary escape from the drudgery of their daily routines, and a chance to play at turning the social order upside down, with plenty of all-around carousing. The potential for disturbances such as the 1692 Mexico City riot were appreciable. These "time out" settings may also have served to reinforce rather than destabilize existing social and political hierarchies. Those who witnessed the lavishly staged processions of Corpus Christi and other holidays may well have come away convinced that the existing order of things was inevitable, even if they entertained questions about its legitimacy. Then too, the opportunity to "let off steam" at festival time may have served as a useful safety valve in keeping the lower classes in their subordinate places. When the party was over, they went back to work and their accustomed outward show of deference to those who ranked above them.

Slice of Life   CORPUS CHRISTI IN CUZCO

THE FEAST of Corpus Christi in early modern Europe and Latin America was a celebration of Catholicism's victories over its enemies. Everywhere the processions included figures representing Muslims, Turks, and others vanquished by militant Christians. In South America, the Spanish city of Cuzco, built literally on the foundations of the Inca capital, provided an ideal platform on which to stage this annual tribute to the faith triumphant. The immense fortunes generated by silver mining permitted local elites to put on a lavish show, and the willing participation of native Andeans seemed to signify that Spanish hegemony and the Catholic Church rested on firm foundations in Peru.

The bishop, city council, and other dignitaries who presided over the Corpus Christi rituals had definite ideas about which native people should play an active role in the solemn procession of the Eucharist. Like the representatives of Spanish society who took part, those chosen to march were all male. They were also presumed to be direct descendants of the pre-hispanic Andean nobility. Conspicuously absent were those related to Incas who had resisted the imposition of Spanish rule and held out at Vilcabamba for more than 30 years after Pizarro's conquest (see Chapter 3).

Spanish authorities intended that the procession display the social, political, and religious order that had prevailed in Peru ever since the 1530s, but Cuzco's Andean leaders added their own messages to the script. Even though they usually wore Spanish-style clothing as they went about their daily lives, on festive occasions they put on costumes that invoked their glorious past. They dressed as specific rulers, such as the legendary first Inca Manco Capac and his descendant Huayna Capac, the last to occupy the throne at Cuzco before the Spaniards arrived in Peru. On their foreheads the marchers wore red-fringed headbands once reserved for the exclusive use of the Inca ruler himself, but in colonial times these headbands were the ultimate status symbol for native Andeans. Those who claimed the right to wear them carefully guarded their privilege. Each year they elected 24 men whose duties included making sure that no one "illegally" donned the fringe.

Corpus Christi and other public celebrations permitted native Andeans many other ways of publicly reenacting what they understood to be their history. Among Cuzco's native population were descendants of Cañaris from southern Ecuador who had been forcibly relocated to the Inca capital in the late fifteenth century. They had sided with the Spaniards during the conquest and from then on had cited that alliance in claiming special status in the new colonial order. Cañaris served as armed guards to Spanish authorities, and on Corpus Christi and other special days they marched in the processions as military companies, armed with arquebuses and pikes, not just in Cuzco

(continued on next page)

CORPUS CHRISTI IN CUZCO   *(continued from previous page)*

but in Lima as well. They figured prominently, for example, in ceremonies held in the capital to welcome a new viceroy in 1667.

Those who called themselves descendants of the Incas often disputed the Cañaris' exalted position in official ceremonies. Ritual celebrations thus provided natives as well as Spaniards the opportunity to display their own special standing in society. Although the Corpus Christi procession was supposed to symbolize the unity of all Christians in submission to the body of Christ in the Eucharist, the feast also mirrored and perpetuated the many divisions in the social and political order.

Questions for Discussion

Suppose that Felipe Guaman Poma de Ayala (see Chapter 5) had witnessed one of the Corpus Christi celebrations in Cuzco. What would he have thought? Would he have approved of the role given to the descendants of the Incas? Why or why not?

CONCLUSION

Colonial Latin Americans lived in a hierarchical society that assigned privileges and obligations according to ethnicity, class, honor, and gender and attempted to fix everyone in a specific niche based on these criteria. Priests and officers of the law tried to get people to pay proper respect to authority within their households and in society at large, and they seemed constantly on the lookout for violations of the boundaries that separated one group from another. Some authorities even experimented with sumptuary laws that forbade Indians and blacks from wearing clothing supposedly reserved for Europeans and their American-born descendants, but people persisted in wearing whatever they could buy or otherwise acquire.

Other rules proved somewhat easier to enforce, but everywhere people of all social classes got away with far more than laws, sermons, court rulings, or Inquisition proceedings might imply. Racial labels were attached to people whenever they appeared in the official records of church or state, and whiteness counted for a lot, but in fact all ethnic identities were quite flexible, especially for those who were economically successful. Many slaves found ways to escape their bondage. Often out of practical necessity and sometimes out of personal choice, women disregarded the strict standards that theoretically placed them firmly under the thumbs of husbands and fathers. People of the lower classes found periodic release from their workaday routines and occasions when they could safely mock or even challenge those who claimed precedence over them. However rigid and specific the rules of social interaction might seem to have been, they were everywhere subject to constant renegotiation.

LEARNING MORE ABOUT LATIN AMERICANS

Andrien, Kenneth, ed. *The Human Tradition in Colonial Latin America* (Wilmington, DE: Scholarly Resources, 2002). Brief biographies of "ordinary" men and women in colonial Latin America.

Bennett, Herman. *Africans in Colonial Mexico: Absolutism, Christianity, and Afro-Creole Consciousness, 1570–1640.* (Bloomington, IN: Indiana University Press, 2003). Looks at free blacks and slaves, and the ways their lives were affected by the government and the church.

Boyer, Richard. *The Lives of the Bigamists: Marriage, Family, and Community in Colonial Mexico*, abridged ed. (Albuquerque, NM: University of New Mexico Press, 2001). Examines the lives of people tried by the Inquisition for bigamy, giving details about family life, education, and migration.

Burns, Kathryn. *Colonial Habits: Convents and the Spiritual Economy of Cuzco, Peru* (Durham, NC: Duke University Press, 1999). An insightful case study of Cuzco's nunneries and their relationships with the larger society.

Curcio-Nagy, Linda A. *The Great Festivals of Colonial Mexico City: Performing Power and Identity* (Albuquerque: University of New Mexico Press, 2004). A richly detailed history of the public civil and religious rituals in the capital of New Spain.

Few, Martha. *Women Who Live Evil Lives: Gender, Religion, and the Politics of Power in Colonial Guatemala* (Austin, TX: University of Texas Press, 2002). Shows how mestiza, black, Spanish, and indigenous women wielded power through witchcraft and healing.

Gauderman, Kimberly. *Women's Lives in Colonial Quito: Gender, Law, and Economy in Spanish America* (Austin, TX: University of Texas Press, 2003). Probes various aspects of women's lives in colonial Ecuador, including their economic activities and their responses to domestic violence.

Johnson, Lyman L., and Sonya Lipsett-Rivera, eds. *The Faces of Honor: Sex, Shame and Violence in Colonial Latin America* (Albuquerque, NM: University of New Mexico Press, 1998). Eight different historians explore such issues as homosexuality, insult, illegitimacy, and honor in Spanish America and Brazil.

Katzew, Ilona. *Casta Painting: Images of Race in Eighteenth-Century Mexico* (New Haven: Yale University Press, 2004). Hundreds of color and black-and-white illustrations provide a fascinating visual tour of colonial Mexico.

Myers, Kathleen, and Amanda Powell, eds. *A Wild Country Out in the Garden: The Spiritual Journals of a Colonial Mexican Nun* (Bloomington, IN: Indiana University Press, 1999). The writings of Madre María de San José, a nun who lived in Mexico from 1656 to 1719, edited and annotated by two well-known literary scholars.

Socolow, Susan Migden. *The Women of Colonial Latin America* (Cambridge, MA: Cambridge University Press, 2000). A comprehensive survey that draws on the best recent scholarship.

Sweet, James H. *Recreating Africa: Culture, Kinship, and Religion in the African-Portuguese World, 1441–1770* (Chapel Hill, NC: University of North Carolina Press, 2003). Shows how slaves in Brazil were able to maintain African religious beliefs and practices and use them to mitigate the suffering of slavery.

7

THE SHIFTING FORTUNES OF COLONIAL EMPIRES

IN 1700, THE CROWNED HEADS of Europe waited anxiously as King Charles II of Spain lay dying without a direct successor ready to assume his throne and his vast colonial possessions. The last of the Spanish Hapsburgs, Charles had ruled since 1665, but his reign bore little resemblance to the brilliant successes of his namesake who had presided over the realm in the time of the great conquests of Mexico and Peru. Spain's population was actually smaller than it had been a century before, the flow of American treasure to the royal coffers had fallen off precipitously, and Spanish merchants reaped diminishing profits in trade with the colonies. Spain's rivals, especially England and France, stood by eager to enrich themselves at its expense, and soon fell to fighting one another over who should inherit Charles's domains.

Thus began a long struggle between France and England, the superpowers of the eighteenth century, a conflict that ended only with the final defeat of the French general Napoleon Bonaparte in 1815. The wars of the eighteenth century and the resulting emergence of Great Britain as the premier economic, political, and military power in Europe and the world had profound consequences for Latin America. Spain often sided with France, even while trying to thwart French incursions in North America. The English therefore viewed the Spanish colonies as fair game for attack, while also coveting entrance into the huge markets of Spanish America. Portugal, on the other hand, maintained close economic and political ties with England, which made Brazil the occasional target of French assaults. Spain had always accused Portugal of encroach-

212

ing on its territory in South America beyond the line of demarcation that the two nations had agreed upon in 1494, but clashes between them accelerated as they found themselves on opposite sides of the conflict between the superpowers of their time. The conflict between France and England also led indirectly to three great revolutions, the first in England's North American colonies, the second in France, and the third in the French sugar colony of Saint Domingue, today's Haiti. Each each of these upheavals was so significant that historians often refer to this period as the "Age of Revolution." Latin America's destiny changed profoundly during these years.

Spain and Portugal had to overhaul their colonial empires to shore up their own competitive position in the high-stakes game of eighteenth-century world politics. New imperial policies coming out of Lisbon and Madrid reordered everything from taxes and trade to the position of the church, to the benefit of some and the detriment of many others. Representatives of many different social classes voiced their opposition to these changes in written petitions, town meetings, riots, and armed uprisings.

THE SPANISH AND PORTUGUESE EMPIRES IN EIGHTEENTH-CENTURY POLITICS

The opening round in the wars of the eighteenth century was the War of the Spanish Succession, which lasted for 13 years following the death of King Charles II in 1700. Charles had named Philip, the French Duke of Anjou and a member of the House of Bourbon, as his heir. Philip was a grandson of King Louis XIV of France, and other European powers feared that one day a single person might rule France and Spain and their huge colonial empires. England and Austria therefore went to war to prevent Philip from assuming the throne. For England, however, the War of the Spanish Succession was about much more than who would occupy the throne in Madrid. As King Louis XIV proclaimed in 1709, "The main object of the present war is the Indies trade and the wealth it produces." British access to the growing markets of Latin America was a major objective in this and all of the other conflicts of the eighteenth century.

Great Britain and Latin America

The eighteenth century witnessed the beginning of the Industrial Revolution in Great Britain. British makers of textiles, tools, and other manufactured goods eagerly sought new customers among the growing population of Latin America. Some of this trade operated legally through Spanish intermediaries, and England's colonies in North America and the Caribbean provided ideal bases for

TIMELINE

1700
Death of King Charles II of Spain, accession of Philip V and beginning of the Bourbon dynasty

1700–1713
War of the Spanish Succession

1703
Commercial treaty between England and Portugal

1718
Founding of San Antonio, Texas

1739
Creation of viceroyalty of New Granada

1739–1748
War of Jenkins' Ear, War of the Austrian Succession

1740
Spain begins abandonment of fleet system

1756–1763
Seven Years' War

1759
Expulsion of Jesuits from Brazil

1763
Treaty of Paris: France surrenders North American possessions; Spain gets Louisiana; England gets Florida

1767
Expulsion of the Jesuits from Spanish America

1776
Separate military command created for northern frontier of New Spain; creation of viceroyalty of Río de la Plata

1776–1783
American Revolution

1780–1781
Revolt of Tupac Amaru II; Comunero revolt in New Granada

1788–1789
Conspiracy in Minas Gerais, Brazil

1789
Beginning of the French Revolution

1791
Haitian Revolution begins

1798
Conspiracy in Bahia (Salvador) in northeastern Brazil

1803
United States acquires Louisiana

1815
Defeat of Napolean

1819
Spain cedes Florida to the United States

smuggling additional merchandise, but Great Britain also flexed its political and military muscle to gain greater direct access to these lucrative markets. In 1703, England and Portugal signed a treaty that guaranteed preferential treatment for British woolens in Portugal and Brazil. Although Portuguese winemakers received similar concessions in British markets, this arrangement crippled Portugal's already struggling textile industry, and Brazilian gold flowed northward, helping to underwrite Great Britain's continued economic growth. According to one estimate, fully 80 percent of the gold that circulated in Europe in the eighteenth century came originally from Brazil.

In 1713, the Treaty of Utrecht formally ended the War of the Spanish Succession. England and its allies agreed to accept Philip as King of Spain, but in many other ways England came out the victor. The Spanish and French Bourbons agreed that the two nations would never be united under a single monarch,

North America in 1750

Map legend:
- Spanish settlements and claims
- British settlements and claims
- French settlements and claims
- Disputed or unclaimed
- - - Present-day political boundaries

and England gained other concessions crucial to its entry into Latin American markets. King Philip V granted British merchants permission to send one ship bearing African slaves and other cargo each year to the Spanish colonies, a concession that continued until 1748. The ship was authorized to call at the most important ports on the Caribbean and the Gulf of Mexico, including Cartagena, Portobelo, Veracruz, and Havana. Eager traders used this privilege as a cover to import a wide variety of merchandise to Latin America and to scout out additional prospects for contraband. Portugal got control of Colônia do Sacramento, a settlement in present-day Uruguay on the Río de la Plata estuary directly across from Buenos Aires. British merchants and Brazilian cattlemen used this port to smuggle goods into the Spanish colonies in southern South America throughout the eighteenth century, even after Portugal ceded it back to Spain in 1777.

Continued contraband trade involving British and a growing number of Anglo-American merchants brought Britain and Spain to armed conflict in 1739 in the War of Jenkins' Ear, so named because Spanish authorities had captured English sea captain and smuggler Robert Jenkins and cut off his ear. British naval forces held Portobelo for 2 months and nearly seized Cartagena, while North American vessels serving as privateers captured numerous Spanish ships at sea. The contest later merged into the larger conflict between England and France and their respective allies known as the War of the Austrian Succession, which lasted until 1748. During the brief interval of peace that followed, the flow of British and North American merchandise into Spanish America continued unabated.

The Seven Years' War

The Seven Years' War of 1756 to 1763 brought a decisive shift in the colonial empires of Britain, France, and Spain. Fighting actually began in 1754, as British colonists clashed with the French and their Indian allies for control of North America. The war then spread to Europe, where the principal point of contention was the long-standing rivalry between Prussia and Austria, allies of Britain and France, respectively. In the end it, became a significant turning point in the long Anglo-French battle for world hegemony. The British won decisively, capturing Quebec in 1759, and defeating French forces in India. They also seized France's Caribbean sugar colonies of Guadeloupe and Martinique. Spain's belated decision in 1762 to join France had enormous consequences for its colonial empire. The British now had an excuse to attack key Spanish possessions. They quickly took Havana, linchpin of Spain's mercantile system, as well as Puerto Rico and even Manila in the Philippines.

The Treaty of Paris of 1763 ended the war and redrew the map of North America. The French withdrew completely from North America, ceding Canada and their claims to everything east of the Mississippi River to Great Britain, but got their Caribbean islands back. The British also received Spanish Florida, which they had long coveted. In compensation, Spain was given the huge and vaguely defined former French territory of Louisiana, extending from New Orleans and the Gulf Coast to Canada and from the Mississippi River westward to the Rocky Mountains. The British returned Puerto Rico and Manila to the Spanish. They also agreed to leave Havana, but only after instituting important economic changes that would have far-reaching effects on Cuba's subsequent history. During 11 months of the British occupation, more than 700 merchant ships from Britain and the North American colonies called at Havana. Hoping to hold Havana indefinitely, the British also stimulated the local sugar industry and the slave trade, and Cuba became one of the world's leading producers of sugar.

North America after 1763

Map legend:
- Spanish settlements and claims
- British settlements and claims
- French settlements and claims
- Disputed or unclaimed
- - - Present-day political boundaries

Map labels: Boston, New York, Philadelphia, Baltimore, San Francisco, Monterey, San Luis Obispo, Santa Barbara, Los Angeles, Santa Fe, San Diego, Tucson, El Paso, Charleston, Natchez, Pensacola, St. Augustine, Florida reverts to Spain, 1783, San Antonio, Mobile, New Orleans, St. Louis, Mississippi R., Missouri R., Ohio R., St. Lawrence R., Rio Grande, Gulf of Mexico, Havana, CUBA, HAITI, NEW SPAIN

The American Revolution and Latin America

Britain's stunning victories in the Seven Years' War were expensive, and as a result Parliament imposed new taxes on the colonies, including the notoriously unpopular Stamp Act of 1765 that required Americans to buy government-issued stamps for all legal documents, and new duties on tea, glass, and paper. Parliament also forbade Americans to settle west of the Appalachian Mountains and stationed British troops in Boston to subdue the city's unhappy residents. These measures and a growing sense of American nationalism drove the colonists to open revolt. Armed clashes began in Massachusetts in 1775, and representatives of the 13 colonies signed a formal declaration of independence in 1776.

The French saw an opportunity to avenge their losses in the Seven Years' War by aiding the North American rebellion. They allied with the 13 colonies in 1778, and a year later encouraged Spain to declare war on Britain. Although King Charles III of Spain could not openly support American independence for fear that his own colonial subjects might follow the example of their neighbors to the north, he welcomed the chance to regain some of the ground Spain had lost in 1763. Most United States history textbooks pay relatively little attention to the Spanish role in the American Revolution, but both Spain and France contributed to the colonists' victories on the battlefield that culminated at Yorktown, Virginia, in 1781, and at the conference table in Paris 2 years later. The Spanish smuggled guns, ammunition, and crucial information to the Anglo-American rebels even before they officially declared war on Britain, and beginning in 1779 they also struck at strategic British positions in North America and the Caribbean. Led by Bernardo de Gálvez, the energetic young governor of Louisiana, Spanish troops dealt decisive blows to the British at Pensacola and Mobile and at Natchez on the Mississippi River. They also repelled an assault on Saint Louis and defended New Orleans against a possible attack.

In the Treaty of Paris of 1783, Great Britain formally recognized the independence of the United States and returned Florida to Spain. The success of the American Revolution certainly encouraged Latin Americans to think in terms of one day forming their own independent nations, but Spain's involvement in the struggle had other more immediate consequences as well. Spanish military operations were financed with steadily mounting taxes paid by colonial subjects from California to Buenos Aires and with silver from the mines of Mexico. The Spanish Caribbean colonies also furnished large amounts of supplies to the American cause, further cementing their economic ties with the new republic to the north. Ironically, then, Latin Americans contributed to the creation of a nation that would one day seize half of Mexico's national territory, intervene militarily in Mexico and several Caribbean and Central American nations, and exert economic and political dominance throughout the hemisphere.

The French Revolution and Latin America

The end of the American Revolution provided only a brief respite from war and social upheaval in Europe and the Americas. The French people labored under mounting tax burdens, brought on by their monarchs' repeated involvement in the wars of the eighteenth century. The uprising that officially began with the storming of the Parisian prison known as the Bastille in the summer of 1789 was much more than just a tax revolt, however. The revolutionaries became more and more extreme in their demands over the next few years. They deposed King Louis XVI and in 1793 put him and Queen Marie Antoinette to death. They also attacked the nobility and the church and even their old comrades in arms who failed to embrace the increasingly radical agenda of the revolution. Thousands of people faced execution by guillotine. On the other hand, the revolution's appeal to the ideals of "liberty, equality, and fraternity" had widespread appeal throughout Europe and the Americas.

By 1793, the French revolutionaries were ready to export their ideas to the rest of Europe, much to the terror of kings, nobles, churchmen, and other privileged classes across the continent. So alarmed were Kings Charles IV of Spain and George III of Great Britain that they reversed their usual policy and sided with one another, and numerous other European powers, in a war against revolutionary France. This temporary alliance again opened the markets of Spanish America to British goods. Cotton textiles from England found enthusiastic buyers in Venezuela, for example. Trade between Latin America and the United States flourished during this period as well. In 1795, Spain reverted to its customary tie with France and the following year declared war on Britain once again.

Meanwhile, Spain's position in North America eroded further. Although Spanish missionaries, soldiers, and settlers had recently occupied California as far north as San Francisco, they could not keep the British and North Americans away from the coast of what is now Oregon, Washington, and British Columbia. In 1789, a Spanish officer arrested the captain and crew of a British naval ship at a remote location on Vancouver Island and sent them to Mexico City for trial. Great Britain threatened war, knowing that internal turmoil in France would prevent Spain from turning to its traditional ally. The following year, Spain agreed to share the region north of California with the British.

Trouble also loomed with the young and expansive United States. After 1783, Americans poured into the area between the Appalachian Mountains and the Mississippi River. Farmers in the Ohio River Valley needed an outlet to the Gulf of Mexico through Spanish New Orleans, and a disagreement over the northern boundary of the Florida territory created additional friction between the two countries. Here too, Spain adopted a policy of appeasement, just as it had done with the British in the Pacific Northwest, ceding the disputed part of Florida to the United States and granting Americans permission to use the port of New Orleans. As Anglo-Americans cast covetous eyes on Louisiana, Spain returned that territory to France, now headed by Napoleon Bonaparte, on the condition that it would never be given to a third party. Napoleon quickly went back on his word and sold the heartland of North America, from New Orleans north to Canada and west to the Rocky Mountains, to the United States in 1803. Spain yielded all of Florida to the United States in 1819. Its once proud empire was clearly in retreat.

Under Napoleon, French armies again took the offensive against the other nations of Europe. War continued with only brief interruptions until he was finally defeated in 1815 and England emerged as the world's undisputed power. Spain sided with France until 1808, when Napoleon invaded the Iberian Peninsula and imposed his brother Joseph Bonaparte as king of Spain, an event that led indirectly to the independence of Latin America. The Napoleonic Wars disrupted Spanish trade across the Atlantic, and Spain opened its colonies to ships coming from neutral powers. Yankee traders from the United States eagerly took advantage of this opportunity to strengthen their position in Latin America.

The Haitian Revolution

The French Revolution's most profound repercussions in the Americas took place on Hispaniola. In 1697, Spain had formally ceded the western portion of the island to France, and the colony known as Saint-Domingue became one of the world's leading producers of sugar over the next several decades. Thousands of slaves were imported from Africa to work the plantations. By 1789, nearly 90 percent of the colony's 520,000 people were slaves, another 28,000 were free people of color, and about 40,000 were white. Events in France divided the colony's whites between those loyal to the king and those who sympathized with the revolutionaries, while free people of color seized on the more radical ideas of the French Revolution, the notions of liberty and equality, and demanded an end to various forms of discrimination.

In August of 1791, the slaves of Saint Domingue took advantage of these splits within the upper and middle classes. They revolted, slaughtering their former masters and torching a thousand plantations. White reprisals were equally vicious. Great Britain and Spain sent forces to intervene, each hoping to seize control of the colony for itself. The revolutionary government of France declared the abolition of slavery in 1794 and rebuffed the British and Spanish attacks with the help of François Dominique Toussaint L'Ouverture, an ex-slave and a key leader of the rebellion. The rise of Napoleon Bonaparte to power inaugurated a shift in the mother country's racial policies, culminating in his public reinstatement of slavery in 1802. Meanwhile, Toussaint L'Ouverture declared independence from France, whereupon Napoleon dispatched a military expedition to crush his revolt. Although the French forces captured him, new black leaders emerged to fight in his place. They defeated Napoleon's troops and killed or expelled all remaining whites from the colony. On January 1, 1804, they proclaimed the independence of the new nation of Haiti—using the name the original Taino Indians had used for their land. The declaration voiced their determination "to enjoy the liberty consecrated by the blood of the people of this island" and to "forever renounce France, to die rather than to live under its domination."

Events in Haiti terrified slaveowners and, indeed, all privileged classes throughout the Americas, while inspiring slaves and free people of color. As early as 1805, just a year after the proclamation of Haitian independence, Afro-Brazilian soldiers were wearing medallions with images of Jean-Jacques Dessalines, one of the new republic's leaders. Afro-Cubans invoked the Haitian example in their own unsuccessful revolt less than a decade later. Napoleon's failure to hold Haiti also led to the transfer of Louisiana to the United States. He had hoped to use the North American territory as a source of food and other supplies for the plantations of Saint Domingue, but now Louisiana was just an attractive target for Great Britain or the United States and more a liability than an asset to France.

THE BOURBON AND POMBALINE REFORMS

The dramatic shifts in world power politics during the eighteenth century moved the Bourbon kings in Spain and the Braganzas in Portugal to change the way they ruled at home and in their colonies. They adopted governing philosophies and practices from the absolutist Bourbons of France and they attempted to bring the Catholic Church more firmly under royal control. They tried to stimulate trade and economic development and imposed new taxes in an effort to generate more revenues to underwrite offensive and defensive military operations. Crown monopolies on such commodities as tobacco, gunpowder, and playing cards constituted another major source of revenue for the Bourbon kings of Spain. As the American, French, and Haitian revolutions unfolded, the Spanish and Portuguese governments attempted to suppress the spread of seditious ideas among their colonial subjects.

Above all, the monarchs of Spain and Portugal worked to tighten their hold on their overseas territories in the face of mounting foreign pressure to gain access to the thriving markets of Latin America. They reorganized colonial administration and sent growing numbers of peninsular bureaucrats to keep potential rebels in line. The Spanish kings revamped colonial defense policies, especially in areas vulnerable to British intrusions. They built stronger fortifications in ports such as Havana, San Juan, and Veracruz and promoted the settlement of California to ward off Russian fur traders moving southward from Alaska, as well as the British and the North Americans.

All of these changes, collectively known as the "Bourbon Reforms" in the Spanish empire and the "Pombaline Reforms" in Portugal and Brazil, carried huge consequences for the people of Latin America. Although the first of these changes occurred during the reign of Philip V, the most sweeping innovations took place during the second half of the eighteenth century, as the conflict between Britain and France reached its climax and Spain's position in the Western Hemisphere became increasingly precarious as the young United States began its westward expansion. King Charles III, who assumed the Spanish throne in 1759 and reigned until 1788, spearheaded the reforms in his empire, with the energetic assistance of his minister of the Indies, José de Gálvez (see Plate 12). In Portugal and Brazil, Sebastião José de Carvalho e Mello, better known as the Marquis of Pombal, served as chief minister during the reign of King José I (1750–1777) and masterminded the overhaul of the Portuguese colonial empire.

The fortified port of Havana, captured by the British in 1762.

Defending the Spanish Empire

Prior to the eighteenth century, Spain maintained a rather minimal military presence in its American colonies. The Hapsburg kings were reluctant to spend much money on colonial defense, even as they squandered huge sums on their military exploits in Europe. In New Spain, as of 1700, fewer than 6000 poorly equipped regular army troops guarded the northern frontier and strategically located ports that had been traditional targets of foreign pirates. The crown preferred that career soldiers from Spain man these garrisons. By the late seventeenth century, however, not enough Spaniards were willing to serve overseas, so growing numbers of creoles, mestizos, and free blacks filled the ranks, often conscripted from among vagrants and criminals. Citizen militias, organized in cities and small towns throughout the empire, supplemented the regular army forces. Often, the militia members had to supply their own uniforms and weapons.

As imperial rivalries accelerated in the eighteenth century, the kings of Spain devoted more resources to the defense of their colonies. In the aftermath of the Seven Years' War, sturdier fortifications were built at San Juan, Cartagena, Havana,

Veracruz, and other ports that had been such tempting targets for the British. In 1767, the king created a standing colonial army to augment the meager frontier garrisons and local militias. Sales taxes were increased from 2 percent to 6 percent to offset the cost. Young men of all social classes except Indians were liable for conscription. Throughout the empire, militia forces were also expanded, with regular army officers assigned to monitor these units. Ambitious creoles found new opportunities as officers in the regular army and the militia units. Growing numbers of career military officers were appointed to administrative positions.

The Bourbon monarchs also sponsored new settlements to bolster Spanish claims to frontier regions. Even though they often allied with France in the world conflicts of the time, they actively resisted French encroachments on their territory in North America. The presence of French missionaries and fur traders in the Mississippi Valley and the establishment of substantial French settlements at New Orleans and along the Gulf Coast prompted Spain to tighten its grip on Texas. King Philip V made the permanent occupation of Texas a top priority, fostering the establishment of missions, military garrisons, and civilian communities clustered around what is now the city of San Antonio, founded in 1718. Settlers were recruited from adjacent parts of northern New Spain and from as far away as the Canary Islands.

Although the French presence in North America was clearly a menace to Spain, it also served as a buffer against the even more troublesome British. After 1763, however, Spain found itself face to face with Great Britain along the Mississippi River. The situation called for a thorough revamping of defense policies all along the northern frontier. In 1776, King Charles III ordered the creation of a separate military command to oversee the security of the entire northern frontier of New Spain. Meanwhile, Franciscans were setting up a chain of missions up the coast of California from San Diego to San Francisco and military presidios and civilian settlements appeared at select locations, all in an effort to secure Spain's hold on the west coast of North America.

Administrative Restructuring and New Viceroyalties

Both the Spanish and the Portuguese governments also reorganized colonial administration. Beginning in 1764, Spain installed men known as intendants to represent the crown's interests, supervise fiscal and military affairs, and implement the Bourbon reforms at the local level. The intendants were like miniature viceroys operating out of major provincial towns. Mexico, for example, had 12 intendants, stationed in cities such as Puebla, Zacatecas, and Guadalajara, while Peru had 8. Subordinate to the intendants were *subdelegados* (subdelegates) in charge of Indian villages. The intendants and subdelegados received better salaries than the old alcaldes mayores and corregidores they were supposed to replace, so that they might be less tempted to corruption. In fact, they appear to have continued the same old practices, and many of them were military officers and peninsulares who alienated local creoles. They also proved to be more efficient tax collectors than their predecessors, to the consternation of the taxpayers.

The Spanish government also created two new viceroyalties in South America. The first, known as New Granada, was established at Bogotá in 1739 and had jurisdiction over present-day Ecuador, Colombia, Panama, and much of Venezuela. In 1776, Buenos Aires became the seat of the viceroyalty of La Plata, which included Upper Peru and the mines of Potosí (present-day Bolivia) as well as Argentina, Uruguay, and Paraguay. The creation of new high courts (*audiencias*) in cities such as Caracas and Buenos Aires also signified the crown's desire to increase its presence in areas that were once considered peripheral to the empire but were now of growing economic and strategic importance.

Meanwhile, comparable developments were occurring in Brazil. The discovery of gold in Minas Gerais at the end of the seventeenth century shifted the colony's economic axis southward, away from the sugar-growing region of Bahia. Accelerating conflict with Spain heightened the strategic importance of the south as well. Although all of Brazil remained under the jurisdiction of a single viceroy, in 1763 he moved his headquarters from Salvador to Rio de Janeiro in the south. Salvador continued to be the seat of a high court (*relação*), but a second court was set up in the new capital. Like his counterparts in Spain, Prime Minister Pombal also appointed peninsular military officers to many high-level government posts in Brazil.

The Power of the Church

The absolutist kings of eighteenth-century Europe increasingly viewed the Catholic Church as a rival power. Although the Pope had long ago conceded the Spanish and Portuguese monarchs the right to name bishops and otherwise supervise church affairs in their colonies, the wealth and political power of the church had grown steadily from its humble missionary origins in the sixteenth century. From the perspective of Lisbon and Madrid, the church enjoyed far too tight a hold on people's loyalties and its extensive property might be better diverted to more utilitarian ends.

The Society of Jesus represented a particularly great threat to ministers of state like the Marquis of Pombal and José de Gálvez. The Jesuits had accumulated enormous real estate holdings and thousands of slaves. From Paraguay in South America to Sonora, Baja California, and Arizona on the northern frontier of New Spain, Jesuit missions constituted veritable kingdoms outside the sphere of crown control, while Jesuit colleges trained the sons of colonial elites throughout Spanish America and Brazil. Moreover, along with the customary monastic commitments to poverty, chastity, and obedience to superiors, they took a special vow of loyalty to the Pope. Ambitious monarchs throughout Europe feared that the Jesuits might work in concert with the pope to subvert their own power. Members of the order were accused of inciting popular riots in Madrid and plots against the king in Lisbon.

Slice of Life THE ROYAL TOBACCO FACTORY IN MEXICO CITY

THE CREATION OF A CROWN monopoly on tobacco in 1765 was a key component of the Spanish Bourbon Reforms. Tobacco production was restricted to specified areas, growers were required to sell their crops to agents of the monopoly, and royal factories were established to replace independent makers of cigars and cigarettes. The monopoly's most obvious objective was to increase crown revenues, but it served other purposes too. The reformers saw the cigarette factories as vehicles to control the growing masses of poor people in the major cities of America and to use their labor for the betterment of the empire. As one monopoly official put it, "The man without an occupation is a dead man for the State; those who work are like living plants which not only produce but propagate ... wherein lies the true increase of the population and prosperity of the State." Although they couched their objectives in terms of men, in fact the Bourbons hoped to tap women's productive potential as well. They believed that women's small hands and manual dexterity ideally suited them to the task of rolling cigarettes, and that women workers were more conscientious and less likely to get drunk or steal from their employers than men. The reformers also hoped that factory jobs would get women off the streets, away from prostitution and into useful activity.

The tobacco factory of Mexico City, the largest of six established in New Spain, employed up to 9000 workers, many of them women and children. Factory jobs were especially appealing to single women and widows without other means of support. Most employees were either españoles or mestizos, but some were Indians and mulattos. They worked Monday through Saturday, with the exception of religious holidays, and they were paid on a piecework basis. A workers' cofradía provided burial insurance and other benefits, and there was even a kind of on-site day care for young children.

Factory work usually implies a fixed routine. Employees show up at a specific time and work more or less nonstop for a stipulated number of hours. Administrators of the tobacco factory aimed to impose this kind of modern industrial discipline on the riffraff they recruited from the streets of Mexico City. In theory, workers arrived on the job early in the morning and stayed for a 12-hour shift, but in fact they often came and went as they pleased. Many subcontracted their daily quotas to family members or dependents and then went about other, more profitable activities. They also took some of their work home so they could attend to household responsibilities along with their paid employment.

Nor were tobacco workers always the obedient, docile labor force envisioned by Bourbon planners. They voiced their concerns in frequent petitions to monopoly administrators and other crown officials and occasionally took to the streets to get their grievances heard. Their most notable success came in 1794 in the so-called paper riot. The imported paper used for making

(continued on next page)

THE ROYAL TOBACCO FACTORY IN MEXICO CITY *(continued from previous page)*

cigarettes was becoming increasingly expensive as war in Europe disrupted shipments from Spain. In an attempt to prevent waste and theft of this precious commodity, factory managers forbade the workers' usual practice of taking paper home in the evening and preparing it for the next day's work. Outraged workers marched in protest to the viceroy's palace and got their customary rights restored. The Bourbons wanted to reorder colonial society to the benefit of the state, but they often had to make concessions to reality.

Questions for Discussion

The Bourbon Reforms have sometimes been portrayed as a second Spanish conquest of America. Would the people who worked in the Mexico City tobacco factory have agreed? Why or why not?

In 1759, the Marquis of Pombal ordered the society expelled from Portugal's overseas territories, and a similar decree went out to Spanish America in 1767. The Jesuits were given just a few days to gather up their personal belongings and embark for Europe, while crown officials seized the order's assets and began selling them off to the highest bidders, many of them drawn from local elites who had long coveted these choice properties. Jesuit missions were placed under the control of secular clergy or other religious orders. In northwestern New Spain, for example, Franciscan priests took over the missions of Sonora, Baja California, and present-day southern Arizona.

The eighteenth-century kings of Spain and Portugal also attempted to curb the wealth and power of other ecclesiastical institutions. The early evangelization of the native peoples of Latin America had been entrusted largely to the regular clergy—that is, the Franciscans, Dominicans, Augustinians, Jesuits, and other religious orders. Their control of these mission parishes was supposed to be temporary, with secular clergy expected to replace them within a decade or two of the initial conversion of a given area. The regulars would then move on to new mission fields on the frontiers of Spanish settlement. In practice, however, the regular clergy continued ministering to many centrally located Indian parishes well into the eighteenth century.

Because the secular clergy answered directly to their bishops, who were in effect royal appointees, the absolutist monarchs of the late colonial period renewed their efforts to secularize Indian parishes. High-handed Spanish bureaucrats forcibly ejected Franciscans, Augustinians, and Dominicans from their sixteenth-century monasteries, and the secular priests who succeeded them often rented out portions of the mission complexes to serve as stables and tenements. Pombal removed the regular clergy from their control over the assets of Indian villages (*aldeias*) in Brazil, although they were allowed to remain as

San Xavier del Bac mission, Tucson, Arizona, built by Franciscans in 1776.

pastors. The Spanish crown restricted the jurisdiction of church courts, forbade the establishment of new nunneries, and tried to convince nuns residing in existing convents to adhere more closely to their vows of poverty.

Economic Development

The Spanish and Portuguese monarchs of the eighteenth century also endeavored to stimulate economic development at home and in the colonies and generate a greater stream of revenue into the royal treasuries. To increase silver mining in Spanish America, the Bourbon kings offered tax incentives, reduced the price of mercury used in processing silver, and even established a college for training mining engineers in Mexico City. Mining guilds patterned on the merchants' organizations were also created, with special tribunals set up in Mexico City and Lima to handle litigation involving miners.

These changes failed to bring any great bonanza in South America, but the output of Mexican silver mines in 1800 was eight times what it had been a century earlier, and Mexico was producing as much silver as the entire rest of the world. Other measures targeted those select places in the Spanish colonies where gold could be

How Historians Understand	REVISIONISM AND THE DEBATE OVER COMPARATIVE SLAVERY

Virtually every European colony in the Americas resorted to African slave labor to one degree or another. For many years, historians assumed that slavery in the Spanish and Portuguese colonies was somewhat more benign than in British America. To support this view they cited the differing legal and religious traditions of the respective mother countries. On the Iberian Peninsula, they argued, slavery had existed more or less continuously from ancient times down to the sixteenth century, and a body of law and custom had developed to define the rights of slaves and their position in society. The Catholic Church regarded slaves as the equals of free people in the eyes of God and recognized the right of everyone, regardless of status, to receive the sacraments. The many laws stipulating ways in which slaves could earn their freedom reflected the notion that slavery was a temporary misfortune rather than a lifelong condition, and a misfortune that could befall many people, not just Africans. According to these historians, English law and religion granted no legal or religious privileges to slaves, leaving them entirely at the mercy of their masters. Because English colonists in the Americas had little prior experience with the institution of slavery, they tended to associate chattel slavery exclusively with Africans, even though whites endured indentured servitude and other temporary forms of bondage.

Other historians, known as revisionists because they have revised the prevailing view on a particular subject, have asserted that these interpretations rely too heavily on laws that were on the books but may have been disregarded by real people in real-life situations. They have suggested that economics was at least as important as law or religion in shaping the conditions under which slaves lived. In particular, they cite the expansion of slavery in Cuba after 1763 to support this argument. Demand soared in the rapidly growing markets of the United States, especially after the destruction of plantations in Haiti in the 1790s, and Cuban sugar cultivation expanded to meet it. In the process, slavery in Cuba began looking more and more like slavery in the British sugar colonies of the Caribbean. As historian Franklin Knight has concluded, "the cumulative

Year	White (%)	Free People of Color (%)	Slave (%)	Total (%)	
1755	no data	no data	28,760 (17)	170,000	Cuban Population Figures, 1755–1817.
1774	96,440 (49)	30,847 (18)	44,333 (26)	172,620	
1792	133,559 (49)	54,152 (20)	84,590 (31)	272,301	
1804	234,000 (46)	90,000 (18)	180,000 (36)	[504,000]	
1810	274,000 (46)	108,600 (18)	217,400 (36)	600,000	
1817	239,830 (43)	114,058 (21)	199,145 (36)	553,033	
1817	259,260 (41)	154,057 (24)	255,131 (35)	638,448	

Source: Matt David Childs, "The Aponte Rebellion and the Transformation of Cuban Society: Race, Slavery, and Freedom in the Atlantic World," PhD dissertation, University of Texas at Austin, 2001, p. 159.

effect of tradition and habit quickly became corroded by the newer mores of the plantation." During the so-called Age of Revolution, Cuba became a slave society, and the crown jewel in Spain's overseas empire after most of its other colonies gained independence in the 1820s. Slavery endured in Cuba until 1886, well past the abolition of slavery in the United States.

Recent research on Florida, on the other hand, has shown that a more lenient attitude toward slavery sometimes served the interests of the Spanish crown and its subjects. After British settlers began setting up slave societies in the Carolinas and Georgia in the late seventeenth and early eighteenth centuries, runaways fled southward to Florida, where colonial authorities welcomed them and encouraged their baptism into the Catholic Church. Some of these runaways remained slaves in Spanish Florida, but others attained their freedom and helped Spanish forces defend the colony against repeated attacks launched by the British from Georgia and Carolina. In 1738, Florida's governor granted freedom to all fugitives from the British colonies and allowed them to establish their own town, Gracia Real de Santa Teresa de Mose, just to the north of St. Augustine. Spain's practice of offering sanctuary to runaways from Anglo America continued after the United States gained its independence. In 1790, however, Spain bowed to pressure from United States Secretary of State and future President Thomas Jefferson and abandoned the policy. For more than a century, however, blacks from the Carolinas and Georgia had "voted with their feet" in favor of Florida's much more tolerant slave regime.

The revisionists and those who have questioned their interpretations have done what any good historian must do. They have examined many different kinds of sources in an effort to understand each historical context on its own terms, realizing that no single factor can explain why societies develop the way they do. In the case of Cuba, slavery reached its apogee in the nineteenth century, after the Haitian Revolution and as strong anti-slavery lobbies were emerging in Great Britain and the United States, but also at a time when huge profits could be made selling sugar in an easily accessible and rapidly growing market. In Florida, Spanish authorities had more to gain by offering asylum to those who fled the emergent slave regimes in Georgia and the Carolinas. The institution of slavery, while always oppressive, varied considerably according to economic, legal, and cultural factors throughout the Americas. Historians must always remain sensitive to the particular characteristics of each specific time and place.

Questions for Discussion

Historians have shown that the conditions of slaves varied according to the specific economic, political, cultural, and religious circumstances of where and when they lived. Can the same be said about the fate of native peoples in the Americas under Spanish and Portuguese rule? Why or why not?

found. Miners in certain parts of present-day Colombia, for example, were permitted to import greater numbers of slaves to assist them in panning for gold.

In both Spanish America and Brazil, royally chartered companies were created to boost production of desired commodities and to lure Spanish, Portuguese, and colonial investors into new ventures. The Basque merchants of the Caracas Company, for example, received a monopoly on cacao exports from Venezuela, a trade that grew substantially as demand for chocolate spread in Europe during the eighteenth century. Pombal created the Companies of Pernambuco and Grão Pará e Maranhão to stimulate the northern regions of Brazil. The latter company received a 20-year monopoly on slave imports to the area.

The Bourbons also experimented with liberalizing trade within the Spanish empire. As we saw in Chapter 4, policies adopted in the sixteenth century had limited trade with the colonies to a single port in Spain, required ships to travel in convoy, and permitted them to call only at Havana, Cartagena, Portobelo, and Veracruz. First to be abandoned was the fleet system. The last convoy bound for Panamá sailed in 1740. A new era of *comercio libre,* or free trade, began after the Seven Years' War, and eventually merchant vessels were permitted to sail from anywhere in Spain to any port in the colonies. Meanwhile, as we have seen, foreign trade with the colonies also increased, sometimes legally permitted, sometimes not.

Pombal's economic policies aimed at reducing Portugal's dependence on Great Britain, but within the constraints posed by the strategic alliance of the two nations. He sent inspectors to Brazil's chief ports to impose quality control standards on the colony's exports of sugar and tobacco, thus hoping to guarantee a favorable world market share for these traditional products. In 1773, he ordered an end to discrimination against New Christians, whose capital and mercantile experience he hoped to enlist for his economic development schemes. He also imposed tighter controls aimed at forcing gold miners to pay their taxes.

The relaxation of trade restrictions within the Spanish empire and other policies of the home governments in Lisbon and Madrid brought spectacular growth to certain regions that had previously been considered marginal parts of the colonies. Buenos Aires, now capital of the viceroyalty of La Plata and the seat of a newly created high court, was especially favored in the new commercial order. The city became the principal outlet for silver from Upper Peru and hides and salted beef from the vast plains known as *pampas* in Argentina, Uruguay, and southern Brazil. The population of Buenos Aires soared from about 10,000 in 1750 to almost 40,000 by the beginning of the nineteenth century.

Havana, of course, had long been important as the hub of the Indies trade, but the rest of the island had remained an economic backwater. Once its deposits of placer gold were exhausted in the early sixteenth century, Cuba's exports had consisted principally of tobacco and hides. The shipbuilding industry was the only other major employer. The British occupation of 1762 inaugurated a new phase in Cuba's economic history that continued after its return to

Spanish control. Hoping to hold the island indefinitely and turn it into another lucrative colonial possession, the British fostered sugar production during their brief tenure, and Spain continued to encourage the industry after it regained control of Cuba. The destruction of plantations in Haiti after 1791 gave an additional stimulus to Cuban production. The island rapidly became one of the world's leading sources of sugar, a position it held during a good part of the century to come. With the expansion of the sugar industry came a huge influx of African slaves to Cuba—more than 300,000 between 1780 and 1820 and another 200,000 in the next 40 years. Cuba would remain a slave society for much of the nineteenth century.

Under the auspices of the Company of Grão Pará e Maranhão, the region near the mouth of the Amazon in northeastern Brazil also developed rapidly. Pombal sent his own brother to the area as governor, explicitly assigning him the task of building a plantation colony to replace the old mission complexes manned by Jesuits and other religious orders. These efforts proved exceptionally successful in Maranhão, where cotton plantations developed rapidly, worked by a fresh supply of slaves imported from Africa. "White cotton turned Maranhão black," people said. Rio de Janeiro also flourished in its new status as capital of Brazil after 1763. Its population grew from just over 20,000 in 1775 to more than double that figure by 1800 and climbed to more than 100,000 in the next 20 years. The city became Brazil's most important port, exporting gold, cotton, rice, coffee, and indigo while importing slaves and manufactured goods.

Other areas experienced marked downturns in the new economic order. Panama, for example, declined following the dismantling of the fleet system, and even its audiencia was abolished. Cartagena's prosperity declined for the same reasons. Some industries in the colonies could no longer compete with the increased volume of imports that accompanied the relaxation of trade restrictions. The textile trade of Quito and the region known as the Bajío, northwest of Mexico City, were among the most severely affected as British and other foreign cloth flooded American markets in the age of free trade. Other manufacturers weathered the changes more successfully, as population growth generated new markets for their wares.

LATIN AMERICAN PEOPLES IN THE AGE OF REVOLUTION

The reorganization of colonial government, the promotion of economic development, new intellectual currents, and the shifting world politics of the "Age of Revolution" brought important changes to the people of Latin America. Economic growth and an influx of immigrants from Spain and Portugal added new dimensions to the region's already complex hierarchies of class and ethnicity. Intellectuals in the colonies eagerly read and discussed the works of Enlightenment philosophers despite the efforts of the Inquisition to thwart the circulation of these potentially subversive ideas. At the same time, the kings of Spain and Portugal actively promoted the Enlightenment's more pragmatic, strictly scientific side. They encouraged innovation in agriculture and industry and sponsored research expeditions to learn more about the flora, fauna, and physical environment of their colonies. They also undertook a systematic makeover of urban space in the Americas, in an effort to make Mexico City, Rio de Janeiro, and other cities look more like the sophisticated metropolises of Europe. Even if they had no access to the news coming out of Philadelphia or Paris, the people of Latin America could find plenty of other evidence that they were living in an Age of Revolution.

Social Change in the Late Colonial Period

One of the most visible social changes of the late colonial period was the marked influx of peninsulares. During the seventeenth and early eighteenth centuries, growing numbers of creoles had gained entry into the ranks of the bureaucracy in the Spanish colonies. Between 1700 and 1759, 108 of the 136 men appointed judges of the audiencias were American-born. As part of their effort to bring the colonies under firmer control of the mother country, the Bourbons began to reverse that trend, especially during the reign of Charles III. In Lima, for example, there were 13 creoles and only 2 peninsulares on the audiencia in 1765, but by 1800 European judges outnumbered the Americans 12 to 2. Choice positions in the church also increasingly went to peninsulares. Twelve of Bogotá's 15 archbishops between 1704 and 1810 were Spanish-born. The growing volume of trade between Spain and the colonies attracted other Spaniards, many of them Basques, eager to make their fortunes as merchants. Ambitious creoles perceived a clear threat to their own chances for political and economic advancement, and the divisions between Spanish-born and American deepened.

In Brazil, the numbers of Portuguese immigrants also increased in the late colonial period, especially in the rapidly developing frontier regions. The Marquis of Lavradio, a Portuguese nobleman who served as viceroy of Brazil during the Pombal regime, often accused Brazilians of being lazy and ill-suited to carrying out the crown's agenda. In general, however, tensions between foreigners and those born in America were not as marked in Brazil as in the Spanish colonies.

If the distinctions between creoles and peninsulares became sharper in many places, other social barriers were undermined by the economic and political changes of the times. The newly rich eagerly spent their fortunes on landed estates and other status symbols, including titles of nobility and certificates of legitimate birth issued by the crown. Even people of questionable social and ethnic backgrounds sported elegant clothing, built impressive townhouses for themselves, and aspired to marry into prestigious families. More Spanish Americans were using the titles "Don" and "Doña" in front of their names, an indicator of social prestige. Some of the older established elites felt threatened by these changes, and attempted to protect their privileged status against these upstarts by exerting even greater control over the marriage choices of their children. The Spanish crown obliged them in 1776 by issuing a law requiring anyone under the age of 25 to have their parents' consent and permitting parents to disinherit any son or daughter who disregarded their wishes.

In many places—with the notable exception of Cuba and some parts of Brazil—the number of slaves declined in the late colonial period. Just about everywhere, the number of free blacks and mulattos grew. In the gold mining region of Antioquia in New Granada, for example, free blacks outnumbered slaves three to one according to a census compiled in the 1770s. In Venezuela and elsewhere, slave revolts and runaway communities became more numerous. It was even possible for a select few free blacks to obtain official government documents granting them the legal status of whites regardless of their color.

Military necessities of the Age of Revolution also chipped away at old social distinctions between blacks and whites. Blacks and mulattos who helped defend the Spanish empire won new privileges in colonial society. In Mexico, the people of the maroon community of Nuestra Señora de los Morenos de Amapa, most of whom were slaves who had run away from sugar plantations in the area around Veracruz received their freedom after their men joined the forces defending the port city against a possible British attack in 1762. Mulatto soldiers in Spanish Louisiana also gained recognition for their service in the capture of British-held posts in Florida during the American Revolution. In other ways, however, the defense reforms of the late colonial period undermined the role of free blacks in the military. In Mexico, white regular army officers were put in charge of free colored militias, undermining the authority of black officers who had previously commanded these forces, and in the 1790s the black units were disbanded altogether.

The cultural differences between Indians and others continued to erode as well. Late colonial censuses show declining numbers of Indians as growing numbers of people "passed" into other ethnic categories and participated more fully in the market economy, while more non-Indians took up residence in Indian villages. These changes were welcomed and encouraged by the Spanish and Portuguese crowns. Hoping to increase the population of the sparsely settled frontier regions, Pombal promoted intermarriage between Indians and non-Indians. He also encouraged Indians in these areas to work for wages and to speak Portuguese. The secular clergy who replaced the religious orders in many Indian parishes were seldom proficient in indigenous languages, and many of them probably agreed with the newly appointed bishop of Oaxaca who in 1803 lamented the fact that the people of his diocese still spoke 18 different "rough, unknown tongues." Teaching Spanish and Portuguese therefore became a matter of practical necessity, and schoolmasters were appointed to Indian villages in central and southern New Spain for precisely that purpose. By the end of the eighteenth century, few Indian villages kept official records in Nahuatl, Mixtec, or other indigenous languages.

In rapidly developing frontier regions, the distinction between "Indians" and non-Indians was even less pronounced than in Mexico or the Andes. By the beginning of the nineteenth century, Indians comprised only 13 percent of the population of central Venezuela, for example. Two-thirds of the people in Buenos Aires were classified as españoles, one-third as black or mulatto, and only about 1 percent as Indians.

The Changing Face of Colonial Cities

The economic changes of the late colonial period spurred a marked increase in the size of cities and towns all across Latin America. Mexico City, for example, had a population estimated at 137,000 in 1803, easily dwarfing such North American cities as Philadelphia, Boston, and New York. Urban growth presented city councils and imperial authorities with mounting challenges in the areas of food supply, public health, and safety. The Bourbon monarchs attempted to end what they considered the insalubrious practice of burying the dead in churches and promoted the use of new cemeteries located outside of town. After Edward Jenner developed the smallpox vaccine in Britain in the late 1790s, the practice quickly spread to Latin America.

Numerous other measures addressed the problem of crime in the streets. Mexico City expanded the capacity of municipal jails and divided the city into 32 police districts, each with its own magistrate. The number of arrests increased from about 1000 per year in 1783 to ten times that number a decade later. Bogotá established its first police force in the 1790s. Mexico City, Veracruz, and other cities also began lighting the streets at night and providing for more efficient garbage disposal. Many town councils enacted ordinances against vagrancy and begging in the streets and attempted to gather the destitute into orphanages, poorhouses, and other social welfare institutions. They also tried to control public drunkenness by imposing tighter controls on taverns.

The Bourbon kings of Spain were also concerned with the threat to public order posed by the many popular religious festivals held in cities and towns throughout the empire, and their determination to lessen the influence of the church added further incentive to reduce the number and extravagance of these observances. Efforts to suppress pre-Lenten carnival festivities began in Mexico City early in the eighteenth century. Other campaigns followed, but with limited success, for the city's elite continued as before to use festivals as a chance to flaunt their wealth, the lower classes looked forward to a change in their daily routines, and people of all social classes viewed religious holidays as a central part of their spiritual lives. Twenty-one separate processions passed through the streets of Mexico City during Holy Week in 1794.

Meanwhile, urban residents enjoyed more amenities. Streets and plazas at the center of many towns were now paved, and public fountains made water more easily available. Mexico City doubled the size of the Alameda, its public park, and inaugurated a new theater known as the Coliseum in the 1750s. Caracas even

A 1763 drawing of Mexico City's central park, the Alameda.

boasted a symphony orchestra. The naming of city streets and the numbering of buildings reflected the growing concern with imposing order on urban space.

The Enlightenment in Latin America

Cities and towns were also hubs of intellectual activity in the late colonial period. Educated elites avidly read and discussed the new ways of thinking coming out of Europe and North America. The United States Declaration of Independence, Tom Paine's pamphlet *Common Sense,* and the Federalist Papers circulated throughout Latin America, along with the British economist Adam Smith's highly influential *The Wealth of Nations,* a book that argued for free trade, and the French revolutionaries' Declaration of the Rights of Man and of the Citizen. Many others read Voltaire, Rousseau, Montesquieu, and other French Enlightenment philosophers, as well as Spanish writers who also disseminated the new ideas.

The kings of Spain and Portugal tried unsuccessfully to stop the spread of such potentially subversive ideas, especially after the French Revolution took its radical turn in the 1790s, but they enthusiastically embraced the Enlightenment's practical side and actively promoted scientific research. In 1737, Philip V sent a team of French scientists to Quito to measure degrees of latitude near the equator. Between 1799 and 1804, the German scientist Alexander von Humboldt traveled throughout Latin

America. He explored Venezuela's Orinoco River and a good portion of the Amazon Basin, climbed Mount Chimborazo in Ecuador, and reported on mining and other industries in Mexico. The Marquis of Pombal dispatched investigators to learn about the flora and fauna of Brazil, including one to the Amazon region headed by Alexandre Rodrigues Ferreira, a native Brazilian educated in Portugal. The presence of so many scientists helped Latin American intellectuals stay abreast of the latest developments in Europe.

Educational institutions also began placing greater emphasis on science and reason in place of theology, especially after the ouster of the Jesuits. Many secular and regular clergymen were in fact quite receptive to these new ideas and introduced them into the curricula of the schools they operated. The Bishop of Pernambuco, for example, set up a seminary with a program of study modeled after that of Portugal's University of Coimbra, which had become a center of the new learning under Pombal's influence. Schools operated by the Franciscans in Rio de Janeiro began offering courses in physics and natural history. New universities established at Caracas and Santiago, Chile, had medical schools.

Alexander von Humboldt.

By the late colonial period, newspapers disseminated scientific learning throughout Spanish America. The *Mercurio Peruano,* edited by the physician Hipólito Unanue, carried numerous articles on medicine, while José Antonio Alzate y Ramírez used the *Gaceta de México* to discuss ways of coping with widespread famine that resulted after a premature frost destroyed much of the maize crop in central Mexico in 1785. The papers also included political news, including substantial coverage of the events of the American Revolution that appeared in Lima's *Gaceta.* European and North American newspapers brought by trading vessels kept Spanish Americans and Brazilians informed about current events.

Meanwhile, intellectuals in the Spanish colonies and in Brazil met in informal gatherings called *tertulias* to discuss the political and scientific ideas of the age. They also established more formal clubs to explore ways stimulate local economic development. In Spanish America, these associations were usually called "Societies of Friends of the Country." The Havana society established Spanish America's first public library in 1793, and within a year it had 1500 circulating volumes. The group in Cartagena sought ways to promote the cultivation of cotton in the surrounding region.

RESISTANCE AND REBELLION IN THE LATE COLONIAL PERIOD

The enormous economic, political, and social changes of the late colonial period, the increased flow of information, and the critical spirit of the Age of Revolution prompted Latin Americans from a variety of social backgrounds to take a hard look at the situations in which they found themselves. Privileged classes objected to the high-handed tactics of colonial administrators, the preferential treatment given to peninsulares, and the taxes and other restrictions imposed on their economic activities. Creole intellectuals expressed a new pride in their homelands and looked for ways to promote true prosperity and progress at the local level. A select few suggested that their compatriots borrow a lesson or two from the North American and French revolutionaries.

People further down the social ladder had neither the education nor the leisure to ponder the works of French philosophers or the latest news from Philadelphia and Boston, but many of them were clearly aware that the changing times were making life more difficult. Taxes and military conscription hit them hard, while population increase strained land and water resources and depressed their real wages. They expressed their dissatisfaction in quite a few popular revolts in the late colonial period. For Latin Americans, the Age of Revolution was a time to evaluate their status as colonial subjects and to resist injustices both old and new.

Developing Creole Consciousness

As they became more familiar with the leading thinkers of the European Enlightenment, Latin Americans were appalled to learn that some of these great minds held the Western Hemisphere and its people in disdain. The French natural historian George-Louis Leclerc Buffon, for example, argued that the New World's climate and environment made people lazy and decrepit. For Buffon, the pre-Columbian inhabitants of the Americas were "stupid, ignorant, unacquainted with the arts and destitute of industry," and creoles were not much better. Another French writer, Guillaume-Thomas Raynal, questioned the accounts of early Spanish conquistadors who were dazzled by what they saw at Tenochtitlan and Cuzco. The Aztec capital, he wrote, was not a great city but "a little town, composed of a multitude of rustic huts," and its highly touted temples and palaces were crudely thrown together.

Creole intellectuals took these criticisms personally. They wrote lengthy treatises on the grandeur of ancient American civilizations in an effort to prove that the Western Hemisphere could nurture cultural achievements second to none. Homesick Jesuits exiled in Italy were among the leading proponents of these views. Francisco Javier Clavijero penned what he called "a history of Mexico written by a Mexican, expressly designed to answer the slanders" of writers like Buffon and Raynal. He drew on his fluency in Nahuatl to counter charges that indigenous languages lacked words to express abstract concepts and praised the intellectual abilities of Indian students he had taught at the Colegio de San Gregorio in Mexico City. His fellow Jesuit, the Ecuadorian Juan de Velasco, wrote a history of the kingdom of Quito that extolled pre-hispanic society in the Andes. The Chilean Juan Ignacio Molina cited the fertile soil and benign climate of his homeland and pointed out that Araucanian poets rivaled those of the Celts in Europe.

Creole intellectuals also grappled with the question of why the Americas had seemingly been overlooked by the Twelve Apostles after Jesus had told them to go out and "preach to all nations." They revived the sixteenth-century notion that St. Thomas had in fact traveled to the New World, and that he was the person that Mesoamericans called Quetzalcoatl. Others, including Clavijero, argued instead that the greatness of pre-Columbian Mexico owed nothing to any outside sources, not even an apostle.

Still another manifestation of growing creole self-awareness was the spread of the cult of Our Lady of Guadalupe in Mexico. Tradition claims that the Virgin Mary appeared to an Indian named Juan Diego on a hillside near Mexico City in 1531. Although historians have confirmed that some kind of shrine had been built on the site by the latter part of the sixteenth century, they have found no evidence that the Juan Diego story actually circulated in New Spain before 1648. Thereafter, however, devotion to the Virgin spread, not initially among Indians but rather among creoles who viewed the apparition as proof of divine favor for Mexico and its people. In 1754, Pope Benedict XIV proclaimed her as the patroness of all New Spain.

Resistance to the Bourbon Reforms

The new taxes and other administrative changes ordered by Charles III sparked protest and debate throughout Spanish America. In towns and cities throughout the empire, leading male citizens convened to discuss issues of concern. One such gathering took place in the town of Concepción in Chile in 1794. Those present voiced their objection to new taxes proposed by the audiencia in Santiago. Concepción's town council had not been consulted, and they were protesting taxation without representation. Throughout the empire, creole elites argued that as descendants of conquistadors and early settlers they should be appointed to government posts in place of upstarts just off the boat from Spain. Meanwhile, merchants' guilds in many towns called for an even greater liberalization of trade.

Other protests were more violent. Riots occurred in Quito in 1765, following the introduction of new taxes and other "reforms." Mobs attacked the customs house in Arequipa, Peru. In Mexico, popular uprisings followed the expulsion of the Jesuits in 1767. Spanish officials responded with exceptional force in the mining district of San Luis Potosí, ordering the execution of 85 people and the imprisonment of hundreds more.

In 1781, the people of New Granada staged a somewhat more successful opposition to the Bourbon Reforms in the so-called Comunero Revolt. They attacked tax collectors and agents of royal monopolies on tobacco, cane alcohol, and playing cards, while also demanding the appointment of more creoles to government offices. Some 20,000 rebels threatened to march on Bogotá, which was poorly defended because most of the Spanish military forces had been sent to the coast to guard against British attacks. They won a reprieve from certain taxes, and a general amnesty for all participants in the rebellion who agreed to return to their homes, except for four alleged ringleaders who were executed.

Conspiracies in Brazil

Brazilians also registered their complaints in the volatile climate of the Age of Revolution. An attempt by zealous bureaucrats in Lisbon to collect overdue tax revenues in the mining district of Minas Gerais prompted a few dozen landowners, military officers, heavily indebted tax contractors, and intellectuals in the town of Ouro Preto to conspire to revolt in 1788 and 1789. Influenced by the example of the American Revolution, the rebels proposed to create an independent, democratic republic in Minas Gerais and to do away with colonial taxes and restrictions on diamond mining and manufacturing. They offered freedom to slaves who joined the plot and planned to defend their government with a citizen militia made up of blacks and mulattos. They also hoped to establish a university and to provide various social services. When colonial authorities got wind of the plot, they exiled five of the conspirators to the Portuguese African colony at Angola. The principal ringleader, a military officer named Joaquim José da Silva Xavier, alias Tiradentes ("tooth-puller"), was publicly executed in 1789.

LATIN AMERICAN LIVES

JOSÉ GABRIEL CONDORCANQUI, TUPAC AMARU II

BORN ABOUT 1742, the mestizo José Gabriel Condorcanqui was the hereditary kuraka of the province of Tinta, south of Cuzco in the Peruvian Andes. He was fluent in Spanish and literate, and he counted numerous creoles, as well as the Bishop of Cuzco, among his wide circle of friends and associates. A muleteer with some 350 animals, he traveled widely on business, as far as Potosí in the highlands of present-day Bolivia and down to the capital at Lima on the coast. In 1780, he began a revolt that directly threatened Spanish authority in the Andes for the next 3 years and hardened the divide between native Andeans and outsiders for decades and perhaps centuries to come.

Personal grievances evidently contributed to Condorcanqui's decision to revolt against Spanish authority and the abuses of the colonial system. Back in 1766, his uncle, also a kuraka and a muleteer, had suffered confiscation of his goods because the consignment of forced (*mita*) laborers he sent to the mines at Potosí had been one man short. But Condorcanqui also concerned himself more generally with the abuses that native people throughout the greater Cuzco region had suffered under Spanish rule.

Memories of the Inca past became increasingly important to Condorcanqui as the years passed. He petitioned the audiencia in Lima for documentation of his claim that he was a direct descendant of Tupac Amaru, the native emperor executed by Spanish authorities in 1572. Although the court failed to act on his request, he proclaimed himself Tupac Amaru II and proceeded to portray himself as the heir to Peru's rightful rulers. He drew heavily on the writings of "the Inca" Garcilaso de la Vega, a sixteenth-century mestizo who had also glorified his native Andean heritage and portrayed the pre-hispanic past as a golden age of harmony and prosperity. He commissioned a portrait that showed him and his wife arrayed as the Inca royal couple and invited people to his home to witness performances of a Quechua-language drama featuring Inca characters.

Tupac Amaru II's rebellious activity cost him his life, and his death in Cuzco's central plaza on May 18, 1781, was a gruesome spectacle. First, he had to witness the executions of his wife, Manuela Bastidas, his 20-year-old son Hipólito, and six other relatives and associates. Then, the executioners cut out his tongue and fastened his legs and arms to the saddle-girths of four horses whose riders took off in four directions, eventually tearing his body to pieces. His head and other body parts and those of his companions then went on display throughout the region where the rebellion had raged, as ominous reminders to anyone who might be tempted to follow their example.

Among those forced to watch the grim ceremony was Condorcanqui's 9-year-old son, Fernando. A few years later, he and some 90 other relatives were rounded up, taken to the coast, and placed on the *San Pedro Alcántara,* a ship bound for Spain and loaded with silver and gold. The vessel wrecked off the coast of Portugal, a tragedy immortalized in 1793 by the Spanish artist Francisco de Goya in his painting *El naufragio* ("The Shipwreck"). Sixteen members of the Condorcanqui family were among the 152 people who died. Young Fernando survived, but lived the rest of his life in Spain, never returning to Peru.

Questions for Discussion

Compare Tupac Amaru II's response to Spanish colonialism to that of Felipe Guaman Poma de Ayala (see Chapter 5). Would Tupac Amaru II's protests have been more effective if he had chosen to emphasize his mestizo identity rather than his indigenous identity? Why or why not?

Another abortive conspiracy occurred about 10 years later in northeastern Brazil, when handwritten proclamations of the "supreme tribunal of Bahian democracy" appeared on churches and other public buildings in Salvador. These rebels came from lower ranks of society than their counterparts in Minas Gerais. Echoing the rhetoric of the French Revolution, they promised freedom for slaves, abolition of monasteries, and equality of all people. They also proposed free trade and an end to the "detestable metropolitan yoke of Portugal." The leader of the group was João de Deus do Nascimento, a 27-year-old free mulatto tailor. Asked about his visions for the future, he proclaimed that with "everything being leveled in a popular revolution, all would be rich, released from the misery in which they were living, discrimination between white, black, and mulatto being abolished; because all occupations and jobs would be open and available without distinction to each and every one."

Local authorities moved quickly to thwart the conspiracy, arresting 49 alleged participants. Most of those apprehended were free mulattos in their 20s, many of them tailors or other artisans, although 11 were slaves, and 10 were white; 5 of those detained were women. The movement also included a number of enlisted military personnel and militia members. Many of the conspirators were able to read and write, in a city where 90 percent of the population was illiterate. In 1799, colonial authorities ordered the public execution of Nascimento and three other key participants, while others received public whippings and some were exiled to Africa.

The Great Rebellion in Peru

The most widespread and violent of the late colonial rebellions occurred in the Andes of Peru and Bolivia in the early 1780s. The uprising had multiple causes. Population growth over the past several decades had left many native communities without sufficient land for everyone. Many Indians also harbored long-standing resentments over their continuing obligation to provide labor at the silver mines of Potosí and over the *repartimiento de mercancías,* the system that allowed local officials to profit from the sale of merchandise to native communities. Specific policies recently introduced by the Bourbon monarchy fueled additional unrest among creoles and mestizos. Buenos Aires rather than Lima had become the principal outlet for the silver of Potosí in 1776, stifling economic activity along the traditional trade routes linking Upper Peru with the Pacific Coast. Greater efficiency of local administrators meant that it was harder for everyone to evade payment of taxes both old and new.

The trouble began at Tinta, just south of the old Inca capital of Cuzco, where rebels led by the mestizo kuraka José Gabriel Condorcanqui killed the corregidor Antonio de Arriaga in November of 1780. For the next 6 months, they threatened much of highland Peru and nearly took Cuzco. The movement's leadership included many other mestizos and creoles, including many muleteers and Condorcanqui's mestiza wife, Manuela Bastidas, but Condorcanqui chose to tout his native Andean heritage. He changed his name to Tupac Amaru II, after his putative ancestor who had resisted Spanish domination and faced execution on orders of Viceroy Francisco de Toledo in 1572, and attracted thousands of Indians to his cause.

In May of 1781, Spanish authorities captured Tupac Amaru, along with several of his close associates, and sentenced him to death in the main plaza of Cuzco, precisely where his namesake had met a similar fate 200 years before. The death of Condorcanqui did not restore peace to the region, however. The rebellion continued for another 2 years in Upper Peru, where it became more radical, marked by repeated calls for the extermination of what Quechua-speakers called *puka kunka,* or "red necks," their derogatory term for Spaniards. Sometimes they indiscriminately killed anyone caught wearing Spanish-style clothing. Order returned only in 1783, when forces loyal to the regime rounded up the movement's ringleaders and put them to death.

Not all native Andeans took part in the rebellion. Ethnic rivalries dating back hundreds of years left some groups reluctant to join a movement that championed the cause of the Incas. Many natives simply saw it to their advantage to support Spanish authority, or found that they could continue get their needs met through traditional, less radical means, such as legal petitions and face-to-face dealings with local authorities. Notable kurakas remained loyal to the crown and even helped defeat the rebellion. One such leader was Mateo García Pumacahua, who provided decisive logistical support in turning back the rebels' march on Cuzco.

The rebellion of Tupac Amaru and his successors terrified Spanish authorities in the Andes. After 1783, they tried to suppress native historical memory that exalted the Incas. They banned the reading of the sixteenth-century mestizo historian Garcilaso de la Vega because his book idealized the old days and drew too critical a picture of the Spanish colonial system. When the new audiencia was established in Cuzco in 1788, local Andean nobles were invited to participate in the inauguration ceremonies, but only if they agreed to leave their traditional costumes at home and dress as Spaniards. From this point onward, racial tensions deepened in the Andes, with disastrous consequences for the formation of any kind of national unity after Peru and Bolivia became independent from Spain.

CONCLUSION

The changing political climate of the eighteenth century, especially in the period after 1763, drove the governments of Spain, Portugal, and Great Britain to reorganize their overseas empires, often to the consternation of their American subjects. In 1776, Anglo-Americans declared their independence and won it on the battle-field a few years later, but their neighbors to the south responded much more cautiously to the changes in colonial administration. Despite their numerous and highly vocal complaints and occasional recourse to violence, few Latin Americans supported a complete break with Spain or Portugal before 1800. A familiar refrain used by Spanish colonists was *"Viva el Rey y muera el mal gobierno"* ("Long live the king and death to bad government"), signifying their continued allegiance to the crown while protesting against specific abuses and particular officials. Even Tupac Amaru II invoked this rhetoric.

Various reasons have been cited to explain why Latin Americans were slower to assert their independence than Britain's North American subjects. Some have suggested that English colonists had more experience in self-government and were therefore less willing to accept new rules imposed by Parliament after 1763, but perhaps we should not carry this interpretation too far. After all, the Spanish and Portuguese colonial systems allowed considerable latitude for local officials, city councils, and ad hoc citizens' groups to protest, ignore, modify, or defy edicts sent from Madrid and Lisbon. In theory, any subject could address his or her grievances directly to the king, over the heads of colonial bureaucrats.

In any event, other more compelling factors definitely favored the cautious stance of Latin Americans. Geography played an important role. The British settlements were clustered along the Atlantic seaboard, making it relatively easy for news to travel by ship from one town to another. Most major cities of Spanish America were located inland, separated by weeks or months of arduous overland travel. South Carolinians could coordinate plans with New Englanders far more readily than residents of Mexico City could share concerns with their counterparts in Lima or Bogotá. Even in Brazil, where many important settlements were located near the Atlantic coast, the vicissitudes of ocean currents prevented towns from communicating easily with one another. Indeed, residents of Pará and Maranhão could send messages more quickly to Portugal than to Bahia or Rio de Janeiro.

The self-perceived vulnerability of Latin American elites also made them hesitant to tamper with the status quo. Many of them lived surrounded by Indians, mestizos, mulattos, and other groups whom they despised and feared, and the gap between rich and poor tended to be much wider than in the British colonies. George Washington was a wealthy slaveholder, but his three-story residence at Mount Vernon in Virginia was quite modest in comparison with the splendid homes of the great landowners and silver miners of Mexico. The slightest suggestion that the dispossessed masses might be unleashed was enough to terrify anyone with anything to lose. The ferocity of Tupac Amaru II's rebellion triggered a conservative backlash in the Andes, and Toussaint L'Ouverture's uprising in Haiti alarmed slaveholders everywhere.

Moreover, many of Latin America's elites both old and new managed to prosper in the troubled times of the Age of Revolution. Brazil, for example, experienced an economic boom as competing sugar plantations in Haiti were destroyed and wartime conditions in Europe created a huge demand for all manner of tropical produce. As we shall see in Chapter 8, only when events in Europe appeared to provide them with few other options did Latin American elites turn to the formation of independent republics.

LEARNING MORE ABOUT LATIN AMERICANS

DuBois, Laurent. *Avengers of the New World: The Story of the Haitian Revolution* (Cambridge, MA: Harvard University Press, 2004). A detailed recreation of the day-to-day events in Haiti revolution in the context of the "Age of Revolution."

Maxwell, Kenneth R. *Pombal: Paradox of the Enlightenment* (Cambridge, U.K.: Cambridge University Press, 1995). Biography of the mastermind of the Portuguese imperial reorganization of the eighteenth century.

Stavig, Ward. *The World of Túpac Amaru: Conflict, Community and Identity in Colonial Peru* (1999). A close look at the lives of ordinary men and women in the region that spawned Tupac Amaru II's rebellion.

Vinson III, Ben. *Bearing Arms for His Majesty: The Free-Colored Militia in Colonial Mexico* (Stanford, CA: Stanford University Press, 2001). Traces the formation of Mexico's black and mulatto militias and explores the roles they played in the larger society.

Viqueira Albán, Juan Pedro. *Propriety and Permissiveness in Bourbon Mexico* (Wilmington, DE: Scholarly Resources, 1999). An examination of popular culture in eighteenth-century Mexico City, including bullfights, dancing, gambling, ball games, and popular religious devotions.

Weber, David J. *Bárbaros: Spaniards and Their Savages in the Age of Enlightenment* (New Haven: Yale University Press, 2005). A leading scholar of the Spanish American frontier examines attitudes and policies toward unsubdued Indians in the eighteenth century.

8

THE NEW NATIONS
OF LATIN AMERICA

FOR 300 YEARS, Spain and Portugal ruled their enormous American empires with few serious challenges from people living in the colonies. But within less than two decades between 1808 and 1824, Brazil and most of Spanish America won independence, leaving Spain with just two islands, Cuba and Puerto Rico, and Portugal with nothing. From Mexico to Argentina, the new nations of Spanish America emerged from drawn out, hard-fought wars, costly both in terms of lives lost and damage to the economic infrastructure (roads, buildings, mines). Brazil's independence came somewhat less violently, in 1822, when a son of Portugal's king agreed to become emperor of the new nation, but there too the years since 1808 had witnessed considerable political turmoil.

The movements for independence in Latin America resulted from the convergence of two sets of factors, one international and the other internal to the individual colonies. Although the most important cause of the rebellions for independence was the demand from Latin Americans to obtain more control over their daily lives, as manifested in local governance and practice of traditions, the timing of the independence movements depended to a considerable extent on events that occurred in the metropolises and in the rest of Europe.

The specific character of the struggles for independence and the kinds of nations that emerged varied greatly across Latin America, reflecting the tremendous geographical and historical diversity of the region. The independence movements were bitterly divided along class and racial lines. Wealthy creoles (people who claimed European descent, though born in the Americas) needed tactical support from the lower classes to win the battles against Spain and Portugal and in the

245

TIMELINE

1788
Charles IV takes the throne of Spain

1789
French Revolution

1791
Haitian Revolution

1807–1808
Napoleon's armies invade Portugal and Spain

1810
Hidalgo begins Mexican War of Independence

1812
New Spanish Constitution

1821
Mexican independence

1822
Brazilian independence

1824
Battle of Ayacucho ends wars of independence

political struggles of nation-building that ensued. But they despised the masses of poor Indians, blacks, and *castas* (racially mixed people) that surrounded them. One of the principal reasons why the Spanish and Portuguese empires endured so long was that upper-class whites were terrified that any act of rebellion against the mother country might unleash popular unrest that could easily turn against them.

Creole fears were anything but groundless. The colonies were sharply split between the haves and the have-nots, and the gap had widened in many parts of Latin America during the last few decades of the eighteenth century. Popular discontent had mounted accordingly, usually meeting brutal repression by colonial governments and the creole upper class. When external events finally began unraveling the ties that bound the colonies to Spain and Portugal, lower classes joined the battles, but with their own agendas in mind. Their specific objectives varied from place to place, but included the abolition of slavery, an end to special taxes levied on Indians, and land reform.

The movements for Latin American independence divided on geographical lines as well. The racially and ethnically diverse people of the countryside thought mostly in terms of local autonomy at the village level and at least initially paid relatively little heed to the ideas of nationhood being hatched by the creole upper classes in the larger cities and towns. The upper classes had their own local and regional loyalties as well. Peruvians and Venezuelans and Argentines all distrusted one another, and people who lived in towns across southern South America resented the domination of Buenos Aires. All of the divisions—racial, social, economic, and geographical—that became so evident during the wars for independence were to shape Latin American politics for much of the nineteenth century.

SPANISH AMERICA AND THE CRISIS OF 1808

The external events that precipitated Latin American independence had their roots in the profound transformations that occurred in Europe and North America during the last half of the eighteenth century and the beginning of the nineteenth century, a period known to historians as the Age of Revolution. The American Revolution, the French Revolution of 1789, and the slave uprising in the French colony of Saint Domingue, which gave birth to Haiti, the world's first black republic, affected how Latin Americans viewed their world and the perceptions and actions of metropolitan monarchs and colonial administrators. Napoleon Bonaparte's campaigns to extend French control throughout Western Europe, and the struggle of Great Britain and its allies to thwart him, had profound consequences for Spain, Portugal, and Latin America. Napoleon's invasion of the Iberian Peninsula in 1807 and 1808 provided the catalyst for the Latin American movements for independence.

Spain and the Napoleonic Invasion

In the 20 years leading up to Napoleon's decision to cross the Pyrenees, Spain experienced considerable political turmoil, beginning in 1788 with the death of King Charles III, an energetic monarch who had spearheaded major changes in the administration of his vast empire during his 29-year reign. His successor, Charles IV, proved much less capable, and he had barely assumed the throne when revolutionaries in France overthrew King Louis XVI and inaugurated a "reign of terror" that sent thousands of their countrymen to the guillotine, including the king himself. In 1793, Spain joined its traditional enemy England in a 2-year war to stop the new French regime from exporting its radical ideas to the rest of Europe. After 1796, however, the regime in France took a more conservative turn, and Charles IV and his ministers reverted to their traditional policy of supporting France against the British.

Spanish subjects at home and abroad then endured more than a decade of nearly constant war and the heavy burden of taxation that war demanded. British naval blockades interrupted trade between Spain and the colonies. Confronted with rising domestic opposition and a French invasion in 1808, Charles IV abdicated in favor of his son Ferdinand, who in secret had plotted against him. Napoleon, however, forced both to surrender their claims to the throne and installed his brother Joseph Bonaparte as king of Spain.

Most people in Spain and the colonies did not regard Joseph as their rightful monarch and instead asserted that sovereignty lay in the hands of the people as long as their rightful king remained captive. They experimented with various forms of representative government from 1808 until Napoleon was defeated and Ferdinand VII returned to power in 1814. The 6-year interlude of self-rule convinced many colonists that they were fully capable of governing themselves. Creoles, in particular, came to the realization that Spanish governance only siphoned off revenues better used at home and that the cost of colonial administration was so detrimental that it was worth the risk of rebellion.

Representative Government in Spain and America, 1808–1814

As French troops advanced into Spain in the spring of 1808, Spaniards waged guerrilla warfare against the invading forces. Cities and towns throughout the country

How Historians Understand   WERE THE WARS OF INDEPENDENCE THE TURNING POINT?

Periodization—the dividing of history into segments and identifying crucial turning points—is a major device historians use to explain and simplify the past. Traditionally, historians have considered the Latin American wars of independence between 1808 and 1825 as the crucial watershed in the region's history, and many Latin American history courses are divided into terms focusing on the colonial and national periods. This interpretation inferred that Latin America abruptly ended its colonial era and entered into modern times with a sharp break from Spain and Portugal. We know, however, that while independence hastened many transformations already underway during the previous century, all vestiges of the colonial order did not disappear in the 1820s. Slavery and discrimination against indigenous peoples endured well past independence, and many laws and government procedures carried over from the colonial regimes to the new nation states. Puerto Rico and Cuba remained colonies of Spain until after 1898. The traditional division of eras obscured critical continuities and made it difficult to assess the effects of change.

During the 1960s, an alternative approach arose, viewing the independence era as part of a broader period stretching from approximately 1720 or

Bernardo O'Higgins, Chilean leader who symbolized the efforts of the colonial elite to maintain its power after Independence.

1750 to 1850. This "Middle Period" incorporated the transition from traditional to modern society and from colonial to independent politics. The newly configured century allowed historians to trace the evolution of the trends and forces that caused the independence movements and to evaluate the impact of the end of colonial rule.

Investigating the half-centuries before and after independence has elucidated a number of new themes and hypotheses. First, traditional assumptions that the Spanish Empire was peaceful in the century before 1810 were incorrect. In the Mexican countryside, for example, there was constant unrest. Second, colonial rule was far from omnipotent. Historians had long ago documented corruption and inefficiency, but recent explorations have revealed the considerable extent of local autonomy. We have only scratched the surface of understanding to what degree the innovations introduced by the Spanish Bourbon kings and their counterparts in Portugal not only disrupted accommodations reached earlier, but also began processes of change that independent governments built on after 1830. The Iberian monarchs of the eighteenth century, for example, took steps to reduce the power and political influence of the Catholic Church in Latin America. Many independent governments in the nineteenth and twentieth centuries continued to pursue this objective. Economic development, especially that of frontier regions, was a major concern of late colonial kings and independent governments alike.

While the inclusion of the wars of independence as part of a longer period and as part of longer historical processes has provided much new knowledge and many new insights, the more traditional periodization (adopted by the authors of this text) has considerable advantages. First, the break with Spain and Portugal had an enormous political impact. As we will see in Chapter 9, it set off decades of conflict over who was to rule and how. Independent governments tried for a century to establish their legitimacy and control. Moreover, there is little doubt that the wars of independence were economically cataclysmic. The damage to property and people over the course of nearly two decades of sporadic (and in some places incessant) fighting was enormous. It required nearly the entire century to recover to the level of production and prosperity in 1800. Independent Latin America had broken significantly from the past and begun a new era.

Questions for Discussion

What examples of significant historical turning points can you think of that have occurred during your own lifetime? What has changed? What continuities are there? Is periodization a useful tool for understanding history? Why or why not?

formed political bodies known as *juntas* to govern in place of King Ferdinand. They also established a central junta that claimed to speak for the entire Spanish nation and presumably the overseas territories as well. Politically active Spaniards soon began calling for the reestablishment of the Cortes, a parliamentary body that had existed in medieval times but had not met for three centuries. Anxious to win support from Spanish subjects in the colonies, they invited Americans to send representatives to the meetings of the central junta and the Cortes. The latter body first convened in the city of Cádiz in September of 1810, and over the next few years it enacted sweeping political changes for Spain and Spanish America. The most important of these was the writing of a constitution in 1812, a document proclaiming that even if Ferdinand VII were restored to power, he would henceforth rule as a constitutional monarch, in consultation with representatives chosen by the people, thus ending the days of absolutist monarchy.

Americans needed no prodding from Spain to take matters into their own hands in this time of political crisis. Juntas comprised mostly of creoles appeared in cities and towns throughout the empire as soon as news of Ferdinand's captivity reached them. All of these bodies proclaimed their loyalty to Ferdinand. Many, however, objected to any form of subservience to the ad hoc government in Spain, arguing that they were not colonies but separate kingdoms fully equal to Castile, León, Navarre, Catalonia, and the other peninsular territories that comprised the realm of the Spanish monarch. They were technically correct, for only in the time of Charles III had Spanish bureaucrats begun using the term "colonies" in reference to the overseas possessions.

This sentiment for autonomy gathered strength in early 1810, when a series of French victories forced the Spanish central junta to dissolve itself in favor of a five-member Council of Regency. Americans favoring local autonomy feared that the French armies might overwhelm all Spanish resistance and then Napoleon might impose his regime on the overseas kingdoms. In some places, politically active groups moved quickly to an outright break with Spain. Town councils in Venezuela, for example, convened a national congress that declared independence in July of 1811.

Other Americans preferred to cooperate with the ad hoc government in Spain and welcomed the opportunity to send spokesmen to the sessions of the central junta and the Cortes. Men in cities and towns all over Spanish America participated enthusiastically in elections. The Constitution of 1812 permitted the formation of elected municipal councils (cabildos) in all towns with 1000 or more residents. Hundreds of cities exercised that option. In Mexico, for example, only 20 communities had had cabildos prior to the enactment of the Constitution, while afterwards that number rose to nearly 900. Eighteen new cabildos were formed in Puerto Rico, and dozens more in the highlands of Ecuador. This process empowered men in Latin America as never before.

Women, however, were excluded from participating in elections until well into the twentieth century.

The "American Question"

The disruptions to the rule of the monarchy between 1808 and 1814 provided the first practical demonstration of the principles of popular sovereignty and a taste of active political participation for the colonies. Autonomy without independence, however, proved impractical. Moreover, the inherent distrust that both creoles and Spaniards felt toward indigenous and casta peoples permeated the discussions.

The first objections to American autonomy arose in the heated debates over how many American delegates the Cortes would include. Authors of the Constitution of 1812 assumed they would allocate representation according to population. Americans easily outnumbered Spaniards, but they included large numbers of Indians and racially mixed people. Were all of these groups to be allowed to vote or even to be counted for purposes of representation? The Constitution of 1812 gave the franchise to Indian and mestizo men but not to castas, whom it defined as people with any trace of African ancestry (Latin Americans themselves used this term to describe many types of racially mixed people). It also excluded felons, debtors, and domestic servants—provisions that might eliminate many Indians and mestizos, and even some people of Spanish extraction, from the political process. Many American upper-class people feared the empowerment of castas and others they considered their social inferiors. Thus, the creoles were torn between their need to assure that their own concerns would receive ample hearing in the emerging political debate and their overwhelming fear of the lower classes. Full representation of all people regardless of ethnicity would have given the Western Hemisphere a three-to-two majority in the Cortes. Not surprisingly, Spaniards opposed this prospect.

The Spaniards prevailed on the question of representation, retaining control of the new parliament and using that advantage whenever their position differed from that of the Americans. One particularly divisive issue was the freedom to trade with all nations, a right that Spain's American colonies had never enjoyed. Spanish merchants preferred to maintain existing rules that allowed Americans to trade legally only with other Spanish subjects. Other American demands included the abolition of crown monopolies and, most crucially, equal access to jobs in the government, the military, and the church.

As they witnessed Spanish intransigence on issues such as representation and freedom of trade, even those Americans who initially favored some degree of cooperation with the new government moved toward a stance of greater self-determination for the overseas territories. Once they began to assert themselves politically, few Spanish Americans were willing to go back to old routines of subservience to the mother country. In the words of Simón Bolívar, a major leader of the independence movement in South America, by 1815 "the habit of obedience … [had] been severed."

SPANISH AMERICAN GRIEVANCES AND THE CRISIS OF 1808

The uncertainty caused by the French invasion of the mother country exacerbated political and social tensions that had festered in the Spanish colonies for several decades. In many places, eighteenth-century population growth had magnified pressures on relatively scarce land and water resources and heightened tension between Indian villages and wealthy landowners. One historian counted at least 150 village riots between 1700 and 1820 in central Mexico, two-thirds of them after 1760. A major uprising led by a man who claimed to be descended from the last Inca emperor spread throughout a good part of present-day Peru and Bolivia in the early 1780s.

Administrative changes introduced by Kings Charles III and IV added to the tensions in the colonies. In a sweeping series of innovations known collectively as the Bourbon Reforms, so named because the kings belonged to the same extended Bourbon dynasty that ruled France, they restructured the way they governed the overseas territories. They wished to bind the colonies more closely to the mother country, step up the defense of the empire from foreign enemies, curb the wealth and power of the Catholic Church, and increase the flow of revenue into the royal coffers. New taxes hit everyone regardless of class or ethnicity. Lower-class men feared conscription into new standing armies created for the empire's defense, while creoles chafed under the administration of newly arrived Spanish-born bureaucrats, who cared little for either past practice or American interests. Angry about the new royal monopolies on tobacco, cane alcohol, playing cards, and gunpowder, mobs pillaged government buildings and attacked royal officials in Mexico, the highlands of Ecuador, and New Granada (present-day Colombia). The expulsion of the powerful religious order known as the Jesuits in 1767 spurred additional violence, especially in Mexico. Crackdowns on popular religious expression, political dissent, and labor unrest added to the general climate of discontent.

The disruption of Spanish sovereignty in 1808 brought all of these grievances to the forefront and sparked different kinds of revolts in the colonies. Three of the most important of these upheavals, each with its own special character but all with important implications for the future independence of Latin America, occurred in Mexico, Argentina, and Venezuela.

Mexico

The kinds of political, social, and economic changes that Latin Americans experienced at the beginning of the nineteenth century were especially apparent in the region of Mexico known as the Bajío, located between 100 and 200 miles northwest of Mexico City. As the colony's population grew in the late colonial period, wealthy individuals had invested in the commercial production of wheat, maize, and other crops, taking advantage of the area's rich soil and its proximity to the principal urban markets of New Spain. To expand their estates, these landowners forced many poor sharecroppers and other small farmers off the land.

At the same time, people who had worked in the region's many cloth factories and artisans who had made textiles in their own homes lost their livelihoods when the Spanish crown eased trade restrictions and opened the Mexican market to cheaper merchandise manufactured abroad. Production at the Bajío's silver mines also declined sharply as the new century began, leaving thousands of workers without jobs. Meanwhile, droughts and crop failures added to the misery. In the worst of these agricultural crises, from 1785 to 1786, almost 15 percent of the Bajío's population died of hunger. A new round of crop failures struck the region in 1809. The combined effects of economic change and natural disaster left thousands of people with little left to lose as the nineteenth century began.

An 1812 flyer recruiting Mexican women to join in the struggle for independence. The caption reads: "To war, American women, let's go with merciless swords to kill Callejas [a royalist commander] and to join up with Señor Morelos."

Father Miguel Hidalgo y Costilla was a priest in the Bajío, in the town of Dolores, about 20 miles from the old silver mining town of Guanajuato. Born in 1753 to a middle-class creole family, Hidalgo had his own grudges against Spanish authority. He had received his early education at the hands of the Jesuits, and their expulsion from Mexico angered him and many others of his class. As an adult, he read the books of French Enlightenment thinkers who disputed the divine right of kings to exact unquestioning obedience from their subjects. His unorthodox ideas got him dismissed from his position as rector of a college in Valladolid (today, Morelia), one of the principal towns of the Bajío, and he narrowly escaped prosecution by the Inquisition. Policies of the Spanish king also hurt him in the pocketbook. He owned a small hacienda, but in 1804 royal officials seized his property when he could not pay special taxes levied to meet Spain's rising costs of defending itself against Napoleon. Meanwhile, Hidalgo took up his post as parish priest in Dolores. There he tried to promote new industries such as ceramics, tanning, and silk production to help his parishioners to weather the economic hard times they were facing. He also continued to meet with other intellectuals conversant with Enlightenment ideas and disgruntled with the Spanish monarchy.

Hidalgo's concerns and those of many other people in the surrounding region merged with the international crisis provoked by Napoleon's invasion of Spain. Since 1808, the government in Mexico City had been in the hands of conservative forces who favored maintaining ties with Spain at all costs. Father Hidalgo joined one of many conspiracies to overthrow them, and when authorities learned of his plans he decided to take the preemptive strike of declaring open revolt in his famous "Grito de Dolores" on September 16, 1810. Word of his rebellion quickly spread among the desperate and dispossessed classes in the Bajío. Within a few days, Hidalgo enlisted thousands of supporters who held a variety of grievances against the status quo. At its height, his army included 60,000 people, of whom about 55 percent were Indians and 20 percent were mestizos. In the words of historian Eric Van Young, many rural people joined Hidalgo's insurgency, and the many revolts that followed because they were "driven by hunger and unemployment, pulled into the maelstrom of violence by the prospect of daily wages in the rebel forces, the easy pickings of looting, or simply to escape from depressed conditions at home." The Indian rebels also wanted to retain control over their own communities, and for the most part, they did not stray far from their homes to fight. Their concern was less with independence from Spain than with local power and traditional values.

Hidalgo's forces sacked several towns and killed hundreds of Spanish men, women, and children who had taken refuge in the municipal grain warehouse in Guanajuato. Creole elites, some of whom had once flirted with the cause of autonomy, recoiled in horror at the violent turn of events and joined forces with pro-Spanish authorities in Mexico City to crush the insurrection. Within a few months, they captured and executed Hidalgo, but another priest, José María Morelos, continued the fight, controlling virtually all of southern Mexico from 1811 until his defeat in 1815. Followers of Morelos, in particular the casta Vicente Guerrero, then continued guerrilla operations against Spanish authorities for several more years, but continued Spanish control seemed almost certain. It would take another round of events in Spain to propel Mexico toward the final step of independence.

Venezuela

The Bourbon Reforms included an emphasis on the economic development of formerly peripheral parts of the empire. Venezuela was one such region. Cacao production flourished as the popularity of chocolate grew in Europe during the eighteenth century. Its principal city, Caracas, became the seat of a new audiencia, or court of appeals, created in 1786.

Creole upper-class men in Caracas began efforts to create a self-governing junta in 1808 but succeeded only in the spring of 1810, when they overthrew the audiencia and the Spanish governor. A year later, they officially declared independence, created a three-man executive body, and drafted a constitution that excluded the lower classes from political participation. The new government lasted just a year. After a powerful earthquake hit Caracas in 1812, royalists regained control after convincing the popular classes that God was punishing Venezuela for its disregard for divinely constituted authority.

The young creole aristocrat Simón Bolívar took command of the forces favoring independence and began a campaign to retake Venezuela in the spring of 1813. Like so many others of his social standing, Bolívar detested the lower classes, and his enemies eagerly took advantage of this situation. In 1814, he suffered a humiliating defeat by royalist armies led by a black man named José Tomás Boves and comprised largely of black and mulatto *llaneros* (plainsmen, cowboys by trade) angered at the harsh treatment they had received at the hands of those favoring an independent republic. Boves himself had suffered imprisonment by the insurgents in 1810. Now 4 years later, his "Legion of Hell" slaughtered wealthy creoles. Boves died on the battlefield, but his troops routed Bolívar and forced him into exile. In Venezuela as in Mexico, the outlook for independence looked grim as Ferdinand VII returned to power in Madrid in 1814.

Argentina

Like Venezuela, southern South America and the port town of Buenos Aires reaped significant benefits from the Bourbon kings' efforts to develop the empire's periphery. Formerly subject to the authority of the Spanish viceroy in Lima, Peru, in 1776 Buenos Aires became the seat of a newly created viceroyalty. The port now became the principal outlet through which silver from Bolivia and hides and tallow from the vast plains of Argentina and Uruguay reached markets abroad. The town's merchants also enjoyed abundant opportunities for contraband with British and Portuguese traders. The population of Buenos Aires quadrupled in the last half of the eighteenth century, reaching almost 40,000 by 1800.

Merchants and civic leaders took pride in the growing prosperity of their community. That sentiment deepened in 1806, when local citizens organized themselves and many of Buenos Aires's blacks and mulattos to drive out a British naval force that had taken control of the city. The following year, this combined militia thwarted yet another British invasion and forced the British to evacuate the city of Montevideo, across the Río de la Plata estuary from Buenos Aires, as well.

Creole militia officers thus positioned themselves to play key roles in the politics of Buenos Aires in the volatile years that followed the Napoleonic invasion of Spain. They figured prominently in a gathering of some 250 members of the town's upper class in May of 1810. That meeting produced a new governing junta that proclaimed nominal allegiance to Ferdinand VII, but in fact Spanish authority had ended in Buenos Aires, never to reappear. Those who dared to voice opposition to the patriot agenda were soon silenced.

SPANISH AMERICAN INDEPENDENCE

Buenos Aires was the exception, however. Only there, at the southernmost extreme of the empire, did prospects for the political independence of Spanish America seem good when Ferdinand resumed the throne. Everywhere else, the cause of independence appeared doomed. Hidalgo and Morelos were dead in Mexico, and within a few years thousands of those who had fought beneath their banners accepted amnesty from the crown. Bolívar had fled to Jamaica and King Ferdinand sent new armies to crush the Venezuelan rebellion once and for all. Once again, however, the determination of Latin Americans to assert control over their own affairs combined with events in Europe to bring about independence.

The Final Campaigns

When Ferdinand returned to power, he dissolved the Cortes and rejected the Constitution of 1812. These actions reinforced the determination of those Americans who had decided to break with the mother country and disillusioned those who had hoped he would be a just and fair monarch attentive to the concerns of all his subjects. Despite the many setbacks they had experienced, Americans persisted in their efforts to wear down the strength and morale of Spanish military forces.

Meanwhile, in Spain, Ferdinand's absolutist policies and the unpopular war in America led liberal politicians and army officers in 1820 to force the king to

accept the 1812 Constitution and reconvene the Cortes. This led to the formation of provincial governments and elections to the Cortes supervised by those
governments in areas loyal to Spain. But Spain's new leaders proved unwilling
to grant the overseas kingdoms an equal voice in government or the liberalization of trade that Americans had long demanded.

The way now lay open for the Americas to make their final break with Spain.
In Mexico, the flurry of political activity among the lower classes, once again
enfranchised by the resumption of constitutional government, alarmed Mexican
conservatives who remembered the excesses of Hidalgo's forces in Guanajuato
and elsewhere. At the same time, the upper classes began contemplating a pragmatic partnership with lower-class groups. A decisive moment came in February
1821, when the royalist general Agustín de Iturbide switched sides, forming an
alliance with the rebel leader Vicente Guerrero, who had carried on guerrilla operations against royalist forces following the death of Morelos. Iturbide's proclamation of independence, known as the Plan de Iguala, was designed to calm
conservatives. He proposed independence for Mexico and the creation of a constitutional monarchy. He also promised protection to the Catholic Church and to
all Europeans in Mexico who agreed to support him. Over the next several

ENTRADA TRIUNPAL DE ITURBIDE EN MEXICO

Iturbide's triumphal entrance into Mexico City, 1821.

JOSÉ ANTONIO APONTE, SCULPTOR OF HAVANA

THE EARLY MONTHS OF 1812 were difficult ones for Spanish authorities in Latin America. José María Morelos's rebellion raged in Mexico, self-governing juntas controlled major cities throughout the hemisphere, and political activists in the mother country contemplated a new constitutional form of government that could bring major changes to colonial administration. Meanwhile, Cuban elites and government officials faced the particularly frightening prospect not only of a pro-independence movement (indeed, they had quashed one such conspiracy already), but also of a series of slave revolts then sweeping across the island. They feared a reenactment of the revolution that had violently ended slavery in the neighboring French colony of Saint-Domingue 20 years previously and ultimately resulted in the creation of the independent nation of Haiti, governed by people of color.

Cuba had changed dramatically in the half-century prior to 1812. The expansion of sugar cultivation had transformed the island from a relatively poor colony, whose greatest importance to Spain lay in its strategic position along shipping routes connecting the two hemispheres, into a thriving plantation colony dependent on slavery and the continued importation of new slaves from Africa. The possibility of a massive slave revolt threatened to destroy Cuba's newly found prosperity.

On March 19, 1812, local officials in Havana arrested José Antonio Aponte, a free black man in his early 50s, and charged him with coordinating the rebellions. Aponte was literate and a carpenter and sculptor by trade. His carved religious statues and altarpieces graced many of the city's churches. Like many other black artisans of his generation, he had served in the free black militia, a force that over the preceding decades had played an increasingly important role in defending the Spanish colonies against foreign adversaries. Aponte attained the rank of captain prior to his retirement in 1800. A highlight of his military career was his participation in a campaign against the British in the Bahamas in 1782, when Spain had joined France in supporting the United States war for independence. Aponte took considerable pride in his military service and the special status that it conferred. He possessed copies of royal ordinances outlining the specific rights that militia members enjoyed in Spanish colonial society.

A key piece of evidence against Aponte was a *libro de pinturas,* a scrapbook found in his home. Although the book itself has been lost, historians have reconstructed its contents from thousands of pages of testimony that he and other alleged conspirators gave at their trials. There were sketches of his own military exploits and those of his father and grandfather and maps of Havana showing the location of military garrisons. Another series of illustrations, hand-copied by Aponte from printed engravings or cut from published books, revealed his considerable familiarity with the revolutionary events that had transpired in Europe and the Americas during his lifetime. Alongside a portrait of George Washington were the likenesses of Toussaint L'Ouverture and other leaders of the Haitian Revolution. Perhaps even more disturbing to Spanish authorities were the drawings that depicted black soldiers fighting whites and a crown and scepter overrun by vipers. Another image showed the king of Spain meeting with two black soldiers and informing them that they need not remove their hats in his presence–an open challenge to militia regulations that required black members to show signs of deference to white soldiers. The subversive nature of Aponte's scrapbook convinced colonial authorities that he had been the ringleader of the entire series of rebellions.

Other circumstantial evidence confirmed Aponte's guilt in the eyes of his accusers. Among his neighbors and known associates were several persons active in groups known as the *cabildos de nación.* Organized along ethnic affiliations of African origin, the cabildos brought together free blacks and slaves, both men and women. They put on festivals and dances that drew the Afro-Cuban community together, and served as mutual aid societies, helping members buy their freedom or pay funeral expenses. The cabildos also provided a vehicle for maintaining African cultural and religious traditions. Some historians have claimed that Aponte was a leader of a cabildo, but the most thorough recent study finds no concrete evidence that he even belonged to one of the organizations.

Prosecuting authorities evidently considered the question of his cabildo membership of no importance, for they declined even to question him on the matter. For them, it was enough that he was an outspoken black man whose personal papers suggested a willingness to challenge the status quo. With the expansion of Cuba's slave-based plantation economy, the social position of free blacks like Aponte had deteriorated. While not all free blacks supported the abolition of slavery, and a few even owned slaves themselves, Cuban elites panicked at any suggestion that the two groups might collaborate in a revolutionary enterprise. José Antonio Aponte served as a convenient scapegoat and was sentenced to death by hanging. On April 9, 1812, he and several alleged coconspirators went to the gallows, and afterwards their severed heads were prominently displayed as a warning to others who might harbor similar ideas.

The so-called Aponte rebellion helped convince several generations of white elites in Cuba that they needed the continued presence of Spanish authorities to prevent the island from going the way of Haiti. The phrase "worse than Aponte" signified extreme brutality in the minds of nineteenth-century white Cubans. While the rest of Spain's American colonies became independent by the 1820s, Cuba and Puerto Rico–another burgeoning slave society–retained their colonial status until 1898. The importation of slaves continued until 1867, and slavery itself was not abolished until 1886. Government concessions to Cuban elites on issues such as taxes and trade

(continued on next page)

JOSÉ ANTONIO APONTE, SCULPTOR OF HAVANA *(continued from previous page)*

further sealed their loyalty. But if José Antonio Aponte and thousands of other Afro-Cubans had had their way, Cuba might have joined the ranks of independent Latin American nations much sooner, and people of color would have become full participants in the island's new government.

Questions for Discussion

Suppose that José Antonio Aponte had had the opportunity to meet with the various leaders of Latin American independence movements discussed in this chapter. With which leaders would he have had most in common? With which leaders would he have had least in common? Brazil and the United States became independent yet remained slave societies. Was this a viable option for Cuba? Why or why not? Why would free people of color such as Aponte support a slave revolt? Why might they oppose such a revolt?

months, Spanish authority simply collapsed in New Spain, as entire units of the army defected and joined Iturbide. In September of 1821, exactly 300 years after the Spanish conquest of Mexico, Iturbide entered Mexico City in triumph. Meanwhile, the people of Guatemala and the rest of Central America declared their independence from Spain and temporarily became part of Mexico.

In South America, Simón Bolívar returned to Venezuela in 1816 and scored major victories against the Spanish. A key reason for his success was his decision to use black troops, a tactical reversal of his prior refusal to allow them a role in the struggle for independence. Forces that Bolívar recruited with the assistance of Haitian president Alexandre Pétion, in return for a promise that he would abolish slavery in the new nation, helped turn the tide in Venezuela after 1815. Thousands of llaneros also joined with Bolívar at this critical juncture. By 1822, he had assured the independence of the Republic of Gran Colombia, consisting of present-day Colombia as well as Venezuela and Ecuador. He liberated Quito, Ecuador, in 1822.

Meanwhile, the cause of independence won new victories in southern South America, led by José de San Martín, an Argentine-born officer in the Spanish army who had fought against Napoleon in Spain but returned home to join the independence struggle in 1812. San Martín's army set up camp at Cuyo at the base of the Andes in western Argentina, gathering to its side many refugees who had fled Chile after the Spanish had quashed an independence revolt there. After 3 years of careful preparations, in January of 1817, San Martín led 5500 troops through treacherous mountain passes, some at altitudes approaching 15,000 feet above sea level, to Chile. Decisive victories over Spanish forces then paved the way for Chile's final independence in 1818.

A monument at the waterfront in Guayaquil, Ecuador, commemorating the meeting of South American independence leaders Simón Bolívar and José de San Martín there in 1822.

Chile in turn became the launching pad for San Martín's naval assault on Peru, an expedition that failed to yield immediate results because royalist forces were well entrenched and many Peruvians who supported independence distrusted Argentine and Chilean patriots. In 1821, however, Peruvian creoles declared independence and accepted San Martín as military and civil ruler for the time being, but royalist forces remained firmly in control of much territory in Peru.

San Martín and Bolívar were both strong-willed men and rivals for control of the independence movement in South America. They met in Guayaquil, on the coast of Ecuador, in 1822. At issue was the status of Guayaquil itself, whether this valuable port and naval base would be part of Gran Colombia, under Bolívar's control, or Peru, which San Martín obviously preferred. The Argentine general also hoped that Bolívar would provide troops to assist him in his campaigns against royalist forces in Peru. Bolívar's military position was far stronger, and he won the debate on both counts. In fact, the Guayaquil encounter led to San Martín's withdrawal from the independence struggle. Undisputed leadership of the movement then fell to Bolívar, who occupied Lima in September of 1823. Bolívar's lieutenant, Antonio José de Sucre, won the final victory for South American independence at Ayacucho, high in the Peruvian Andes, in December of 1824. A few months later, royalist troops stationed in Upper Peru (present-day Bolivia) accepted a general amnesty and agreed to become part of a new republican army of Bolivia.

Regional Conflicts in the Spanish American Struggle for Independence

The surrender of the royalist armies in Upper Peru in 1825 ended Spanish sovereignty in all of the Americas except for Cuba and Puerto Rico. The new republics that replaced the Spanish empire were taking shape, although their final boundaries underwent numerous alterations throughout the nineteenth century and beyond. The nation-states that emerged were the products of age-old local rivalries that drove Spanish Americans apart even as they fought for the common cause of independence. The movement for independence remained rooted in the desire of people from many different social classes to remain in control of their own communities.

Throughout the struggle for independence, the ad hoc governments created in major cities claimed to speak for entire provinces, but smaller towns resisted their domination. Declarations of "independence" proliferated, but the authors of these manifestos often meant independence from Lima or Buenos Aires or Mexico City, and not necessarily from Spain. Under royalist control in 1810, Quito formed a superior junta to preserve the kingdom for Ferdinand VII, to defend the Catholic faith against godless revolutionaries from France, and, as they put it, "to seek all the well-being possible for the nation and the *patria.*" For them the word "nation" meant all subjects of the Spanish crown, while the "patria," literally translated as "fatherland," was the Kingdom of Quito, free and independent from the viceregal capitals of Lima and Bogotá. Meanwhile, other towns in the Ecuadorian highlands in turn proclaimed *their* independence from Quito.

In southern South America, many places resisted the hegemony of Buenos Aires, where forces favoring autonomy from the mother country were firmly in control. Paraguay declared itself an "independent republic" in 1813, but again, the issue of concern was independence from Buenos Aires. Montevideo also separated from Buenos Aires, paving the way for an independent nation of Uruguay. People in Upper Peru (present-day Bolivia) faced a double threat to their ability to control their own destinies. This silver-rich region had been ruled from Lima for more than 200 years, but in 1776 it became part of the new viceroyalty of La Plata, headquartered in Buenos Aires. Now Bolivians took up arms to win freedom from both their present and their former capitals.

The authoritarian actions of governments established in the major cities contributed to these rapidly multiplying struggles for local autonomy. Leaders who were radical when it came to asserting full and outright independence from Spain often served as mouthpieces for the colonial upper class intent on maintaining a firm grip on outlying provinces and on the Indian and casta masses. They restricted the vote to a select few, stifled dissent, and claimed dictatorial powers for themselves. Ironically, it was in the areas controlled by forces loyal to Spain where the very liberal voting provisions of the Constitution of 1812 were most often enforced. In Quito, for example, the same general who had crushed a local

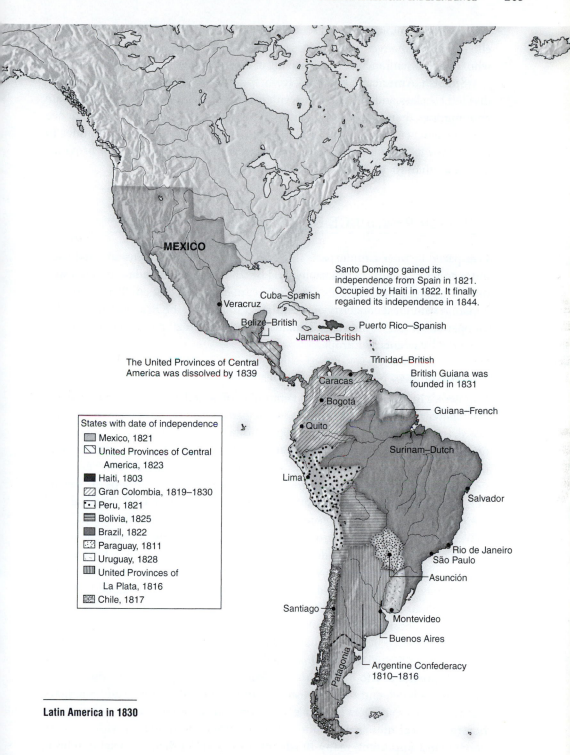

MEXICO

Veracruz

Cuba–Spanish

Belize–British

Jamaica–British

Puerto Rico–Spanish

Santo Domingo gained its
independence from Spain in 1821.
Occupied by Haiti in 1822. It finally
regained its independence in 1844.

The United Provinces of Central
America was dissolved by 1839

Trinidad–British

British Guiana was
founded in 1831

Caracas

Bogotá

Quito

Guiana–French

Lima

Surinam–Dutch

Salvador

States with date of independence

- Mexico, 1821
- United Provinces of Central
  America, 1823
- Haiti, 1803
- Gran Colombia, 1819–1830
- Peru, 1821
- Bolivia, 1825
- Brazil, 1822
- Paraguay, 1811
- Uruguay, 1828
- United Provinces of
  La Plata, 1816
- Chile, 1817

Rio de Janeiro
São Paulo

Asunción

Santiago

Montevideo

Buenos Aires

Patagonia

Argentine Confederacy
1810–1816

Latin America in 1830

movement for autonomy in 1812 supervised elections held throughout Ecuador to choose representatives to the Cortes a year later. He reprimanded a local official who tried to disenfranchise Indians living in remote jungle areas east of the Andes.

Spanish Americans emerged from their wars of independence sharply divided by class and ethnicity and with far more allegiance to their immediate communities than to any larger entity. If anything, the fight for independence may have accentuated those local loyalties by giving people opportunities to articulate why they did not care to be governed by the next town or province any more than they wished to be ruled from Europe.

THE INDEPENDENCE OF BRAZIL

Compared to their counterparts in Spanish America, Brazilians attained their independence relatively peacefully, and Brazil remained united rather than split into many small nations. This does not mean, however, that conflict and preoccupation with local concerns were entirely absent from the Brazilian struggle for independence. As in the case of Spanish America, Brazilian independence was triggered by events in Europe.

The Portuguese Monarchy in Brazil

Napoleon's invasion of the Iberian Peninsula unleashed a chain of events that forever altered Portuguese America as well as Spanish America. The French emperor was determined to sever Portugal's long-standing alliance with Great Britain. For decades, policymakers in Lisbon had toyed with the idea of removing themselves from the vicissitudes of European power politics by making Brazil, rather than Portugal, the center of the empire. The rapid approach of French troops in November of 1807 persuaded the government to consider this radical proposal as a temporary expedient in the face of a national emergency. At the time, Queen Maria wore the Portuguese crown, but her son João actually governed as prince regent, and it was he who made the decision to move his entire household and an entourage numbering as many as 10,000 people to Brazil, sailing with a British naval escort. Arriving in Rio de Janeiro in 1808, Prince João declared his intention to remain until the crisis in the mother country had passed. In 1816, Maria died and he became King João VI, while still residing in Brazil.

The presence of the royal court brought dramatic changes to Portuguese America. Intellectual activity flourished with the long-overdue introduction of printing presses at Rio de Janeiro and Salvador, the expansion of education at the primary level, and the establishment of two medical schools and a military academy to train officers for Brazil's new army. Rio de Janeiro thrived as never before, as local merchants found a market providing the court with its many needs. Most important, many Brazilians took pride in their homeland, touting its greatness in new periodicals that circulated in major cities. As one young man from Bahia put it, "Brazil, proud now that it contains within it the Immortal Prince, … is no longer to be a maritime Colony … but rather a powerful Empire, which will come to be the Moderator of Europe, the arbiter of Asia, and the dominator of Africa." In 1815, Portuguese America was proclaimed the Kingdom of Brazil, fully equal with the mother country.

Other changes proved less welcome, however. Brazilians had to shoulder new tax burdens to pay for the expanded bureaucracy and the costs of waging war against the French in Portugal. Willingly at first but with increasing reluctance as time passed, prominent citizens of Rio de Janeiro vacated their homes to accommodate the courtiers and bureaucrats who accompanied the king to Brazil. People in Bahia in the northeastern part of the country chafed under Rio de Janeiro's growing dominance over them. Although the government in exile officially encouraged trade with all nations, it also bound Brazil more closely than ever before to an economic dependence on Great Britain that stifled the growth of local manufacturing.

Popular Unrest in Brazil

Some Brazilians dared to express their opposition to the adverse effects of the Portuguese occupation, and King João was no more sympathetic to their concerns than King Ferdinand was to the grievances of his American subjects. In

Coronation of Emperor Pedro I, Rio de Janeiro, 1822.

March of 1817, a revolt began in Pernambuco in the northeast after royal authorities arrested a number of army officers and others suspected of harboring trea-
sonous sentiments. The rebels destroyed images of the king and his coat of arms,
proclaimed a republic, and trumpeted ideals voiced by their contemporaries in
Spanish America, among them personal liberty, equality before the law, support
for the Catholic religion, and devotion to their homeland, or patria. They also
expressed their hatred toward the many Portuguese-born Europeans who had
settled in Brazil in the years since 1808, but vigorously denied rumors that they
advocated an immediate end to African slavery, a mainstay of the Brazilian economy. The revolt spread throughout the northeastern part of Brazil, the area that
most resented the heavy hand of the royal government based in Rio de Janeiro.

King João was aghast at what he called "a horrible attempt upon My Royal
Sovereignty and Supreme Authority." His forces suppressed the rebellion within
just 2 months and about 20 of its leaders were executed, but the king could no
longer take his Brazilian subjects for granted. He brought new armies over from
Portugal and stationed them in Rio de Janeiro, Salvador, and Recife. The king
was determined to snuff out any signs of unrest on either side of the Atlantic.

The Culmination of Brazilian Independence

Indeed, King João had cause for concern that the people of Portugal might
attempt to throw off his authority as well. Discontent within the military sparked
a revolt in August of 1820 that strongly resembled the Spanish coup of that same
year. The participants called for the convoking of a Cortes and the writing of a
constitution modeled after the Spanish document of 1812. They also demanded
that King João return to Lisbon, and he prudently acquiesced. Before embarking from Rio de Janeiro in April of 1821, he placed his 22-year-old son, Pedro,
in charge as prince regent of the Kingdom of Brazil.

This was a period of important political change in Brazil. With the blessing of
the Portuguese Cortes, many towns and cities formed juntas, asserting their local
autonomy rather than accepting the continued domination of the government in
Rio de Janeiro, much as Spanish Americans of their time tried to free themselves
from the control of capital cities. The Cortes also ordered the dismantling of superior tribunals created during King João's residency, and the local governing juntas refused to send tax revenues to Rio de Janeiro. The cumulative effect of these
changes was to reduce Prince Pedro's authority, so that, in effect, he functioned as
little more than the governor of the capital city and its immediate surrounding
area. Affluent residents of Rio missed the good times their city had enjoyed
between 1808 and 1821, and those imbued with a sense of Brazilian national pride
fretted over the splintering of the great Kingdom of Brazil into a series of petty
autonomous provinces, each under the jurisdiction of a separate local junta.

Meanwhile, delegates in the Cortes worried with considerable justification
that those opposed to these constitutional changes might rally around Prince

Brazil States and Their Capitals

Pedro. The Cortes therefore commanded the prince regent to return to Portugal, as his father had done several months previously. In January of 1822, Pedro announced his decision to stay in Brazil, evidently convinced that the Cortes's order constituted a supreme disregard for royal authority. Over the next several months, he moved ever closer to those favoring a complete break with the mother country. The final break came on September 7, 1822, and Pedro I became the "constitutional emperor and perpetual defender" of Brazil, a position he held until 1831, when he abdicated in favor of his son, Pedro II, who in turn ruled until Brazil finally became a republic in 1889.

The Meaning of Independence

As they went about setting up governments, leaders of the new nations of Latin America borrowed very selectively from the egalitarian rhetoric of the North

Slice of Life   THE 16TH OF SEPTEMBER: INDEPENDENCE DAY IN MEXICO

THE LEADERS OF LATIN America's new nations not only had to set up governments and rebuild economies disrupted by the independence wars; they also had to convince their people to pay allegiance to the nation. Historians sometimes speak of nation-states as "imagined communities" in which people who do not have face-to-face contact with one another, and who may not have much in common, all see themselves as citizens of the nation. In practical terms, forging these new communities in Latin America meant getting people as diverse as, for example, pampered creole aristocrats in Mexico City, Zapotec-speaking Indians in Oaxaca far to the south, and farmers who eked out a living on the far northern frontier of New Mexico, to set aside their racial, economic, linguistic, and cultural differences and swear loyalty to the new republic of Mexico.

Most Latin Americans of the early nineteenth century, whatever their backgrounds, did in fact see themselves as part of a universal community, that of the Catholic Church. Those who took command of the new national governments strove to persuade their citizens to transfer their loyalties from the church to the nation, and they borrowed some of the tools the church had used for centuries to instill a sense of community among the faithful.

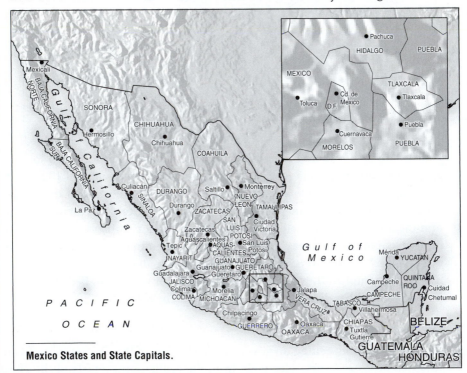

Mexico States and State Capitals.

National holidays now competed with religious ones, and the heroes of the independence wars were invoked as examples of patriotism, much as saints had served as examples of Christian piety.

Leaders of Mexico lost little time in setting up a new ritual calendar intended to enkindle a sense of nationalism from Oaxaca to New Mexico. Foremost among the days they chose to commemorate was September 16, the anniversary of Father Hidalgo's "Grito de Dolores" of 1810, the proclamation that had ignited the first phase of Mexico's wars for independence. The initial celebration of September 16 took place in Mexico City in 1823. The festivities included the ringing of church bells, a splendid parade with music supplied by a military band, and speeches extolling the virtues of the new nation. The remains of national hero José María Morelos were brought to Mexico City for burial. Just as saints' days had offered a variety of secular entertainments in addition to the religious observances, the independence celebrations of September 1823 featured music and theatrical presentations in the Alameda, the city's centrally located park. Fireworks shows at the *zócalo,* the main plaza facing the cathedral, lasted far into the night.

From 1825, a private, voluntary organization supervised the celebration in Mexico City. For 30 years, with only one exception, when U.S. troops occupied the city in 1847, the *Junta Patriótica* (patriotic committee) oversaw the events. Beginning on the night of September 15 and continuing throughout the next day, there were patriotic speeches, artillery salutes, music, theater, and fireworks. The junta, the President of the Republic, and other dignitaries marched through the city's streets on the morning of the 16th. Schoolchildren sang patriotic hymns specially commissioned for the occasion. The people of Mexico City turned out in droves dressed in their best. The junta also marked the day with charitable works such as cash payments to disabled or impoverished veterans and to widows and orphans of rebels who died in the wars. In the 1820s, poor children received new clothes. Every prisoner in the Mexico City jails received a good meal, a packet of cigarettes, a bar of soap, and one *real* (a coin, worth one-eighth of a peso) on September 16. In the provinces, the holiday was marked with equal fervor, if not with equal splendor. In San Luis Potosí, for example, local dignitaries marched and tossed coins to the assembled crowds, who also enjoyed music and fireworks.

From the 1820s to the present, the timing, scale, and specific content of Mexico's independence festivities varied according to the political climate of the time. Sometimes, members of the nineteenth-century upper class muted the celebrations because they feared a rekindling of the same kind of popular unrest that Hidalgo's proclamation had unleashed. On some occasions, they suspended all observances except for a few speeches in Congress. In times when national governments felt more securely in control, they praised the revolutionary aspirations of Hidalgo and Morelos, hoping to win the allegiance of the lower classes. The first celebrations of Mexican independence had commemorated Agustín de Iturbide's triumphal entry into

(continued on next page)

INDEPENDENCE DAY IN MEXICO   *(continued from previous page)*

Mexico City in September of 1821 along with Hidalgo's Grito de Dolores, but later leaders chose to focus exclusively on the first phase of the movement, when Hidalgo and Morelos had so forcefully articulated the grievances of the masses, even though it had been Iturbide's actions that had secured Mexico's final independence from Spain. Iturbide's victory represented the consummation of upper-class negotiations with insurgents—a backroom deal. Subsequent leaders of Mexico had more to gain politically if they claimed to be the heirs of Hidalgo and Morelos, even if their outlook and their means of governance far more closely resembled those of the conservative Iturbide. Ironically, the symbol of the people's movement, Father Hidalgo, triumphed just as governments grew strong enough to encroach upon the very local autonomy for which the people had fought.

Questions for Discussion

Are patriotic holidays effective in promoting a sense of national loyalty? Why or why not? What are some other means that governments use to win people's allegiance? Are there means that are available to governments today that were not available to the leaders of the new Latin American governments in the early nineteenth century?

American and French Revolutions. They eagerly invoked ideas of representation and freedom of expression when it came to claiming a voice for themselves in governing their homelands. Taking their cues from France and the United States, Latin America's leaders forged a new concept of citizenship, calling on all who lived within their borders to place loyalty to the nation above any ties to their church, family, or local community.

The kind of equality proclaimed by the more radical factions of the French Revolution, and the specter of the bloody slave revolt that had brought independence to the former French colony of Haiti, terrified Latin American political elites. At the same time, fighters both for and against independence sought to enlist the lower classes on their side. Various insurgent leaders in Spanish America promised to abolish the tribute, a special tax on Indians and blacks levied by on the colonial state. In Peru, the insurgents also ordered an end to the mita, a highly oppressive system of forced labor that had sent thousands of Indians to work in silver mines and other enterprises. The tribute and the mita both symbolized the power of the colonial state that the insurgents were anxious to destroy. Indians often had few reasons to trust privileged creole patriots and sided with the Spanish. In Peru and Bolivia, for example, Indians comprised the bulk of the royalist armies. After independence, many leaders declared that the people formerly known as "Indians" were now citizens of the new national states.

In practice, however, many forms of discrimination lingered long beyond the end of colonial rule.

Royalist commanders throughout the hemisphere promised freedom to slaves who helped them fight the rebel forces. Similar offers went out from insurgent camps as well, but sometimes blacks were advised that they would have to wait patiently for these promises to be fulfilled. In 1812, for example, the revolutionary junta at Buenos Aires told the city's slaves, "Your longed-for liberty cannot be decreed right away, as humanity and reason would wish, because unfortunately it stands in opposition to the sacred right of individual liberty." By "individual liberty," the Argentine patriots meant the property rights of slaveowners. Even when the offers of freedom were genuine, creole leaders of the independence movement often showed extreme prejudice toward blacks even as they tried to recruit them, and many people of color cast their lot with the royalists. After independence, victorious creoles devised means to deny blacks access to the political process in their new nations. Only in places where slavery was no longer economically viable did they carry through with their wartime promises to abolish slavery.

Both sides in the independence struggle also sought the support of women. Women often accompanied soldiers into battle, preparing meals, nursing the wounded, and sometimes taking up arms themselves. In South America, Bolívar's companion Manuela Sáenz played a prominent role in the final battles for independence. Throughout the Americas, women served as spies for royalist and patriot armies alike. María Josefa Ortiz de Domínguez, wife of a royal official in the Bajío and nicknamed "La Corregidora," alerted Father Hidalgo and his co-conspirators that the authorities had learned of their plot. Women smuggled weapons, and—in one instance in Mexico—a printing press, to insurgents and persuaded soldiers in the royalist armies to desert. In Mexico City, however, a women's organization called the *Patriotas Marianas* drummed up support for the royalist cause. Despite the active involvement of many women in the independence movement, the new leaders of Latin America, like those who commanded the United States and all the nation-states of nineteenth-century Europe, included only males in their definition of who was entitled to play an active role in civic affairs.

CONCLUSION

In most of Latin America, the wars of independence were long, drawn out, brutal contests. The Spaniards had defeated the insurgencies in the first phase by 1815. Popular and creole movements (in New Spain and northern South America, respectively) failed because of the deep-seated mutual distrust between the upper classes on one hand and Indians and castas on the other. Upper-class fear of the indigenous and mixed population cut short Hidalgo's campaign, and the unwillingness of creoles to make concessions to the lower classes in New Granada ensured Bolívar's initial defeats. Undercurrents of class and race war added a vicious, murderous aspect to the fighting.

Beginning about 1817, the tide turned in favor of independence, in part because the creoles learned from past mistakes and reached temporary arrangements with the lower classes, such as the llaneros of Venezuela and Vicente Guerrero's guerrilla forces of southern Mexico. Politics in Europe also played a role in pushing the colonies toward the final break with the mother countries. Following his restoration to the Spanish throne, King Ferdinand VII had paid little attention to colonial concerns, and the representative assemblies that reemerged in Spain and Portugal in 1820 proved intransigent on issues of vital concern to Latin Americans. Colonial upper classes finally felt confident they could declare independence and contain popular discontent without help from overseas. From 1817 to 1824, Spanish and Portuguese authority yielded to independent governments from Mexico to southern South America.

Soon after taking power, leaders of the new Latin American governments began declaring national holidays that honored the heroes of independence and their victories on the battlefield, but more than a decade of war left most Latin Americans with little to celebrate. Parts of the region were in ruins, and hundreds of thousands had died. Many survivors, armed and mobile, had nothing to which they could return. Facing an uncertain future, those who did have resources hesitated to invest in new enterprises. It would take much of Latin America a century to recover economically from the wars of independence. Poverty in turn undermined the political stability of the new republics.

And while it was easy enough to create new symbols of nationhood such as flags, monuments, and coinage, much more difficult was the task of forging new national identities, "imagined communities" in which racially and culturally disunited peoples who thought mostly in terms of their own towns and villages could live together and come to see themselves as Mexicans or Peruvians or Brazilians. As we will see in the following chapters, the resulting tensions would undermine the stability of Latin American politics for a half century.

LEARNING MORE ABOUT LATIN AMERICANS

Chambers, Sarah C. *From Subjects to Citizens: Honor, Gender and Politics in Arequipa, Peru, 1780–1854* (University Park, PA: Pennsylvania State University Press, 1999). A look at how ordinary people in one Peruvian community experienced the transition from colonialism to independence.

Graham, Richard. *Independence in Spanish America: A Comparative Approach*, 2nd ed. (New York: McGraw-Hill, 1994). Comprehensive coverage of the wars for independence.

Kinsbruner, Jay. *Independence in Spanish America: Civil Wars, Revolutions, and Underdevelopment* (Albuquerque, NM: University of New Mexico Press, 2000). Good overview of the process of independence.

Kraay, Hendrik. *Race, State, and Armed Forces in Independence-Era Brazil: Bahia, 1790s–1840s* (Stanford, CA: Stanford University Press, 2001). An examination of independence and early state-building in one of Brazil's historic sugar-producing regions.

Méndez, Cecilia. *The Plebeian Republic: The Huanta Rebellion and the Making of the Peruvian State, 1820–1850* (Durham, NC: Duke University Press, 2005). This study of a rebellion by peasants, muleteers, landowners and military officers shows the kinds of challenges facing the new governments of Latin America in the era of Independence.

Schultz, Kirsten. *Tropical Versailles: Empire, Monarchy, and the Portuguese Royal Court in Rio de Janeiro, 1808–1821* (New York: Routledge, 2001). How the temporary presence of the Portuguese monarchy transformed life in the capital of Brazil.

Walker, Charles F. *Smoldering Ashes: Cuzco and the Creation of Republican Peru, 1780–1840* (Durham, NC: Duke University Press, 1999). Gives key insights into the roles played by the indigenous people of Cuzco in forging independence and a new national state.

GLOSSARY

Alcaldes mayores (ahl-KAHL-days mah-YOR-ays)   In Spanish America, local officials who represented the authority of the king and exercised administrative and judicial functions; similar to corregidores.

Aldeias (ahl-DAY-ahs)   In Brazil, villages of mission Indians.

Audiencias (ow-dee-EHN-see-ahs)   In Spanish America, a court of appeal located in a major city.

Ayllu (ai-YOO)   The basic unit of indigenous society in Peru, a group of people who claimed descent from a single ancestor, worked lands in common, and venerated their own special deities.

Bandeirantes (bahn-day-RAHN-chees)   In Brazil, especially in the region around São Paulo, people who explored the back country and rounded up Indians to be sold as slaves.

Cabildo (kah-BEEL-doh)   A town council in Spanish America.

Cacique (kah-SEE-kay)   Originally, a traditional chief in Caribbean societies; later an indigenous local ruler in Spanish America; this term was also used to describe local political bosses in the nineteenth century, after Latin American independence.

Castas (KAHS-tahs)   In Spanish America, people of mixed race; often specifically referring to people with some evidence of African ancestry.

Chicha (CHEE-chah)   In South America, a fermented beverage made from maize.

Cofradía (koh-frah-DEE-ah)   In Spanish America, an organization of lay people devoted to a particular saint or religious observance; members maintained village churches and sponsored festivals.

Corregidores (koh-ray-hee-DOR-ays)   In Spanish America, local officials who represented the authority of the king and exercised administrative and judicial functions; similar to alcaldes mayores.

Creoles   People who claimed to be descended only from Europeans, but born in the Americas.

Donatário (doh-nah-TAH-ree-oh)   In Brazil, the head of a proprietary colony.

Encomendero (ehn-koh-mehn-DAY-roh)   In Spanish America, an individual who received an encomienda.

Encomienda (ehn-koh-mee-EHN-dah)   In Spanish America, the right granted to an individual to demand tribute and/or labor from the Indians of a specific place; in theory, an encomienda also included the obligation to protect the assigned Indians from abuse and provide for their instruction in the Catholic faith.

Engenho (ehn-ZHEN-yeu)   In Brazil, a sugar mill.

Español (ehs-pahn-YOHL)   A person claiming Spanish lineage, whether born in Spain or the Americas.

Gobernador (goh-behr-nah-DOR)   In Spanish America, the governor of a province or the ruler of an Indian village.

Hacienda (ah-see-EHN-dah)   Any kind of large agricultural property in Spanish America.

Indios ladinos (EEN-dee-ohs lah-DEE-nohs)   In Spanish America, Indians who could speak Spanish and were acculturated into Spanish ways.

Kuraka (koo-RAH-kah)   A traditional chief in Peru and other Andean countries both before and after the Spanish conquest.

Lavradores de cana (lah-vrah-DOR-ehs zhee KAH-nah)   In Brazil, small farmers who produced sugar cane.

Mameluca (mah-may-LOO-kah)   In Brazil, a female of mixed European and Native American descent.

Mameluco (mah-may-LOO-koh)   In Brazil, a male of mixed European and Native American descent.

Manumission   The process whereby slaves could legally obtain their freedom.

Mestiza (mehs-TEE-sah)   In Spanish America, a female of mixed European and Native American descent.

Mestizo (mehs-TEE-soh)   In Spanish America, a male of mixed European and Native American descent.

Mita (MEE-tah)   A forced draft of Indian labor in Peru, both before and after the Spanish conquest.

Mitayo (mee-TAI-yoh)   A worker drafted through the mita.

Mulatta   A female of mixed African and European and/or Native American descent.

Mulatto   A male of mixed African and European and/or Native American descent.

Nahuatl (nah-WAHT-ul)   Language spoken by the Aztecs and other pre-hispanic peoples of Central Mexico; still spoken today.

New Christians   Converts from Judaism to Catholicism and their descendants.

Obraje (oh-BRAH-hay)   Textile factory in Spanish America.

Peninsulares (pay-neen-soo-LAH-rays)   Natives of Spain or Portugal.

Presidio (pray-SEE-dee-oh)   In Spanish America, a military fort.

Pulque (POOL-kay)   In Mexico, a fermented beverage made from the agave cactus.

Quechua (KAY-chwah)   Language spoken by the Incas and other pre-hispanic peoples of Peru, Bolivia, and Ecuador; still spoken today.

Regular clergy   Priests who belonged to a religious order such as the Franciscans, the Dominicans, or the Jesuits; they followed the rules established by the founder of their order.

Relação (ray-lah-SOW)   In Brazil, the highest court in the land.

Repartimiento (ray-pahr-tee-mee-EHN-toh)   In Spanish America, a forced labor draft.

Repartimiento de mercancías (ray-pahr-tee-mee-EHN-toh day mehr-kahn-SEE-ahs)   In Spanish America, a practice whereby local officials engaged Indians in trade, often forcibly.

República de españoles (ray-POO-blee-kah day ehs-pahn-YOHL-ays)   In Spanish America, the Spanish community, supposedly separate from the Indian community.

República de indios (ray-POO-blee-kah day EEN-dee-ohs)   In Spanish America, the Indian community, supposedly separate from the Spanish community.

Secular clergy   Priests who did not belong to religious orders; they were directly under the supervision of their bishop.

Senhor de engenho (sayn-YOR zhee ehn-ZHEN-yeu)   In Brazil, the owner of a sugar mill.

Traza (TRAH-sah)   In Spanish America, the central portion of a city, reserved in theory for residents of Spanish descent.

Viceroy   Chief government official in the colonies; the personal representative of the king of Spain or Portugal.

CREDITS

INDEX